PROTECTING
AMERICAN WORKERS

PROTECTING
AMERICAN WORKERS

An Assessment of Government Programs

Sar A. Levitan
Peter E. Carlson
Isaac Shapiro

The Bureau of National Affairs, Inc.
Washington, D.C.

Library of Congress Cataloging-in-Publication Data

Levitan, Sar A.
  Protecting American workers.

  Includes index.
  1. Labor laws and legislation—United States.
I. Carlson, Peter E. II. Shapiro, Isaac, 1931-
III. Title.
KF3319.L44 1986   344.73'01   86-13681
ISBN 0-87179-521-3   347.3041

Printed in the United States of America
International Standard Book Number 0-87179-521-3 ,

Preface

Federal regulation of the workplace is pervasive, safe-guarding workers throughout their employment career, from the time they are hired until they retire. This network of protection became an integral component of the American welfare system as it evolved during the past half century. It helps prepare employees to gain access to the work force and removes many of the obstacles blocking equal access to productive and rewarding employment. On the job, federal laws guarantee most workers a minimal socially accepted wage and require employers to provide a work environment reasonably free of injury and health hazards. Statutory bargaining rights permit employees to band together to secure additional workplace protections.

Government interventions on behalf of labor do not cease when workers leave the job. Most employees forced into idleness, even after a relatively short work period, are guaranteed temporary income during their period of joblessness. The federal government also provides support to workers and their dependents upon retirement. In cases where employers have agreed to pay pensions, federal laws ensure that the interests of the potential beneficiaries are protected and a federal agency assumes responsibility for paying the pensions if employers do not meet their obligations.

The nation is now debating whether the existing regulations should be relaxed, revised, or rescinded. The Reagan administration favors turning over responsibility for some regulations to state governments or relying upon self-regulating free market forces to protect workers.

While retrenchments have been the watchword of the 1980s, new areas require additional federal involvement. These areas include protecting workers from arbitrary dismissal, reducing the gap in pay between men and women working in jobs of comparable worth, and providing some protection for workers who lose their jobs because of mass layoffs or a plant closing.

The book begins by tracing the development of federal workplace regulations and by surveying the protaganists involved. Eight broad areas of government intervention are then examined. In each case, the forces that led to federal action are scrutinized, the scope of the regulation is summarized, and its impact is assessed. The book concludes with a discussion of probable future federal involvements affecting the workplace.

The usual lament of the evaluator applies to assessing government workplace regulations. The data are often inadequate or contradictory, program administrators are not always cooperative in subjecting "their" operations to scrutiny by outsiders, and the impact of each program cannot be isolated from overall economic developments. Granting these assessment difficulties, the cumulative evidence is nonetheless persuasive that federal interventions have had a positive impact upon the workplace. The industrial jurisprudence that emerged as a direct result of federal regulation, the establishment of a floor under wages, the ban on discrimination, and the provision of income support when unemployment strikes or during retirement, all have contributed to making the workplace more compatible with the democratic ideals of a compassionate and affluent society. In some cases, the federal interventions have also enhanced economic efficiency. In every case, federal intervention occurred after it became clear that the market system did not provide for corrective voluntary action and that state efforts were inadequate.

Numerous experts in and out of government have been helpful in preparing this study. We are particularly grateful to Joseph M. Becker, Richard Belous, Stuart Brahs, Frank Gallo, Charles Hurley, Karl Kronebusch, Leon Lunden, Randy Rabinowitz, Marc Rosenblum, Bert Seidman, and Kathleen Utgoff. They all helped improve the final product. We are also indebted to Barbara Webster for her editorial contributions in preparing the volume for publication and to Peggy Kelly for preparing initial drafts of several chapters.

The study was prepared under an ongoing grant from the Ford Foundation to the Center for Social Policy Studies of The

George Washington University. In line with the Foundation's practice, responsibility for the contents of the study was left with the center director.

The Authors

Ides of March, 1986

Contents

Part IV. Through the Crystal Ball

Part 1

The System and the Policies

1
Federal Worker Protection: The Evolving System

Over the past half century the federal government has played an increasingly active role in shaping the fortunes of American workers. Regulation of the workplace has guaranteed basic rights and protections to workers, shielding them from economic forces over which they have little or no control. In this era when many Americans rally around the slogan of "getting government off our backs," it is worth reflecting on the impact of federal workplace regulation.

Regulation of the workplace represents an uneasy compromise between laissez-faire economic ideals and society's concern for the welfare of its citizens. Opponents believe that government intervention in the workplace impedes the efficient operations of the free market and violates the freedom of employers and, sometimes, of employees. Those in favor of intervention argue that unregulated labor markets lead to working conditions that hamper productivity growth and may be harmful to workers. The debate is as old as the market system but has increased in intensity since the New Deal era. Public support for workplace regulation emerged during the early 1900s; it became stronger in the 1930s, and, again, in the 1960s and early 1970s. More recently, the pendulum has swung in the opposite direction. The renewed conservative movement and the administration of President Reagan have joined forces to weaken government workplace regulations in the name of economic efficiency.

The Need for Regulation

The belief that labor markets should operate unencumbered by federal intervention was widely held by Americans until the Great Depression. Social Darwinism with its strong emphasis on individualism and self-reliance was a widely accepted philosophy—those who made it to the top of the economic ladder deserved to be there; similarly, those who failed received their just reward. The law protected employer interests and employees enjoyed few protections or rights in the workplace.

Although the period before the Great Depression was one of substantial economic growth and immigrants had significantly better opportunities than in their native lands, for every Horatio Alger, there were many workers who remained in destitution. Entire families often worked long hours in sweat shops, but still earned so little that they lived in poverty. Laborers who moved from farms to factories became more vulnerable to economic downturns. The growing interdependence of the economy guaranteed that maladjustments in one sector would cause havoc in other areas. Workers with specialized skills were less adaptable to these economic disruptions and did not raise their own food supply. Because of the growing labor supply created by rural to urban migration and by immigration, workers lacked bargaining power. They had little alternative but to accept difficult working conditions.

The hardships created by industrialization and the unregulated marketplace inevitably resulted in reform movements. The populist movement, with its agrarian roots, was strong in the late 19th century. The socialist movement reached its heyday in the early 20th century. The progressive movement, which flourished at the same time as the socialist movement, accepted capitalism but sought to ameliorate harsh workplace conditions. The union movement was established during this period to advance the interests of labor and to create a more secure and humane work environment.

These reform movements had little success in securing protection for industrial workers. No federal legislation was enacted and even modest state protective legislation was often struck down by the courts. The Supreme Court held the property rights of employers to be paramount and found legislated wage or hourly standards to be an unconstitutional infringement on employers' freedom to contract with their employees. In a 1923 decision striking down a District of Columbia minimum wage law, the Supreme Court held that "The tendency of the times to socialize property rights . . . will prove destructive of our free institutions." The Court ruled that the right of an employee to a living wage was subordinate to the employer's right to determine a "just" wage for services rendered. The Court reasoned that employers would be left without "adequate means of livelihood" if restrained from cutting wages during periods of stress and business downturns.[1] No similar concern was expressed for the economic security of employees.

The Great Depression shook public confidence in the beneficent operations of the free market. Mass joblessness and underemployment, bank and business failures, and the inadequacy of private and state relief efforts convinced the American people of the need for federal regulation. The growing influence of Keynesian economic theory also played a part in the increased role of the federal government. The anticipation of effective federal intervention during sharp economic downturns provided the public with hope and dispelled the prevailing belief that business cycles must run their course no matter the toll in human suffering.

The initiatives of the New Deal responded to the pressing needs of the time. An income support system was established to mitigate the harsh consequences of widespread unemployment and to ease the burden of caring for the nation's elderly. The only direct intervention into the terms of employment were minimum wage and overtime restrictions, which were intended to guarantee minimal socially acceptable compensation for the working population. Federal law legitimized the role of unions to protect worker interests on the job through collective bargaining as an alternative to coercive, sometimes violent, tactics by employers. An institutional structure was established through which unions could operate and thrive.

These interventions were an explicit recognition that unregulated markets could not adequately protect the welfare of the nation's workers. Although opposition to the New Deal reforms persisted, the Eisenhower administration made no serious effort to alter this expanded federal role. Conservatives accepted the public's support for the New Deal programs, and focused their efforts at the margins—restraining the growth of federal programs and chipping away at labor's legislated advantages.

Three decades of adjustment to the deep social reforms of the New Deal were necessary before a second wave of reform was launched. The doors of economic opportunity had opened for the great majority of Americans during the two decades of postwar prosperity, but prospects for advancement for minorities and women remained bleak. Unemployed and underemployed individuals found their opportunities limited by their lack of education, inadequate job skills, or regional isolation. Gradually, evidence mounted that economic freedom and opportunity for all, even in periods of sustained economic growth, can be realized only if barriers to work and advancement are removed through government action. The initiatives of the Great Society as well as those of the Nixon administration were directed at those who had been left behind. The Johnson and Nixon administrations also responded to the expanding aspirations of mainstream Americans. An affluent and better educated work force demanded workplace protection, leading in the early 1970s to workplace health and safety legislation and provisions for safeguarding private pensions.

From Roosevelt to Carter—through five Democratic and three Republican administrations—Americans generally favored federal regulation of the workplace as a necessary protection from the vicissitudes of the free market. The web of existing workplace laws and regulations has benefited millions of workers and has resulted in a more just and stable social order. The right to organize and bargain collectively has promoted industrial democracy by strengthening the economic power of workers and putting them on a more equal footing with their employers. Income support has been provided to the aged and the unemployed. Work conditions—ranging from wages to the length of the workweek to workplace health and safety—have improved substantially. New opportunities have been opened for those previously excluded from the labor force or unjustly denied employment. Workplace regulations are not without costs, but on balance they have improved the quality of life for the bulk of American workers and have helped to create a more just and equitable society.

The Swinging Pendulum

This positive assessment of federal interventions in the workplace is not universally accepted. The quest for equity, fairness, and security is often perceived to be in conflict with the quest for freedom and efficiency. In the mid-1970s, as productivity growth declined and inflation and unemployment rose, analysts increasingly argued that the costs of regulation absorbed resources that would otherwise flow to "productive" investments.[2] These views were not new, but they were fueled by economic change and uncertainty and gained remarkable currency as part of the general opposition to government intervention by the growing conservative movement. Advocates of federal regulation failed to effectively counter this movement with an adequate explanation of the factors underlying the troubled economy.

Conservatives, supported by a well-funded public relations apparatus, launched a sustained campaign against government intrusion in the free market economy. They argued that misguided government policies—ballooning taxes, swelling deficits, overgrown bureaucracies, burdensome regulations, and the spread of frequently ineffective and wasteful government programs—were the cause of economic stagnation. They promoted the image of the United States as an economic power in decline and drifting listlessly. Employer organizations enthusiastically supported this movement and contributed heavily to conveying these ideas to the nation.

This antigovernment campaign was directed at specific workplace regulations. In an attack on the minimum wage, conservatives charged that it denied job seekers, particularly young individuals, the opportunity to work. Conservatives argued that health and safety regulations required costly investments and the adoption of inefficient production methods. They criticized affirmative action programs for promoting reverse discrimination. They also championed the use of private insurance to replace or to supplement social insurance programs for the elderly and unemployed.

The conservative cause was greatly benefited by a sympathetic administration. On assuming office in 1981, President Reagan assigned regulatory relief a central place in his strategy to revitalize the American economy. For the first time, revision and elimination of federal regulations were given an integral part in economic policy, on the same level as fiscal and monetary policies. The zeal with which the administration has attempted deregulation and the depth of its regulatory review reflect its devotion to the cause of reshaping the workplace protection apparatus, as well as the conservative movement's influence on the administration's ideological agenda. One administration official advised his subordinates: "If you can find nothing else to do, then undo."

The Participants

The current battlelines over workplace regulation reflect traditional divisions. On one side, the conservative movement, frequently assisted by business lobbies, fights to deregulate the workplace. Its cause has been advanced by key Reagan administration officials as well as through the expanded conservative think tanks that provide the intellectual underpinnings for the drive to reduce or eliminate regulations. Business relies on its Washington representatives, political action committees, and single-issue coalitions to influence public policy.

On the other side, the labor movement and a large number of liberal and consumer groups fight for the retention of workplace regulations. Although the disparate groups favoring regulation have experienced difficulties speaking with one voice and in countering the invigorated ideas of the Right, federal intervention has continued to enjoy public support. The loose labor-consumer-liberal coalitions have succeeded in thwarting the Reagan administration's attempts to radically restructure federal workplace legislation.

The liberal coalition has been less successful in preventing the erosion of workplace protections through administrative action. The Reagan administration extended executive control over the regulatory apparatus by appointing agency heads either ideologically opposed to their legislated responsibilities or too inexperienced to carry them out. Sweeping across-the-board cuts in budget and staff levels paved the way for increased emphasis on voluntary compliance by business and for reduced enforcement efforts. Concerned that the agencies might be slow to dismantle federal regulations, the administration expanded the oversight powers of the Office of Management and Budget (OMB) so that proposed regulations are subject to OMB review before they are made available to the public.

The Balance Sheet

The conservative drive to deregulate the workplace has had varied effects. The Reagan administration has been forced to tread lightly in sensitive areas such as social security, where program supporters are well organized and wield considerable political clout. A powerful civil rights coalition focused public attention on administration attempts to weaken civil rights enforcement and has challenged Reagan appointees in this area. It has been helped by the notable lack of solidarity in the business community on civil rights issues. Congressional advocates of a strong federal role in the workplace have had to pick and choose their battles carefully, and their actions have been strongly affected by the growing pressure to reduce the federal deficit. The balance sheet shows a net loss, but the basic structure of federal workplace regulation still stands.

Access to Work

For two decades the nation has experimented with different ways to break down barriers to employment faced by individuals who are deficient in education, skills, or work experience. Some efforts that proved too costly or that had limited results have been abandoned. Other programs that were cost-effective have grown under both Democratic and Republican administrations. Education and job training programs are now needed more than ever as the United States adjusts to significant international competition and rapid technological change, and as unemployment remains high during a period of economic growth. Notwithstanding these factors, the Reagan administration has succeeded in its push for sharp program reductions in both education and job training. Congress cut the funding of federal employment and training efforts by half from 1981 to 1986. The administration's attempt to eliminate the Job Corps, a widely acclaimed and highly successful program, was prevented only when bipartisan congressional supporters rallied to its defense.

On the Job

Protection of worker rights on the job has eroded during the Reagan years. Enforcement of federal statutes covering collective bargaining, fair labor standards, equal employment opportunity, and workplace health and safety has been carried out with high sensitivity to employer interests, but little concern for protection of workers.

The New Deal reforms helped spur union growth. In turn, unions have secured improved wages and workplace standards for their members, and have protected them against arbitrary and unfair employer actions. Many of these protections have also spilled over to nonunion workers. Union organizational strength, however, has declined during much of the post-World War II period, in part because of the passage of federal legislation. The actions of the Reagan administration have accelerated this decline and, more generally, have weakened the protections available to all workers.

Minimum wage standards have fallen considerably during the Reagan administration. The purchasing power of the minimum wage rose during the two decades following World War II and the extent of its coverage expanded, providing crucial income support for the working poor as well as increases in income for millions of other workers. Although Congress has blocked the Reagan administration's proposal to lower the minimum wage for teenagers, there has been little effort to raise the minimum wage from its January 1981 level. As a result, the minimum wage in 1986 was at its lowest real level in three decades.

The Reagan administration has also significantly changed federal equal employment opportunity policy. Since the passage of the 1964 Civil Rights Act, the federal government has played a vital role in the progress of minorities and women in the workplace by closely monitoring employer hiring and promotion practices. Reagan administration officials, however, have curtailed enforcement, once again relying on voluntary compliance. Reporting requirements have been scaled back sharply to reduce paperwork and to cut employer costs. Administration attempts to rescind affirmative action regulations threaten to undermine this most successful federal anti-discrimination policy. Significantly, civil rights groups have been joined by employer organizations in opposing the abandonment of affirmative action.

The Reagan administration has also relaxed the enforcement of occupational health and safety regulations. After some start-up difficulties, the Occupational Safety and Health Administration (OSHA) succeeded both in raising employer and worker awareness about workplace health and safety and issuing needed health standards. This progress has been halted, and in some cases reversed, by the Reagan administration. In this area where regulation is largely determined by administrative action, personnel cuts, declining enforcement, and the paucity of new standards have seriously jeopardized worker protection from workplace health and safety hazards.

When Employment Ends

Employer and government responsibility for workers outside the workplace has decreased during the Reagan years. Unemployment insurance was a highly successful and widely acclaimed program which had expanded considerably over time. It helped millions of workers during spells of temporary forced idleness. In 1981 the Reagan administration proposed, and Congress passed, amendments restricting eligibility for unemployment insurance benefits. Since then, the extended benefits program in states with high unemployment has been nearly eliminated. In 1985 the percentage of the unemployed receiving jobless insurance was at a historic low.

A widely publicized struggle has taken place over preservation of the social security program. Social security has grown enormously since its enactment in 1935. Nearly one in every six Americans are now direct beneficiaries of the program. It provides 40 percent of the income of the average elderly person; in fact, for most of the elderly, it is their major source of income. In addition, the welfare system provides nearly universal health care for the aged. In 1981 the Reagan administration proposed to resolve the threatened shortfall in social security funds by reducing benefits, but retreated in the face of intense political opposition. Adopting the recommendations of a broadly representative and distinguished commission, Congress passed legislation that established a sound financial footing for the social security system by raising payroll taxes and taxing one-half of the benefits of more affluent recipients. The level of benefits was left nearly intact.

The Reagan administration also tried to trim disability insurance by encouraging the state agencies to remove undeserving recipients from disability insurance rolls. The courts temporarily halted these removals and in 1984, prompted by public outcry over unfairness in the administrative proceedings, Congress passed legislation limiting denial of benefits by administrative action. In general, efforts by the Reagan administration to limit social security and disability benefits have been blocked by congressional action and by widespread public support for these programs.

Federal pension policy for retired workers has been one of the few areas where worker protection has increased during the Reagan administration. Since the passage of the Employee Retirement and Income Security Act in 1974, pension plan assets have quadrupled to $1 trillion, the number of recipients has increased substantially, and the probability of receiving a promised pension has been greatly improved. In 1981 Congress adopted an administration proposal to allow individuals to defer taxes on income saved for retirement. The administration favored increased private savings as a means both of stimulating the economy and reducing dependence on social security. Since 1981, private retirement accounts have flourished, but they disproportionately benefit high income individuals and involve a substantial loss in tax revenues. In another expansion of the pension system, in 1984 Congress passed legislation to make it easier for women to qualify for pensions.

Continued Workplace Regulation

Evaluation difficulties constrain assessment of government workplace regulations. Agreement on the appropriate databases is difficult to achieve. Employers are often in control of information on the costs of federal programs and they have an incentive to overstate these costs. The benefits are even more difficult to measure. Some, such as the value of saving a human life or the preservation of dignity among the elderly, defy objective quantification.

Sufficient evidence does exist, however, to justify the conclusion that federal workplace regulation has generally benefited the labor force and that the conservative case for deregulation suffers from serious flaws. First, advocates of deregulation tend to overstate the costs and adverse impact of intervention in the workplace. For example, annual investment by business on workplace health and safety accounts for less than 2 percent of all capital expenditures; minimum wage laws and overtime provisions also add only a small cost to doing business. These regulations are hardly the cause of the failure of American industry to compete effectively in world markets—some of the nation's largest trading partners place even greater restrictions on employer activity.

Second, critics of regulation frequently fail to recognize that an insufficiently regulated workplace creates costs that are ultimately borne by the taxpayer. For example, a lower federal minimum wage increases the dependency of low-income individuals on public support. In another example, the inadequate regulation of exposure to coal dust led to numerous cases of black lung disease—100,000 in 1984. Because the victims were unable to work and lacked the resources to help themselves, taxpayers assumed the cost of their support. Federal regulation of coal producers ensures that exposure to this debilitating disease is reduced and that any preventive or remedial costs are paid by those who benefit from the hazardous working conditions.

Third, the critics ignore the tremendous accomplishments of government workplace regulations. The workplace environment is more benign than it was before regulation, and unemployment benefits cushion the harsh impact of forced idleness. Social security benefits bring millions of elderly out of poverty. Over five million individuals benefited from the last increase in the minimum wage, and thousands of lives have been saved by the new health and safety standards.

Workplace regulation also benefits employers and society at large. Federal support for education and skill development ensures an adequate supply of labor for employers. Equal employment opportunity increases the quality of the labor supply. Studies have repeatedly demonstrated that a healthy and secure work force is more productive, indicating that regulation may in fact contribute to economic efficiency. Unemployment insurance allows employers the opportunity to adjust to changing business conditions without losing valuable, skilled employees, and, along with social security, stabilizes demand during recessions.

Fourth, critics tend to idealize the free market. The market imperfections that provoked the initial federal interventions in the 1930s have not been completely eliminated. Employers have little motivation to provide job training to those outside the mainstream of the labor market. Individual firms lack incentive to devote resources to research on health and safety issues. Few employers in the absence of federal requirements would feel compelled to supplement the income of retirees. The free market does not effectively promote all of society's objectives. As a top official in President Nixon's Labor Department quipped, in accomplishing some objectives, "the invisible hand is all thumbs."

Fifth, the conservative call for decentralizing workplace regulation ignores the record of state and local regulation. In practice, prior to federal intervention, state and local laws were either nonexistent (as in the case of social security) or clearly inadequate (as in the case of health and safety regulation). States often fail to regulate workplaces, fearing correctly that employers will flee to unregulated jurisdictions. In addition, companies with multistate operations can adjust more easily to a single national law which often decreases administrative and research costs.

Government regulators occasionally exercise excessive zeal in their implementation of the goals set by Congress. There is a time for regulatory action and a time to absorb the effects of such action. The workplace needs time to adjust to regulations, and modifications are often necessary. The costs of regulation should, of course, be considered, particularly given the intensity of international competition. Together, however, these arguments do not negate the need for intervention—they suggest only that regulation should be undertaken with care and that continual adjustments are necessary to achieve its goals.

Return to Responsibility

Conservatives anticipate continuing public support for their efforts to trim the size and scope of government and to prevent the expansion of federal regulation into areas such as employment-at-will, plant closings, and comparable worth. Public support for regulation of the workplace may, however, once again shift to a desire for greater government involvement. Americans profess to dislike big government in the abstract, but they continue to support a major federal role in specific protections related to the quality of life of the nation's workers.[3]

When the results and costs of the Reagan conservative experiment become apparent, it is likely that the nation will insist that regulation of the workplace return to its previous course. The social costs of the federal flight from responsibility could prove too high a price for most Americans, and the fruits of earlier efforts too important to surrender. The federal rush to deregulate has tended to ignore the need for and merit of workplace regulations. The challenge facing today's political leaders is to undertake a rigorous reappraisal of federal programs affecting the workplace, to acknowledge the many successes, and to rebuild public confidence in government. By adopting this course of action, dignity and security in the workplace can be enhanced.

2

The Politics of Regulation

Persistent high inflation and diminished economic growth in the 1970s weakened the political consensus in support of an activist federal government responsible for stabilizing the economy and protecting the worker. Reflecting the public mood, it became increasingly fashionable not only for politicians, but also for social scientists, to raise doubts about the efficacy of government intervention and to find fault with the sweeping reforms of the Johnson and Nixon administrations.

The ascendancy of conservatism created a favorable climate for a revival of laissez-faire sentiments and the retrenchment of government responsibility for promoting the welfare of workers. By the end of the 1970s the federal government deregulated a number of industries—airlines, trucking, natural gas, and banking. While some of these actions indirectly affected employees in specific industries, those launched by the Reagan administration aimed at wholesale deregulation of the workplace.

The revived conservative movement made a virtue of less government intervention, and the Reagan administration adopted this faith by making deregulation an integral part of its economic policy. Although business had learned to live with government intervention, it considered less government interference a gift it could not refuse and mobilized resources to help the cause. Labor interests, although not as powerful as they once were, have nevertheless helped prevent a more severe erosion of worker protections. They have been aided by public support for specific workplace regulation such as social security and unemployment insurance, to name just two major areas, even though the idea of deregulation seemed to have considerable appeal in the abstract.

Deregulation by Administrative Action

Avoiding confrontation with Congress or, in many cases, public opinion, the Reagan administration relied on its appointed officials to substantially modify workplace regulations without legislative action. Within days after his inauguration, he appointed a task force chaired by Vice President George Bush to review existing and pending regulations, with the goal of eliminating those most burdensome to business. Two weeks after assuming office, he also imposed a 60-day freeze on all regulations issued and under development during the closing weeks of the Carter administration. However, rules that cut costs to the private sector or lightened the regulatory burden were automatically allowed to take effect after the freeze expired. Less than three weeks after imposing the freeze, President Reagan issued Executive Order 12991 requiring that all proposed "major rules" be accompanied by a regulatory impact analysis and establishing OMB as the watchdog over all regulatory agencies.

This general deregulation effort immediately affected regulation of the workplace. In his first official act as Secretary of Labor, Raymond Donovan suspended the effective dates of 22 rules issued near the end of the Carter term. A regulation to extend federal overtime protections to more executives, managers, and professionals was indefinitely postponed because of concern it would raise business costs. Similarly, the secretary withdrew an OSHA "hazard identification" proposal that would have provided more information to employees working with dangerous chemicals.[1] Other regulations that weakened worker protections soon appeared in the *Federal Register*. These included rules to incorporate cost-benefit considerations in applying the cancer policy of the Occupational Safety and Health Administration (OSHA), to decrease the number of air quality samples required at mines regulated by the Mine Safety and Health Administration, and to reduce reporting requirements for company pension programs.

President Reagan's appointments to key agency positions reflected his belief in regulatory relief. During the Carter years the administrators of several regulatory agencies came from the ranks of public interest groups committed to tough enforcement of protective legislation. Reagan administration appointees came mostly from the other side of the tracks: conservatives with a record of opposition to government regulation, and in some cases, individuals with little experience at all. For example, one of Reagan's appointees to the National Labor Relations Board, Donald R. Dotson, argued that unions were a major cause of industrial decline and charged the NLRB with acting as a "legal aid society and organizing arm" for unions during previous administrations.[2] He had also sided with the J.P. Stevens Company in its attempts to avoid unionization. Such appointees profoundly influenced the general direction of boards and agencies regulating the workplace.

The deregulatory tone set in the first few weeks of the Reagan administration has been followed ever since. With the notable exception of President Reagan's second Secretary of Labor, William Brock, and his subcabinet selections, more and more hard-line conservatives have been appointed to key administrative positions. For example, the Attorney General of the second Reagan term, Edwin Meese, has long been a hero of conservatives and has advocated eliminating affirmative action programs.

The ongoing deregulatory efforts of the Reagan administration have also occurred through the consolidation of regulatory oversight within the Office of Management and Budget. Its role in the regulation process can be expected to be even more pronounced during Reagan's second term as a result of an executive order which requires agencies to submit their annual regulatory agendas to OMB and empowers OMB to kill potential regulations. The further centralization of regulatory authority makes it difficult for Congress to exercise meaningful oversight because new approaches may never surface if OMB disapproves of them.[3] Moreover, in 1985 President Reagan appointed James Miller as director of OMB. Mr. Miller has been an avid proponent of deregulation as an academic, as a staff member at the American Enterprise Institute, and as a Reagan administration official.

Sweeping across-the-board cuts in budget and staff levels of executive agencies which weakened enforcement capacity and increased emphasis on voluntary compliance have also contributed to the deregulation of the workplace during the Reagan administration. Between 1980 and 1985, federal appropriations for five major agencies responsible for workplace regulation fell by 9 percent, when adjusted for inflation, and full-time staff levels in these agencies were reduced by 16 percent (Table 1). Early in the Reagan administration, a

Table 1. Federal Agency Budget and Staff Reductions
1980–1985

	Budget in 1980 Dollars (in millions)		Staff (Full-Time Permanent)	
	1980	1985 (est.)	1980	1985 (est.)
Totals:	$760.0	$693.9	18,689	15,735
OSHA	191.3	171.1	3,015	2,323
MSHA	143.6	117.8	3,857	3,107
EEOC	124.3	126.9	3,433	3,125
NLRB	108.2	107.0	3,157	3,000
ESA (DOL)	192.6	171.1	5,227	4,180

Note: MSHA—Mine Safety and Health Administration; EEOC—Equal Employment Opportunity Commission; ESA—Employment Standards Administration.

Source: Budget of the U.S. Government: 1982, 1986.

General Accounting Office study raised the concern that personnel cuts may prevent agencies from performing regulatory reviews.[4]

Career civil servants have often provided effective opposition to deregulatory efforts by arguing within the agencies for carrying out their congressional mandates. The tried and true means traditionally available to civil servants to abort controversial agency initiatives by leaking information to the press and friendly members of Congress was frequently denied to career employees, because the Reagan administration political appointees tended not to trust holdovers from previous administrations and often relied on counsel from conservative think tanks or lobbyists for staff work. Shut out from the decision process and lacking information, career employees could not effectively oppose new policies. In addition, President Reagan and top officials of his administration consistently criticized he purpose and effectiveness of the agencies, playing havoc with staff morale and further contributing to agency problems.

Business Lobbies and Their Allies

With the election of a sympathetic administration, and the growing sophistication and strength of business lobbying efforts, the Reagan years have afforded business lobbies with the best opportunity in nearly six decades to shape workplace regulations more to their own liking. However, despite some sentiment among employers and movement conservatives for repealing or radically modifying protective labor statutes, and despite the initial opposition of most businesses to the establishment of new workplace regulatory agencies, most employer organizations have tended to call for selective deregulation, opposing only what they considered unwarranted and costly federal interference with the operations of their enterprises. They accept the basic structure of workplace regulations and do not advocate that these regulations be dismantled. Employer opposition to affirmative action or safety requirements, for example, emerged as opposition to redundant compliance reviews, long delays in securing administrative guidance, and unfair requirements that jeopardize efficiency, rather than as an attack on the need for any government intervention in this area.

One reason business lobbies have not called for dismantling worker regulations is that they recognize the underlying public support for most workplace regulations. Even when employers view a particular program as objectionable, they have understood that its elimination might be anathema to the general public. As a result, business rhetoric denouncing regulations as "socialistic" or "endangering the foundation of freedom" has given way to attacks on "waste and abuse" and, above all, to an emphasis on costs. In this respect, business lobbies are more closely aligned with the moderate wing of the Republican party.

A second reason why business lobbies have not been pushing for the outright repeal of workplace regulations is that they also can benefit from federal intervention. For example, the same law that imposes costly pension rights for corporate employees also helps establish a more stable work force and generates new sources of investment capital. Reagan administration efforts to weaken affirmative action requirements have received little business support because many companies found that elimination of discrimination expands the labor pool available to them, and many business leaders reject past practices of discrimination on moral grounds. In fact, one survey found that 95 percent of 104 major corporations responded that they would continue their affirmative action plans even if the government abandoned enforcement of goals and time-tables.[5] As a final example, during the debate over social security reform, employer organizations strongly supported preservation of the federal system, no doubt mindful of the pressures they would face to sponsor private arrangements in the absence of social retirement insurance.

Third, employers are not always of one mind when it comes to workplace regulations. In particular, the interests of large and small businesses often diverge. For example, the administration's affirmative action approach is opposed by the National Association of Manufacturers, which tends to reflect the interests of large manufacturing firms, but finds greater favor among small business interests represented by the National Federation of Independent Business. Large firms have implemented formal affirmative action plans, which suit their bureaucratic structures, while small firms object to the costs of these plans.

In contrast to several European nations, no single dominant organization in the United States speaks for business on major policy issues. The number and diversity of employer organizations in America reflect the size and pluralism of our economy. Most prominent of the all-industry organizations are the National Association of Manufacturers and the Chamber of Commerce, while the Business Roundtable and the American Business Conference are also influential. In addition, the Committee for Economic Development and the Business Council emphasize policy statements and the exchange of views between government and business leaders respectively, but do not formally engage in lobbying. Small business is represented by a number of organizations, the largest being the National Federation of Independent Business.

Despite this diversity, one can obtain a sense of the general employers' views concerning workplace regulations by examining the legislative positions of the Chamber of Commerce. The Chamber has supported the Reagan administration's deregulation efforts but has refrained from calling for the repeal of existing legislation. In a summary of its positions on 1985 legislative issues, the Chamber supports legislation that would codify and clarify some of OSHA's recent administrative actions, such as cutting compliance costs and discouraging employee complaints. The Chamber opposes raising the minimum wage and favors establishing a lower minimum wage for youth. It also rejects federal intervention in the policy areas of comparable worth and plant closings, but has gone on record in favor of equal pay for women.[6]

The major national organizations are not the only business players in the lobbying game. Specialized interest groups within the employer community have been increasingly well represented over the past decade by trade and industry associations. Trade associations flocked to Washington in record numbers during the 1970s, reflecting the growing impact of government decisions on industry and the need to influence federal policymakers and program administrators. The number of registered lobbyists plying their trade in Congress has multiplied twelvefold within the past two decades and the vast majority represent business interests. Various workplace policy areas draw the sustained interest of different associations. For instance, the Chemical Manufacturers Association has a vital interest in occupational safety and health.

As long as federal regulation tended to be industry specific—for example, the Interstate Commerce Commission regulating railroads and trucking, or the Civil Aeronautics Board regulating airlines—companies and trade associations had little reason to build political alliances across industrial lines. More recently, however, federal intervention has increasingly cut across industry lines, affecting occupational safety and health, pensions, or employment discrimination, as well as the regulation of environmental pollution and consumer protection. This has led employers to organize around specific issue areas such as unemployment insurance.

The UBA has acted as an advisor and consultant to member corporations in the unemployment compensation area since 1945. While UBA takes no formal policy positions, its experts provide an information clearinghouse, publish bulletins, and engage in research in the unemployment and workers' compensation field that is often the basis for the congressional testimony of employer organizations. To supplement UBA, in 1980 employers established an ad hoc working group to coordinate lobbying efforts. The Chamber of Commerce has been particularly vocal and has set up a council on unemployment compensation within its own organization. Also, representatives of specific industries that have large employee turnover, such as retail or construction, tend to be active in the unemployment insurance area.

This well-organized effort has helped employers tailor the development of the unemployment insurance program to their own interests. Although they have lost the debate over expanding coverage, they have mostly won the debates over benefit adequacy, duration, eligibility, and financing. Employers also generally supported the Reagan administration reforms of the unemployment insurance system in 1981 that cut back federal-state extended benefits substantially.

Another business coalition involves some 150 companies and trade associations that sponsor the Equal Employment Advisory Council (EEAC). Although the EEAC does not lobby on management's behalf, it offers advice to employers on interpretation of affirmative action regulations and provides research ammunition to advance their cause. The council files friend-of-the-court briefs in employment discrimination cases, comments on proposed regulations and legislation on both the federal and state levels, disseminates information, and organizes symposiums.

In contrast to the early sustained employer lobbying on unemployment benefits, the business community missed the opportunity to effectively influence the initial federal regulation of private pensions. By the time the business community entered the fray, the parameters of the 1974 Employee Retirement Income Security Act (ERISA) were well established. Also, the lobbying effort of employers was not well organized and thus less effective than it could have been. Following the Act's passage, business acted to correct the problem of inadequate organization by establishing the ERISA Industry Committee (ERIC), a policymaking and lobbying organization that now represents roughly 100 major companies.

Organized as a forum for the exchange of views on various regulatory and legislative proposals, ERIC presents business views to executive agencies and Congress. The committee has also filed friend-of-the-court briefs in ERISA-related litigation. Since ERIC's establishment, business has been well-prepared to respond to any proposed changes in ERISA. ERIC has also led the recent effort by employers, which has made progress though legislation has not yet passed, to overhaul the single employer plan termination insurance program.

Much of the coordination that occurs among employer associations is informal. As in the unemployment insurance example, ad hoc groups are formed by staff members of those organizations with a direct stake in a particular legislative issue. These groups exchange information and, when appropriate, plan strategy on particular bills. The Chamber of Commerce is often at the center of these coalitions because of its substantial resources, and is an active participant in several dozen "issue strategy groups." In the labor field these include the Washington industrial relations coordinating committee, Washington OSHA group, ERISA breakfast group, benefits overview group, ad hoc immigration reform group, employment and training strategy group, prevailing wage reform group, social security strategy group, and Washington equal employment opportunity group. Although the membership of these groups may change, they play a continuing important role in coordinating the lobbying efforts of hundreds of independent employer organizations.

A coalition approach has proven effective for business interests as has the adoption of more sophisticated lobbying efforts. Employer representatives studied the lobbying methods that had proven effective for their opponents; then, with the help of superior financial resources, employers were able to improve upon these methods. Employer representatives organized popular support, hired consultants, marshalled facts, learned to use the media, made alliances, filled the coffers of political action committees, and applied product marketing techniques to political organizing. They computerized their association membership lists by congressional district and state, and utilized sophisticated telecommunications equipment to keep in touch with their members.

Reagan officials and business lobbyists have been well served by a proliferation of think tanks ranging from mainstream traditional conservative organizations to single issue organizations. These diverse institutions have been the driving force in promoting conservative ideas. They have provided the intellectual underpinnings and reinforced the climate in favor of deregulation, and have supplied a talent pool for the Reagan administration.

The American Enterprise Institute for Public Policy Research (AEI) is the most established conservative think tank. Founded in 1943 as a Republican-oriented research and analytical forum, its reputation was greatly enhanced and its budget swelled following the Nixon and Ford administrations, when it became the major asylum for out-of-office Republican public officials, including former President Gerald Ford, and some neoconservatives who defected from Democratic ranks.[7] By the mid-1970s AEI established itself as the leading center of conservative intellectual thought with an emphasis on providing intellectual backup for conservative activists. Its resources make it possible for AEI to reach out beyond its immediate staff to generate monographs on issues that are in the public domain. These monographs are complemented by published conference proceedings which are made available to policymakers. The magazine *Regulation* has influenced evolving perspectives on market and social regulations.

The institute has been proud of its tolerance of opposing views. However, its analyses and its analysts are almost always right of center. Still, in the 1980s AEI lost favor with committed supply side advocates, who sought uncompromising devotion to their brand of economic analysis. AEI scholars were responsible for the most cogent and penetrating analyses and criticisms of the 1981 economic policies that led to the huge federal budget deficits. Some AEI analysts even raised the fairness issue inherent in the Reagan administration proposals to cut programs in aid of the poor while transfer payments to more affluent groups were left untouched. These criticisms of the Reagan administration excesses testify to the independent thinking that emanates from AEI as long as the views are backed by traditional conservative premises.

In contrast to the moderate AEI, the Cato Institute can be counted on to supply ideas to the far Right. Founded in 1979, Cato advances an essentially libertarian philosophy, and has a marginal but growing influence on the policy debate. Its appeal to business groups assures the institute an expanding budget, and in 1985 it attracted to its staff the former acting chairman of the Reagan administration's Council of Economic Advisors.

Many other conservative think tanks influence the policy debate, but none has had greater influence on the Reagan administration than the Heritage Foundation in championing opposition to government intervention. Established in 1973 with $250,000 from Colorado brewer Joseph Coors, Heritage has expanded rapidly, and in a decade its budget reached that of AEI and it has assumed a leadership position among "movement conservatives."[8] These conservatives criticize the attitudes of "traditional Republicans" as accommodationist. Movement conservatives, in fact, hope to replace the old-time

Republican elite with a new conservative establishment that has unswerving dedication to free market principles.[9]

Heritage prides itself on generating analysis of immediate relevance to the policy debate. It publishes books, reviews, studies, newsletters, digests, monographs, policy papers, and critiques on public policy issues. Copies are routinely distributed to members of Congress, administration officials, agency executives, journalists, and the public, giving Heritage a high profile in the nation's policymaking circles.

Heritage's *Mandate for Leadership,* a massive study detailing policy options for the new administration, was presented to President Reagan ten days after his election. The study received personal praise from President Reagan, and Heritage claimed that almost two-thirds of its 2,000 policy recommendations—many dealing with workplace deregulation—had been or were being adopted by the end of Reagan's first term.[10] Although some of these policies would have been adopted in the absence of its recommendations, Heritage clearly has played an important role in generating, compiling, and advocating conservative ideas that have become administration policy. A *Mandate for Leadership II* was prepared for the second Reagan term; its suggested initiatives included greater White House control of Labor Department appointments, a youth subminimum wage, and a number of proposals to crack down on union corruption and coercion, which Heritage believes are widespread.

The Heritage Foundation has also helped recruit and place movement conservatives in the Reagan administration. Whereas AEI acted as a "government in waiting" for a number of former Republican officials and was able to supply capable and experienced individuals for senior positions, movement conservatives lacked experienced candidates suitable to fill key positions in the first Reagan administration. Since then, movement conservatives have concentrated their efforts on identifying supporters to place in the administration, and the Heritage Foundation has played a central and successful role in finding and then placing these supporters in the administration.[11]

Proregulation Lobbies

Representatives of organized labor, in league with other liberal organizations, have challenged the attempts of the Reagan administration and business lobbies to weaken workplace protections. Locked out of the White House and distanced from most federal executive offices by unfriendly political appointees, labor and its allies have, nevertheless, successfully warded off major legislative changes. Proposals to curtail wages on federal contracts, relax eight-hour-day rules, establish a dual subminimum wage for teenagers, punish picket line violators, and weaken laws governing equal employment opportunity all failed during the first four years of the Reagan administration and are not likely to succeed during the balance of the second term.

The success of regulation advocates in defeating these initiatives has been partly due to the Reagan administration concentrating its efforts on other issues, but it is also due to its friends in key congressional committees. Success in blocking legislation requires only that one committee, or even a subcommittee, reject a proposal. While President Reagan had his way in passing his macroeconomic program, administration labor-related bills have been blocked even in the Republican controlled Senate. The Senate Labor and Human Resources Committee, chaired by Senator Orrin G. Hatch of Utah, had a nine to seven Republican majority in the 97th, 98th, and 99th Congresses, but because two moderate Republicans—Lowell P. Weicker, Jr. and Robert T. Stafford—frequently defected from the administration camp, the committee opposed measures that would have undermined worker protections. Liberal Democrats dominate the House Education and Labor Committee, making legislative sledding for the Reagan administration even rougher on the House side.

Organized labor has attempted to preserve its dwindling political influence by imitating the business coalitions and creating internal unity before lobbying the Hill. Labor renewed its alliances with established civil rights, women's, religious, environmental, and other organizations that had been strained during the Vietnam war. There had also been conflict with these groups in the area of equal employment opportunity, because the seniority rights of white male union members often clashed with the aspirations of female and minority workers. Similarly, environmentalists and labor had parted company over the relative importance of jobs and clean air or clean water.

Since 1981 the sharp cuts in domestic programs and administration proposals to curtail federal responsibilities have helped reunify labor, religious, environmental, educational, and civil rights organizations. Coalitions have formed around specific policy areas; as an example, the periodic threats to cut social security benefits or tighten eligibility requirements for disability insurance have drawn together organizations representing the elderly. This "gray" lobby includes the multi-million-member American Association of Retired Persons as well as the National Council of Senior Citizens, a group created by labor during the battle to enact medicare in the 1960s. Although they sometimes disagree over preferred action on specific issues, these two organizations and a score of related groups have remained steadfast in their attempts to preserve established benefit levels, regulate private pension plans, and secure reauthorization of the Older Americans Act which provides various forms of assistance and protections to able older workers in the labor market. In the debate on the fiscal 1986 budget, Reagan administration proposals to freeze social security cost-of-living increases led to the formation of a broad coalition to protect social security. In the face of this strong opposition, the Reagan administration withdrew its proposals.

In the equal employment field, the Leadership Conference on Civil Rights, an umbrella organization founded in 1950 which now includes 165 groups, has continued to fight for the enforcement of affirmative action agreements. It has successfully blocked Reagan administration nominees opposed to federal intervention aimed at eliminating employment discrimination. Advance work to build broad consensus on issues and bipartisan support has been the key to their success.[12]

The AFL-CIO frequently pulls together groups with common interests for specific legislative battles. These single-issue groups operate on a low budget, often rely heavily on AFL-CIO contributions and staff, and are frequently housed in its headquarters in Washington. For example, labor responded to proposals to lower the minimum wage for youth both with its own lobbying effort and by organizing the Youth Coalition for Jobs and Fair Wages. The coalition represents 40 youth groups, including labor's own Frontlash.

The AFL-CIO may identify causes it supports or opposes, but it cannot always command an equal commitment from affiliated unions. Labor lobbyists are often confronted with the differing priorities and agendas of unions they represent. The labor federation endorsement of specific protection legislation does not commit its affiliates to support the proposals. Driven by the immediate interests of their members, the representatives of the 96 national or international unions may support some causes more fervently than others or even oppose parts of the federation's legislative agenda.

The comparable worth issue is a good example of unions' differing priorities. The AFL-CIO has endorsed the concept of comparable worth, as have a number of its affiliates, particularly those with a substantial number of current or potential women members. The public employee unions have initiated and joined efforts to win pay equity legislation and have won some favorable court decisions. Other unions, particularly those with few women or in declining industries, have more pressing concerns and little direct interest in this issue.

In contrast to the plethora of think tanks, small and big, that generated ideas to support retrenchments of governmental regulation of the workplace, the research support for proponents of intervention has been sadly lacking in the 1980s. It seems that like the Supreme Court, researchers in academia and think tanks follow the latest election returns. This is not just a function of crass materialism; sometimes changing fashions dominate research just like the length of dresses or width of ties. Analysts who were eager to call for federal intervention to regulate the workplace in the 1960s and 1970s and marshalled the evidence to support their beliefs displayed no less enthusiasm in arguing that federal regulation can be ineffective or even counterproductive.

In the 1960s and 1970s liberal legislators could count on the Brookings Institution to provide intellectual support for their agendas. Like the AEI which provided a haven for conservative social scientists exiled from policy positions during periods of Democratic administrations, Brookings provided similar facilities for Democratic officeholders during Republican administrations. During the late 1970s and 1980s the Brookings researchers, with some notable exceptions, moved closer to the AEI. On many issues the products of the two organizations were hardly distinguishable. Brookings Institution products (as distinguished from ad hoc statements by individual staff members) are normally not responsive to the needs of policymakers. For example, the *Brookings Papers on Economic Activity*, the major periodic publication of its economic staff, is highly technical and is clearly intended for the consumption of trained economists. Although its formal purpose is to concentrate on "live" issues, the products of the publication are rarely cited in congressional debate.

The Urban Institute, established by President Johnson as a think tank to fashion cures for urban ills, managed to retain a more liberal position. Funded by the Ford and other foundations, the Urban Institute staff produced the most even-handed analytic studies of the Reagan administration record.[13]

Bereft of resources, the numerous smaller organizations and think tanks on the Democratic left were not in a position to support solid research that would support their contentions. Academics seeking support or outlets for publications or support for their research found that analysis favoring federal regulations did not receive friendly reception. Indeed, in some cases OMB or other federal agencies discouraged investigation of the impact of federal initiatives, and federal funds earmarked for research were sharply curtailed. Ideology dictated that federal intervention was not justified and there was, therefore, no need to investigate the results. The Equal Employment Opportunity Commission and some Labor Department agencies ceased collecting data that would provide analysts the means to evaluate the impact of the regulations they were supposed to implement. Presumably if the data were necessary, individuals in the private sector should find the means to collect, analyze, and disseminate the information.

Supporters of federal workplace regulations were not left without any information. The Freedom of Information Act required federal agencies to release some data, although sometimes at a cost beyond the means of individual analysts. But investigative reporters working for affluent media sources could make use of such data sources. The separation of powers also helped. Congress has its own means of obtaining information independent of the cooperation of executive agencies. Congressional committees and individual members can always turn to the General Accounting Office with its vast resources or to the Office of Technology Assessment (OTA) and the Congressional Research Service to obtain information about federal programs and evaluate their impact. As just one example, in

1985 OTA published a detailed study of occupational illness and injury.[14]

Smaller research organizations also continued to function. For example, the Center on Budget and Policy Priorities focuses its efforts on defending programs that aid the poor. By the mid-1980s, however, there remained only a few small liberal think tanks devoted to the analysis and evaluation of federal programs that are of immediate relevance to policy debates in Congress. Moreover, there is not a liberal equivalent to the Heritage Foundation. No proregulation think tank possesses the resources for churning out quick analyses suitable for congressional consumption.

Money Talks

Advocates of deregulation also enjoy the important advantage of superior financial resources. In recent national elections, business and conservative groups raised more financial support for their candidates than did labor or liberal organizations, and the gap is widening. In the early 1970s, union political action committees (PACs) outnumbered their corporate counterparts by two to one; by 1984 business PACs had achieved a six-to-one advantage. Over the same period, business PAC contributions, including corporate and association funds, have grown to represent three-fifths of all contributions to political candidates, while labor's share has shrunk from one-half to one-fourth.[15]

The importance of PAC contributions to candidates has increased significantly in recent years as the cost of running a campaign has risen sharply, and the funds raised by PACs have multiplied. In the 1984 elections, 38 percent of the contributions to House candidates and 19 percent of the contributions to Senate candidates were from PACs. Some 186 House candidates received more than half their money from PACs, while 17 Senate candidates received more than one-third of their money from PACs.[16] Such contributions offer no guarantee on how a particular candidate will ultimately decide to vote on an issue, particularly when contributions are accepted from a number of different sources, but in this environment PAC contributions are bound to have an effect. The greater financial resources of groups favoring deregulation are an important political advantage.

The Public as Umpire

There is a check on the amount of influence lobbyists and PACs can assert, however—all public officials must eventually stand for reelection. Therefore, the needs and desires of the people they represent cannot be overlooked. President Reagan rediscovered this essential fact in the battle over cutting social security. In addition, public opinion on workplace regulations can be volatile. For example, public opinion on the unemployment insurance program responds rather directly to the national unemployment rate. During the 1982 recession, employers could not stem the tide in favor of the extension of benefits, and the Reagan administration (prodded by Congress) could not ignore the tremendous public concern about the high levels of unemployment and the needs of millions who had exhausted their regular and extended benefits. Similarly, mine disasters or occasional accidents in plants producing toxic products periodically reawaken public concern over workplace health and safety and reaffirm the need for rigorous enforcement of safety precautions in the workplace.

The clash between regulation and deregulation forces in Washington will continue to reflect movements in national public opinion. Perceptions that deregulatory excesses violate the public interest could quickly swing public opinion back in favor of a stronger federal role in the workplace. In the meanwhile, existing public support for the basic structure of workplace regulations will constrain public officials from a wholehearted endorsement of the ideological agenda of movement conservatives.

Part 2

On the Job

3
Gaining Access to Work

Most people work for pay at some time in their lives. Some, however, are better equipped to compete in the labor market than others, either because they meet an employer's requirements, possess superior information about how to obtain employment, or because they were fortunate enough to have parents who could help them with their education and job search. Individuals frequently underinvest in their own training because of a lack of motivation, inadequate information about job opportunities, or because they have insufficient resources to prepare for gainful employment. Private markets also tend to underinvest in employee training, focusing instead on meeting employers' specific needs. By providing assistance to prepare people for work and helping to match workers with job openings, the federal government promotes not only the welfare of individuals, but enhances the economic efficiency of the nation.

Federally supported work-related training is a vast, albeit unintegrated, system that begins with preschool instruction and extends beyond graduate study to encompass the retraining of adult workers. State and local governments carry the brunt of the costs of equipping youth with the basic educational tools needed to compete successfully in the labor market, while the federal government concentrates on providing equal access to productive work. Federal employment and training programs offer individuals who fail or have been failed by mainstream institutions a second chance to adapt to the demands of prospective employers.

An additional federal concern is facilitating the smooth operation of labor markets. Most job seekers successfully find work through a variety of formal and informal means, but

35

those who do not often face economic hardship. Employers also suffer losses for want of qualified applicants. While the availability of jobs and the demand for workers are the major determinants of access to work, a federally supported labor exchange fills gaps left by other labor market intermediaries.

Throughout much of its history, the United States has depended on immigrants to complement the labor supply. When jobs become scarce, however, as they have in recent years, various groups pressure the federal government to restrict the flow of labor from abroad to improve work opportunities for Americans.

Preparation for Work

Preparation and training for work, which begins in childhood and continues throughout life, takes place in the home, schools, workplaces, military services, and through self-study. New workers entering the labor force with only general knowledge and skills require specific job-related instruction, which is most often acquired through on-the-job training. In many cases vocational deficiencies are overcome through additional formal training. Later, employees may require further classroom training to enhance promotional opportunities, adapt to new technologies, or acquire new skills when their current skills become obsolete. Such training is frequently obtained through employer-subsidized educational programs. These opportunities for occupational advancement, however, require that an individual be employed, and many jobs require formal pre-employment schooling. Adequate preparation for work is, therefore, a crucial determinant of future labor market success.

The General Education Route

Since the Jacksonian revolution of the 1830s when the battle for "free" education was won, government efforts to facilitate work-related training have focused primarily on the schools. Education, considered both inherently good and a ladder for upward mobility, has been the main track for bringing the children of immigrants and farmers into the mainstream of industrial society. Today, mastery of the three R's is an indispensable component in work preparation, and a high school diploma is a prerequisite for most jobs. Of the 75 percent who complete a high school education or its equivalent, three of every five enter college, and about one-half of those graduate (Figure 1).

Employers may pick and choose from a diverse pool of applicants to meet their labor needs. Although basic compe-

Figure 1. School retention rates

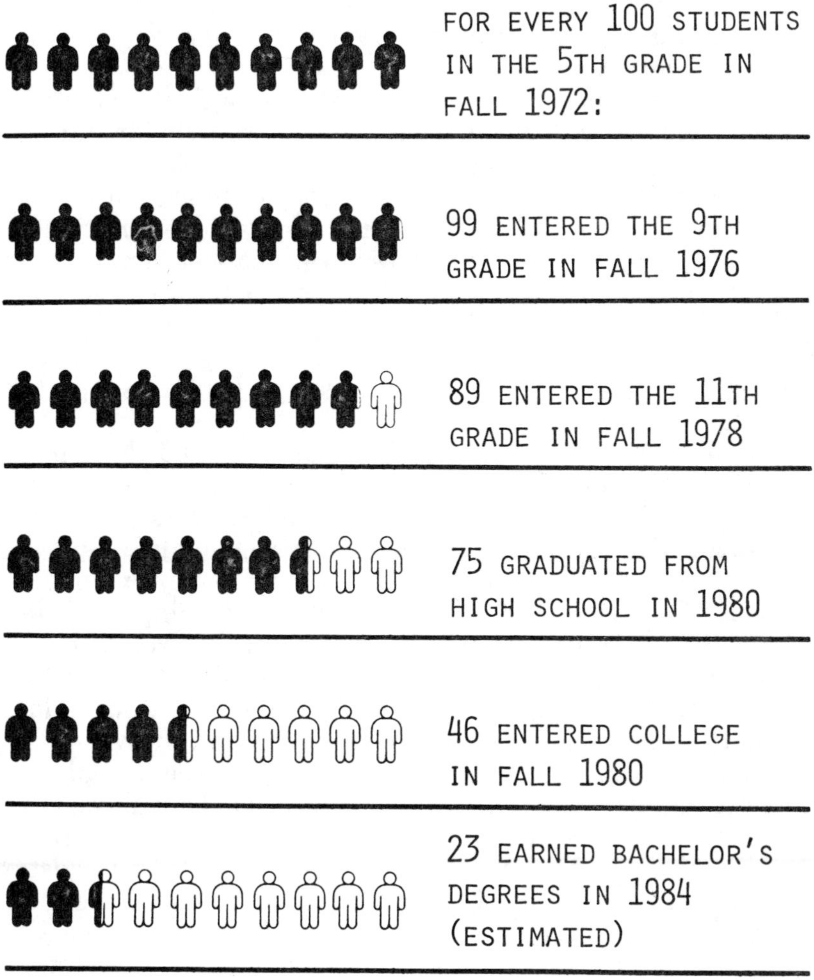

FOR EVERY 100 STUDENTS IN THE 5TH GRADE IN FALL 1972:

99 ENTERED THE 9TH GRADE IN FALL 1976

89 ENTERED THE 11TH GRADE IN FALL 1978

75 GRADUATED FROM HIGH SCHOOL IN 1980

46 ENTERED COLLEGE IN FALL 1980

23 EARNED BACHELOR'S DEGREES IN 1984 (ESTIMATED)

Source: National Center for Education Statistics.

tency and some specialized training is sufficient to perform most jobs, employers tend to insist on credentials such as diplomas and degrees, leaving the deficiently educated at an increasing disadvantage in today's job market.

Responsibility for providing elementary and secondary education remains primarily a state and local function. Since 1965, however, the federal government has augmented the funds of school districts that lack sufficient resources, facilities, and personnel to provide equal educational opportunity to disadvantaged children. For example, the Headstart program prepares disadvantaged preschoolers to compete with more affluent children.

Preparation for many technical, managerial, and professional occupations requires access to postsecondary institutions. For motivated students, federal programs reduce financial barriers to the attainment of longer education through grants, loans, and work-study programs. The emphasis is on equalizing opportunity among racial and socioeconomic groups so that access to higher education is not determined solely by the ability to pay. Special programs for disadvantaged students offer remedial instruction and tutoring, personal counseling, and career development services. Federal support for education is also provided through the Veterans Administration, direct aid to colleges and universities, and through tax incentives for employer-provided education programs.

Evaluations of federal support for education show positive results. Chapter I of the Education Consolidation and Improvement Act (formerly Title I of the Elementary and Secondary Education Act) is credited with narrowing disparities in achievement between poor and nonpoor children, and evaluations of the program conducted for the U.S. Department of Education found significant gains in achievement and educational attainment among low-income children over time.[1] Federal aid appears to have had a cumulative beneficial effect on the cognitive development and educational advancement of children from low-income households, and thus on their future employability. Researchers have also found that Headstart children are more likely than controls to graduate from high school, enroll in college, and obtain a self-supporting job.[2]

Federal student aid programs have also been successful in improving access to a college education during the past two decades. The federal government is (outside the family) the major contributor to student aid and in 1983 provided almost 80 percent of the total financial assistance available to college students.[3] Four of every ten of the nation's 12.5 million full- and part-time college students benefited from one or more federal programs, which covered one-third of the educational expenses incurred by all students.[4] From 1968 to 1978 the enrollment of minorities at the college level more than tripled—from 456,000 to 1,589,000. Federal affirmative action programs have also opened doors to significant numbers of women and minorities who have begun to pursue careers in fields such as medicine, law, engineering, and business that have traditionally been dominated by white males.

Federal aid to students has declined during the Reagan administration and eligibility requirements have been tightened. Adjusted for inflation, the federal student aid awarded in 1984-85 was almost 15 percent less than in 1980-81. This financial retrenchment resulted in a drop in the number of middle-income students enrolling in private institutions. A combination of reduced assistance and lax enforcement of federal affirmative action efforts has contributed to a sharp overall decline in low-income student enrollment.[5]

The Vocational Route

While high schools cater primarily to the needs of college-bound students, not every individual has the interest, ability, or resources to pursue a college education. Although two of every three high school graduates enroll in a postsecondary institution, nearly one in four enters the job market upon graduation.[6] To prepare this group for the labor market, secondary schools offer occupational training as well as general academic training.

Vocational education courses, often narrowly associated with "shop," offer training in more than 150 occupations, usually combined with some instruction in how to find and keep a job. Currently, more than 70 percent of all high school graduates are likely to have taken one or more vocational courses.[7] Many of these students continue their vocational program with more specific technical training in postsecondary schools. Many adults also attend technical schools or community colleges to upgrade their skills or retrain for new employment.

Federal support for vocational education dates to the passage of the Smith-Hughes Act of 1917. A response to perceived skill shortages, the Act was designed to stimulate support for vocational education through grants to the states. Emphasis was initially placed on agricultural education, home economics, and trade and industrial education. The Vocational Act of 1963 expanded the scope of these programs and increased federal support. Later amendments to the Act sharply changed federal policy, emphasizing the employment needs of various population groups rather than the skill needs of employers. The goal of vocational education remained the promotion of occupational training for all students, but it was also seen as a mechanism to overcome the barriers faced by disadvantaged students in competing effectively in the labor market. The amendments singled out the disadvantaged and the handicapped for special concern, reallocated funds from the secondary to postsecondary level—reflecting the need for more sophisticated skills—and encouraged promotion of cooperative efforts between employers and the schools.

In 1984 Congress strengthened vocational education by passing the Carl D. Perkins Vocational Education Act, a comprehensive revision of the 1963 legislation. The Act emphasized programs for underserved populations, prohibited sex stereotyping in occupational counseling, and emphasized program improvement at the local level. Congress chose to concentrate federal efforts on expanding vocational education opportunities for the disadvantaged, an area too often neglected by the states.[8] Congress appropriated funds for the priorities it set and left support of mainstream vocational training programs to state and local governments. The federal contribution of $831 million in 1985 accounted for about a tenth of total state and local outlays for vocational education.

This congressional action was a repudiation of Reagan administration attempts to scale back federal support and involvement in vocational education. The administration, questioning program benefits and claiming that federal efforts to increase access to vocational training for the disadvantaged had failed, had recommended a sharp reduction in funding and consolidation of vocational education into a state-administered block grant.[9] This proposal would have virtually eliminated federal involvement in vocational education except for the provision of funds.

These administration claims have lent support to research questioning the value of vocational education, although reliable comparisons between general or academic and vocational programs are difficult to come by. Vocational students tend to be below average in socioeconomic status and verbal ability,[10] and many find employment in occupations other than those in which they were trained, thus losing some of the value of their education. There is also considerable enrollment overlap between vocational and nonvocational programs.

The occupational distribution of vocational and nonvocational graduates differs significantly. A survey of 1980 high school graduates found that two years after graduation twice as many male vocational graduates as nonvocational graduates were working in craft occupations, while only half as many male vocational graduates were working in professional, technical, clerical, or service jobs. Sixty-one percent of female vocational graduates worked in clerical occupations, compared to 37 percent of nonvocational graduates, while female vocational graduates were underrepresented in professional, technical, sales, and service occupations.[11] Any relative earnings advantage initially enjoyed by male vocational graduates entering the craft occupations appears to be offset by the entry of their nonvocational counterparts into white collar jobs with better opportunities for advancement. While limited job opportunities for female nonvocational graduates also give vocational graduates an initial advantage, it is offset by limited promotion and on-the-job training opportunities in clerical occupations.[12]

The most important criterion for judging vocational education is whether its graduates are better off than they would have been in the absence of such training. Because these students go from secondary school directly into the job market, any assistance in securing and holding a job is beneficial. The availability of vocational courses also encourages some students who might otherwise drop out to remain in school. Considering the high jobless rates prevailing among youth, any effort to open employment opportunities for them deserves continued public support.

Apprenticeship

Apprenticeship, in one form or another, dates back to the guild days. Before the industrial revolution, children were indentured to master craftsmen who fed, clothed, and housed them. The advent of mass production led to the abandonment of apprenticeship in most manufacturing jobs. Current apprenticeship programs provide a route for non-college-bound high school graduates to gain access to the highest-paid manual jobs. Through a combination of classroom and on-the-job training lasting for as long as five years, participants receive progressive wage increases as their skill levels are enhanced. Apprentice-trained workers have portable skills which increase their employability within an occupation.

Although there are a growing number of registered non-union apprenticeship programs, formal programs are concentrated in the heavily unionized industries and trades. Construction accounts for six of every ten apprentices. Of the ten occupations with the highest apprenticeship enrollment, seven are in construction; the other three programs train machinery tool and die makers and automotive mechanics. Altogether, 60 percent of all apprentices are found in these ten occupations.[13]

Federal involvement in the apprenticeship system dates back to the passage of the National Apprenticeship (Fitzgerald) Act of 1937. Its goal was to set minimum standards for occupations requiring skill training. Administered by the Bureau of Apprenticeship and Training (BAT) in the U.S. Department of Labor, the program promotes apprenticeship through technical assistance to unions and employers, who determine their requirements and administer their programs within the framework of broad federal and state standards. Currently, 30 states, Puerto Rico, the Virgin Islands, and the District of Columbia have established state apprenticeship councils to register qualified programs, monitor performance, and certify program graduates. In mid-1985 there were some 250,000 registered apprentices who comprised about 2 percent of the total U.S. craft and kindred workers.

In an attempt to reduce discrimination against minorities and women in the skilled trades and to promote equal opportunity for entry into these high-paying blue collar jobs, the federal government required unions and contractors to initiate affirmative action hiring plans in the construction industry. As a key entry port for several craft occupations, apprenticeship programs received significant federal attention, including the establishment of apprenticeship information centers and outreach programs. During the 1970s, pressure from women's organizations prompted the Labor Department to apply affirmative action goals to female apprentices as well.

Federal efforts to improve the representation of minorities and women in apprenticeship programs have paid off. When the Civil Rights Act was passed in 1964, only an estimated 2.5 percent of apprentices were minorities, compared with nearly one in five two decades later.[14] Female apprentices comprised 6 percent of all program participants in 1982; there were hardly any in 1964. Future progress will be difficult to determine, however, because the Office of Management and Budget has terminated the public surveys and reports needed to produce and disseminate information on female and minority representation in apprenticeship programs.[15] OMB claimed that the government was making no use of the data and that its intent was to eliminate a burden on employers. In addition, Congress cut the BAT budget from $15.1 million in 1981 to $12.6 million in 1985, a 29 percent cut after adjusting for inflation.

Critics cite a number of problems with the apprenticeship system. The most persistent criticism concerns the inadequate number of craft workers who receive apprenticeship training. Craft unions attempt to restrict the supply of skilled workers in an effort to maintain their bargaining strength, while employers primarily train workers for the specialized tasks required in their particular operations. Because employers are concerned with maintaining flexibility in assigning responsibilities that cross craft lines, they have limited interest in comprehensive training in a particular craft. During the 1970s the average number of apprenticeship completions was roughly one-fifth the average annual increase in craft and kindred workers. Since not all skilled workers require extensive training, this one-to-five ratio between apprentice-trained skilled workers and other craft workers may be adequate to meet demand.

Military Training

The nation's military is a major provider of work-related education and training. It offers an attractive alternative to civilian employment to about one-third of all non-college-bound male high school graduates. Although a high school diploma or equivalent is generally preferred, the armed services provide remedial training for those who are deficiently educated. To meets its needs for a supply of skilled personnel to maintain the nation's defense, the military has developed basic and advanced training and education programs in a broad variety of occupations, ranging from auto mechanics to astrophysics.

The military education and training system is a massive $9 billion operation. Altogether, more than a quarter million recruits will participate in education and training courses in 1986. In addition to active duty trainees, the Defense Department will provide varying amounts of support to an average of 106,000 college students through ROTC programs, and to an additional 3,600 persons enrolled in health profession training programs in exchange for future military service. The Defense Department also trains reservists, with an anticipated average training load of 48,000 in 1986.[16]

Military personnel policy is characterized by a closed promotion system with almost no lateral entry. The services recruit into entry-level grades and provide intensive job-specific training. Advanced officer rank may be granted to those with professional skills, such as doctors, other health professionals, lawyers and chaplains, and to a limited number of enlisted personnel entering occupations requiring specialized skills such as musicians. For the most part, however, training is done the military way.

Initial specialized skill training prepares military personnel for a particular job assignment and serves as the foundation for future advanced training for those who enlist for longer service. Given the large number of military occupations, skill training is very diverse and represents the largest part of the military training program. Personnel who sign up for four to six years receive more training up front, allowing the military to capitalize on its training investment. Military job skill training is much narrower than in the civilian sector, however, and prepares an individual to perform a specific task, not to master a skill.

Enlisted personnel usually advance in their skill areas through job experience or on-the-job training. There are also a variety of programs designed to develop officers and groom them for positions of high responsibility. Less comprehensive professional development programs are open to enlisted personnel. These include leadership training for enlisted noncommissioned officers and degree completion programs for selected enlisted and officer personnel. Because advanced study is necessary to help military leaders keep up with changing technology and retain talented leadership in the career force, the services support a system of military schools, cooperative degree programs, and a number of voluntary education programs.

The prime purpose of military training and education efforts is, of course, to meet defense needs, but because turnover is high, it is a matter of vital public concern that military training be useful to veterans returning to civilian life. Approximately 90 percent of the armed forces personnel are employed in occupations that have some civilian counterparts.[17] The transferability potential is obvious for aircraft and vehicle mechanics, medical and dental technicians, and air traffic controllers. Electronics training, particularly important in the Navy and the Air Force, also has many useful civilian applications.

The transferability of military training and work experience ultimately rests on the availability of civilian jobs. Veterans' employment is also influenced by employers' judgments about the quality of military training and their perceptions about the transferability of veterans' work experience. There are many impediments to making the jump from military to civilian life that are unrelated to an individual's capabilities. Most civilian employers follow the military practice of promoting on the basis of seniority. This practice may bar long-term service personnel from transferring their skills into civilian jobs with commensurate levels of responsibility.

Several studies on the effect of military training on subsequent civilian earnings have found that veterans employed in civilian jobs where they were able to use their military-acquired skills earned more than those who could not do so.[18] If the occupational preferences of new recruits receive greater consideration, more veterans can be expected to obtain employment in areas in which they have been trained. The returns to society from military training would then increase.

Even those veterans who do not directly use their military training may gain from the military experience. Many employers consider completion of a military obligation an indicator of general suitability for employment. Veterans are screened mentally and physically before entering the service and they are taught discipline and good work habits. Employers are, therefore, relieved of some of the costs associated with screening applicants when hiring veterans. There is evidence that this "certification" effect works to the particular advantage of minorities.[19] However, substantial pay increases for enlisted personnel in the early 1980s have meant that better-educated individuals are attracted to the military, thus foreclosing enlistment opportunities for the deficiently educated.

Second Chance Opportunities

Many individuals face ongoing difficulty competing in the labor market both in good times and in periods of economic downturn. Some have failed or been failed by the schools, and lack even the minimal requirements for suitable employment. Others face racial and/or sex discrimination, inadequate information about job openings, or geographical barriers that thwart job search efforts.

Employers have shown considerable reluctance to hire undereducated workers with a history of unemployment, assuming that their productivity is too low to justify the costs of employment. Even generous federal subsidies have found few takers in private industry.

Consequently, it has fallen to the government to enhance the employability of these individuals through federally funded employment and training programs, targeted directly to the labor market problems of the poor and deficiently educated. Through improved access to work, these persons have a chance to lead productive lives, and society as a whole benefits.

Employment and Training

The antipoverty efforts of the 1960s spawned a wide variety of employment and training programs. Recognizing that workers at the margin of the labor force, including a growing number of entrants with minimal or no job skills, required assistance to enable them to find sustained employment, Congress funded basic adult education programs and training in a variety of occupations along with supportive services and training allowances.

By the early 1970s there was a clear need to consolidate and coordinate these efforts which had emerged in piecemeal fashion during the previous decade. The response was the Comprehensive Employment and Training Act (CETA) of 1973 which provided for a federal-state-local partnership and allowed increased flexibility at the local level to develop employment and training services responsive to local labor market needs.

In the 1970s, job creation in the public and nonprofit sectors became a major component of employment and training programs, providing 750,000 job slots at its peak in 1978. Individuals who experienced difficulty obtaining employment in the private sector, either because they lacked the attributes valued by employers or because jobs were scarce, were provided a means of self-support. Congress has allocated additional funds to employers during the summer months to employ as many as one million jobless youth and pay them the federal minimum wage.

Since 1981 federal involvement in the employment and training system has been drastically reduced. Employment and training outlays, in 1986 dollars, fell from $11.2 billion in 1981 to $5.6 billion in 1986. The character of the programs has also been transformed by a shift of emphasis to the labor market needs of employers, rather than to the needs of the poor and the unemployed. The Job Training Partnership Act (JTPA), which replaced CETA in 1983, puts greater emphasis on private sector placement, lower training costs, and state responsibility. Stipends are no longer available for participants undergoing training, making it more difficult for the poor to take advantage of training opportunities. Public job creation has been eliminated. Responsibility for program administration has been largely turned over to the states with little federal monitoring or control. Federal technical assistance, program evaluation, and research have been virtually eliminated, while follow-up data collection has been blocked by the Office of Management and Budget's refusal to allocate funds for that purpose. The use of a placement-rate standard of performance directs resources away from those most in need of training to those who require little assistance. In brief, federal employment and training initiatives channeled resources away from those in greatest need who had been the target of federal efforts since the mid-1960s.

Considerable research has been conducted to assess the effectiveness of the CETA programs, many of which have been continued under JTPA. For the most part, the employment and training programs appear to have been reasonable public investments. A 1981 comprehensive review of evaluation data estimated that each dollar spent on institutional training resulted in a $1.14 increase in income per participant. Many individuals who received training for short durations averaging 22 weeks were qualified only for low-wage jobs. Longer-term training for occupations requiring greater skill increased the payoff substantially. Those enrolled for more than 40 weeks had more than six times the earnings gains of trainees enrolled for only 11 to 20 weeks. The resources available to training administrators invariably have been too limited to permit the luxury of longer enrollment to any but a small proportion of participants.

On-the-job training with private employers, with the program paying one-half the wage for a limited period of time, resulted in a 16 percent greater increase in income for enrollees than for comparison groups. Since enrollees were working and producing while earning and learning, the return to society included their training period output as well as the post-training income gain. Assuming that the output during the subsidized training period was worth one-half the wages paid to enrollees, the benefit-cost ratio was 2.3 to 1. The primary problem with on-the-job training programs was persuading employers to participate. When they did, they tended to be selective and particularly reluctant to employ youth, who accounted for only 2 percent of on-the-job trainees.[20]

Participants in public service employment programs, on average, experienced 7 percent greater post-enrollment earnings than those in control groups. The benefit-cost ratio again depends on valuation of the output of the average workers. Work experience enrollees, on the other hand—mostly youth doing rudimentary work—actually had average post-enrollment earnings that were lower than their comparison groups. Yet carefully run projects combining work experience with basic education yielded beneficial results.[21]

The Job Corps, which provides skill training in residential settings, has an outstanding record with young people from the most disadvantaged backgrounds, yielding an estimated $1.39 return on the dollar.[22] After early difficulties, the program is now run by contractors who are under considerable pressure to produce results and minimize costs in order to retain the contract.

Participants in employment and training programs benefit from a variety of services, the importance of which cannot be separately measured by post-training income. The record in providing basic education is particularly encouraging. Ninety hours of adult instruction typically results in a 1.5 year achievement gain in reading ability and a 1.0 year gain in math.[23] Computer-assisted instruction, pioneered by Job Corps centers, produces gain rates twice as high as this. Job-search training significantly increases job finding rates. The English as a second language (ESL) program also has had high payoffs. People with substantial job skills which they are unable to use because of language deficiencies can find jobs using their skills after a short low-cost ESL program.[24]

Work and Welfare

Welfare recipients face perhaps the greatest obstacles to labor force entry—inadequate job skills, little work experience, and the demonstrated reluctance of employers to hire them. These impediments are compounded by the high marginal costs to welfare recipients when they do find a job (they are denied Medicaid and other services). Yet, these individuals are not unable or unwilling to work, nor do they languish forever on public assistance.[25] For many recipients, welfare is a temporary means of weathering personal or financial crises.

Beginning in the early 1960s, the federal government funded a series of work and training programs for welfare recipients with the dual aim of fostering economic independence for those on welfare and relieving the nation's taxpayers of the welfare burden. The Work Incentive (WIN) program, enacted as part of the 1967 amendments to the Social Security Act, was designed to provide institutional training, including basic education, along with child care and other supportive services. The impact of the program was limited because appropriations never matched congressional rhetoric and because of the scarce availability of jobs for welfare recipients who lack skills and education. In 1984 the WIN program registered about 1,015,763 welfare recipients, of whom about 20 percent received structured job search services. Of these registrants,

354,396 found unsubsidized employment, although only one job in four was directly the result of a WIN placement. Moreover, those who did obtain jobs frequently earned too little to remove their need for some continued public assistance.

In 1981 the Reagan administration proposed elimination of the WIN program, substituting reliance on workfare—mandatory job search and other employment related activities for AFDC recipients—in its place. The administration's objective was to separate work and welfare, assuming that those who are able to work can find jobs and support themselves. This approach would have limited AFDC to persons unable to work because of responsibility for preschool children or physical or mental handicaps. Workfare is intended primarily to deter welfare dependency as an alternative to work by mandating work in an amount determined by the benefits received.

Congress has allowed, but has not endorsed, the workfare approach and it continued to fund the WIN program at a reduced appropriation of $267 million in 1985. States have shown limited enthusiasm for implementing workfare programs, however, finding it difficult to develop meaningful work projects without considerably increasing costs. The states have viewed workfare more as a supplemental activity to provide employability development and limited work experience, much like the WIN work experience component which the administration has repeatedly proposed to eliminate.[26]

Experience from the supported work program during the 1970s demonstrates that provision of a supervised job for AFDC recipients can by itself remove barriers to employment.[27] Such findings lent credibility to efforts by the Nixon, Ford, and Carter administrations to combine work with welfare. Given that the jobs available to AFDC recipients are predominantly in the low-wage sector and normally fail to lift them out of poverty, many beneficiaries cannot become totally independent regardless of their work effort. For them, work and welfare must be combined to ensure self-sufficiency.

A Labor Exchange

Employment and training efforts are effective only if job opportunities are easily available. Though employer and employee eventually find each other, the loss of income and production—not to mention the toll in human deprivation—

has led to the establishment of intermediaries to facilitate the process of matching workers with job openings. Such intermediaries may be public agencies, nonprofit organizations, or for-profit firms supported by users. Private labor exchange services are normally restricted to job-ready or highly qualified workers and not all workers and employers can afford these services. There is a need for an effective and free public employment service to match job seekers with job openings.

The Wagner-Peyser Act of 1933 established a national network of state-run, federally financed, employment service offices to match workers seeking employment with job openings. These offices also provide referrals to supportive services, counseling, and testing. An effective labor exchange agency bringing together employers and jobseekers, as envisioned by the designers of the 1933 law, has yet to be realized. From July 1983 to June 1984, local offices registered over 15 million job seekers, of whom 3.7 million were placed in jobs. Nationally, the employment service fills less than 8 percent of all job openings. By 1985 the employment service budget amounted to $830 million—less than 90 percent of 1981 levels adjusted for inflation.

The public employment service has been in the position of having to beg for clients. It must compete with private employment agencies and high school and college placement offices. The employment service's constant challenge has been to justify taxpayer support in the face of this extensive competition. Several factors contribute to its lackluster performance. First, employers tend to hire those applicants recommended by friends, relatives, and employees, or to rely on union hiring halls, civil service examinations, or advertisements. Most job seekers, therefore, follow these routes to find employment. Second, employers may hesitate to list vacancies with the employment service because the agency is not as likely to ignore equal employment opportunity rules as private agencies. Third, the employment service's labor market intermediary mission has been diluted by various compliance functions.

Job openings listed with the employment service tend to be in nonprofessional and low-skill occupations. The General Accounting Office found that in 1981 the hourly wages of jobs filled by the employment service averaged about $1 above the $3.35 minimum wage—half of the jobs listed paid less than $4.00 an hour. Job security and chances for advancement were limited because 40 percent of the jobs were expected to last no more than 150 days and a large percentage lasted as little as three days. Because they assume that few qualified applicants are registered with the employment service, most employers use alternative sources for recruitment. Jobseekers registered with the local offices in 1981 were often deficiently educated and had little work experience. Unemployment insurance claimants, required by law to register for work, constituted 24 percent of the total applicants and were among the least likely to be placed, partly because they tended to be over-qualified for the jobs registered with the employment service, while others may have had continuing recall rights to previous employment.[28]

Increased business involvement would provide greater stability for the employment service. To encourage employers to register vacancies with the employment service, it must have a record of filling orders promptly with job-ready workers. As the focus of employment service activities shifts toward satisfying the needs of the business community, hard-to-employ workers may not be served adequately. This will prevent the employment service from fulfilling its function of serving all applicants.

Regulating Immigration

Although access to jobs for American workers is primarily contingent on their preparation for work, employment opportunities are also affected by the influx of workers through immigration. Throughout the 19th and early 20th centuries, federal policy encouraged immigration to supply labor for an expanding economy. After World War I, legislation resulting from economic strain and cultural conflict restricted the flow of immigration by establishing quotas based on national origin. Four decades later, Congress revised the law: equal treatment of all nationalities and family reunification became the primary considerations in admitting immigrants. In 1984, a total of 544,000 legal immigrants, including refugees, entered this country, mostly from Mexico, the Philippines, and Viet Nam.

The large number of illegal immigrants during turbulent economic times has sparked the recent debate over immigration policy. High levels of illegal immigration have rekindled concern that immigrants may displace domestic workers, depress wages, and contribute to poor working conditions. The magnitude of the problem is subject to debate and centers on the impact of undocumented immigration on the labor market. Reliable data are limited and the number of resident illegal immigrants, as well as the number of entrants per year, is difficult to ascertain. Estimates of undocumented immigrants range from 3 to 10 million.

Sample data indicate that illegal immigrants today, like immigrants of the past, tend to be young, unskilled adult males in search of economic opportunity. Although most of the jobs they obtain are menial or low-wage, they are not excluded from better paying jobs, primarily in construction where formal job applications are rare and detection is improbable.[29] Surveys of apprehended illegals have estimated that only about one-fifth are employed in farm work; substantial numbers find work in manufacturing, construction, and services. This wide range of jobs means that some undocumented workers obtain relatively good wages. One study concluded that, in the Houston area, a third of all commercial construction jobs were held by undocumented workers. According to another report, the average hourly wage for these illegal immigrants was one-third higher than the minimum wage; only one in ten earned less than the minimum wage.[30]

The presence of large numbers of illegal immigrants in broad sectors of the labor force raises policy questions during periods of high national unemployment. One estimate is that legal and illegal immigrants (including refugees) contributed more than half of the nation's net labor force growth during the early 1980s, indicating that many of them are holding jobs that could be filled by some of the nation's unemployed.[31] Requirements that immigrants receive Labor Department certification that their presence will not adversely affect the labor market opportunities of U.S. workers apply, at best, to a fraction of legal entrants. For the 80 percent of legal immigrants admitted under family reunification regulations, labor market conditions are not a factor. Occupational preference admissions are given primarily to those with high skills or extensive educational backgrounds.[32] A 1983 Census Bureau survey indicates that the labor market profile of foreign-born workers closely resembles that of their U.S.-born counterparts.[33]

There is also little information about refugees. Prior to the 1970s, the small number of refugees were predominantly well-to-do and middle class persons fleeing social upheaval. The large infusion of refugees during the past several years included large numbers of unskilled and uneducated persons and increased competition with U.S. workers for low-wage jobs. A high concentration of refugees in certain local areas intensifies job competition—over one-third of the 640,000 Indochinese refugees have resettled in urban areas in California and over two-thirds of the 155,000 recent Cuban and Haitian entrants live in Florida, particularly in the Miami area.[34]

Contending points of view about the effects of illegal immigration have flourished in the absence of reliable data. Some investigators argue that the impact of illegal immigration on American labor markets is exaggerated and dispute the contention that undocumented immigrants displace significant numbers of domestic workers or depress wages, claiming that the immigrants typically fill jobs U.S. citizens are unwilling to take.[35] Analysts also contend that immigrants pay more in taxes and payroll deductions than they withdraw in social services. These arguments are also advanced by employers, particularly in the West and Southwest, who depend on legal and illegal immigrants for seasonal agricultural labor. Similarly, operators of hotels, restaurants, and other service facilities in urban areas assert that they are unable to fill low-paying menial positions with U.S. workers. A last argument in favor of expanding immigration quotas is that humanitarian concerns require the nation to admit as many foreign workers as it can. The United States has traditionally served as a haven for the politically and economically oppressed.[36]

Advocates of restricted immigration contend that immigrant labor, particularly illegal immigrants, adversely affects the labor market conditions of American workers. They argue that undocumented aliens often work under harsh conditions for low pay and thus tend to depress wage rates, impede improvements in working conditions, hamper unionization efforts, and even drive U.S. citizens out of labor markets. Employers, according to this view, prefer undocumented workers who are not in a position to challenge managerial authority. Proponents of restricting immigration further argue that because immigrants tend to concentrate in central cities, their presence adversely affects low-wage and minority workers and forces some who might otherwise be employed to depend on welfare. Labor unions have traditionally backed measures to curb immigration, instinctively opposing anything that might depress the living standards of American workers. This struggle has left labor and organizations representing ethnic groups, particularly Hispanics, at odds over immigration policy.

Legislation pending before Congress in 1985 provided increased enforcement funds for the Immigration and Naturalization Service, sanctions against employers who knowingly hire illegal immigrants, amnesty for illegal immigrants residing in this country for a given period, and an expanded foreign worker program to meet the needs of the nation's agricultural industry. A major stumbling block to passage has been the fact that restricting illegal immigration would require strong sanctions that would both infringe on free market operations and erode cherished democratic traditions.

The resolution of the immigration debate may depend on the health of the nation's economy. If high levels of unemployment persist, pressure will mount for tighter restrictions on legal immigration and imposition of stiff sanctions to prevent employment of illegal aliens. Improvement in the job market, however, might expand immigration opportunities for those seeking to enter this country.

Expanding Opportunities

During the last two decades the nation has made substantial progress toward increasing access to work for all Americans. Federal compensatory education programs have helped children in poor families acquire the basic skills necessary to compete in today's job market. For those who have dropped out of the race or have been left behind, a system of employment and training initiatives has offered a second chance. Federal efforts have focused on skill training to increase the employability of persons who experience difficulties in securing sustained employment, and aid to college students has opened opportunities in professional and managerial occupations. The price tag of these federal activities has been high, but the results have been well worth the expense.

With record federal budget deficits, all federal programs must be closely examined to eliminate questionable outlays. Nevertheless, the problems the federal human resource initiatives were designed to solve have by no means disappeared. Preparing young people and adults to effectively compete for jobs remains a challenge. Some need federal programs to acquire basic competency and others need assistance to attend college or obtain other advanced training. Periodic recessions, new technology, foreign competition, and lagging areas of the economy all result in unemployment for some workers. For these individuals and for others entering the labor force, federal employment and training programs can make a crucial difference in reducing the hardship associated with joblessness.

Expanding equal opportunity for employment remains an important federal responsibility. One remedy for the prevailing high jobless rates, particularly among minority youth, is adequate preparation for work. Expanded vocational training efforts can assist those having difficulty in the labor market. A revamped public employment service can provide timely information to job seekers, including displaced workers, about openings in a wide variety of occupations across the country, while increasing its efforts to serve those facing the greatest labor market disadvantage. Finally, a new federal immigration policy is needed to protect the employment opportunities of American workers while carefully preserving cherished freedoms and humanitarian traditions.

American society needs these federal efforts both to avoid the waste of human resources and to offer opportunity to all who seek to earn a living through productive jobs. A recommitment to the goal of equal access to work is the appropriate federal response.

4

Equal Employment Opportunity

Qualified minorities and women face a range of barriers to equal employment opportunities in the workplace. These discriminatory practices unfairly prevent them from obtaining jobs for which they are qualified and have led to higher poverty levels among minorities and among female-headed families. The underutilization of these groups also diminishes the total potential wealth and productivity of the nation.

Analysts disagree on the role the federal government should play in providing remedies. Some believe that the free market alone provides sufficient incentive to reduce discriminatory practices. Milton Friedman, as an example, has argued that discrimination is self-defeating because ". . . there is an economic incentive in a free market to separate economic efficiency from other characteristics of the individual."[1] In this view, employers would not tolerate the inefficiency of paying higher wages to white male workers over equally qualified minorities or women because competitive pressure would favor the employers who broke with this practice. Other employers would either follow suit or suffer loss of business.

The free market, although in theory a highly effective mechanism for preserving individual freedom, has not eliminated social inequities. An entrenched system of discriminatory attitudes and institutions is not easily corrected. The efforts of employers who oppose discrimination and are inclined to hire minorities or women may be frustrated by a limited supply of qualified applicants, resulting from their unequal access to the institutions that would prepare them for available jobs. The free market tends to reflect and support traditional social attitudes, some of which favor certain groups over others.

Employment opportunities for traditionally excluded groups are expanded in sustained tight labor markets. When the existing supply of labor fails to meet demand, employers do hire, train, and promote members of previously discriminated against groups. This process does not automatically ensure, however, that women and minorities either gain access to jobs at all occupational levels or accrue enough seniority to survive cyclical downturns and business readjustments. When left to market forces, the rate of progress in expanding employment opportunities is uneven and sometimes painfully slow.

Federal intervention is needed, therefore, to speed up this process and to establish rules leading to the expansion of employment opportunity. By outlawing discrimination, federal regulation can directly influence action and indirectly influence attitudes. By expanding access to labor market information, education, and training, the pool of qualified minority and women applicants is enlarged. Where resistance to change persists, government regulatory activity can help achieve a more open labor market.

Evolving Public Policy

Breaking the ingrained pattern of occupational segregation and discrimination has required a transformation in social attitudes, as well as an alteration of the underlying institutional forces that perpetuate discriminatory practices. The New Deal programs which addressed many social ills of the 1930s did not focus on the grave employment problems of black workers, three-fourths of whom lived in the South. Blacks who moved North after World War II found declining job opportunities in many industries and occupations that traditionally had absorbed large numbers of semiskilled and unskilled workers. Because discrimination in employment was widespread, federal legislation was required to adequately deal with the problem. Public support for such legislation was forthcoming, however, only when the demands of minorities and women for equal opportunity could no longer be ignored.

During the 1950s, federal court decisions set new precedents covering public policy in education, voting rights, and public accommodations, but in the absence of legislation prohibiting discrimination in the workplace, employers continued to pursue discriminatory hiring and promotion practices through selection procedures favoring white employees. Despairing of prompt legislative action, President Kennedy issued an executive order in 1961 requiring all federal government contractors to "take affirmative action to ensure that all applicants are employed, and that employees are treated during employment, without regard to their race, creed, color, or national origin."[2]

The growing number of women who entered the work force during and after World War II found only a narrow range of jobs open to them, although many were qualified for a broader range of occupations. Social norms sharply restricted the jobs open to working women to those emphasizing nurturing and helping roles. Employers—who tended to presume that a woman's labor force participation would be temporary, ending with either marriage or childbirth—defended the low wages paid to women by pointing to their status as secondary earners who worked only to supplement their husband's income.

Increasingly, these assumptions conflicted with reality as women delayed marriage and childbirth, reduced their time away from work for childrearing, and remained in the work force longer. Increasing numbers of married women entered the work force despite their restricted opportunities. In 1947 only 21 percent of married women worked outside the home; by 1963 their participation had increased to 33 percent, and by 1985 to 55 percent.

These developments lent considerable weight to demands that women receive equal pay for equal work and that job opportunities be opened to all qualified applicants. State laws, which protected women in the workplace from arduous or dangerous working conditions, were based on the premise that women needed special care but not necessarily the pay or promotion opportunities enjoyed by men. The federal response to this continuing discrimination was the Equal Pay Act of 1963, which requires employers to pay all workers the same wages for the same job.

Voluntary Equal Opportunity

By the early 1960s pressures had mounted for federal legislation which would bar discriminatory job practices. In the two preceding decades more than 200 fair employment measures had been introduced in Congress, but they had been steadfastly resisted by southern Democrats. The fair employment practice laws enacted in 34 states had proved inadequate in the face of deep-rooted and pervasive discriminatory employment patterns and in the absence of a national policy.

The clamor for federal action resulted in the comprehensive Civil Rights Act of 1964 which specifically addressed equal employment opportunity. Signing the bill on June 26, 1964, President Johnson declared, "For the first time in world history we have the abundance and the ability to free every man from hopeless want, and to free every person to find fulfillment in the works of his mind or the labor of his hands." President Johnson's rhetoric reflected the prevailing optimistic spirit of the times.

Title VII of the Civil Rights Act of 1964 outlaws discrimination on the basis of race, color, religion, sex, or national origin in hiring, compensation, and promotion. The law applies to all private establishments, employment agencies, and labor organizations employing or serving 25 or more persons. The Equal Employment Opportunity Commission (EEOC) was created to enforce the provisions of the Act, but its role was limited to gathering information, mediating disputes to encourage voluntary compliance, and providing "friend-of-the-court" support in antidiscrimination suits.

The EEOC was unable to resort to the courts during its first eight years and relied on the conciliation process—seeking compliance with Title VII standards through voluntary agreements. These procedures were time consuming and had only limited results. When conciliation agreements were reached, they had no legal force and, therefore, produced negligible changes in the marketplace. At best, the process benefited only the complaining parties. There was no continuing influence on black or female employment as a whole.[3]

A typical example of EEOC's limited effectiveness involved the complaint of two black women who in 1966 were twice refused sales jobs in a small southern general merchandise store. After an initial investigation established "reasonable cause" to suspect discrimination, the EEOC negotiated an agreement with the home office of the parent company, which offered the two women jobs and $1,300 in back pay. The company also agreed to treat the job applications of blacks and whites equally and to develop plans to recruit and promote blacks. By 1971, however, no substantial changes had occurred although the home office of the store had issued several policy statements on equal employment opportunities. The two women had ultimately refused the jobs they were offered, blacks had not filled the two positions, and only one black employee had been promoted. The EEOC had not checked back to monitor the terms of the agreement and, in any event, lacked enforcement authority.

President Johnson also acted to strengthen the federal contractor program. Federal agencies had failed to resort to contract cancellation—a key sanction in the Kennedy executive order—in cases of employers who persisted in discriminatory practices. Contractors claimed that they were uncertain of the actions they were expected to take, and enforcement was scattered among different agencies. By executive order President Johnson created an Office of Federal Contract Compliance (OFCC) in the Department of Labor and added women as a protected group.[4] Regulations promulgated by the OFCC required contractors to examine their utilization of minority and women workers, to establish affirmative action goals and timetables for reaching those goals, and to collect data to document their progress.

By the mid-1960s it was widely recognized that it was both necessary and desirable to combat discriminatory practices in the workplace. It was not clear, however, how best to implement this goal. President Johnson articulated the problem in a 1965 commencement address at Howard University: "You do not take a person who, for years, has been hobbled by chains and liberate him, bring him up to the starting line of a race and then say you are free to compete with all the others, and still just believe that you have been completely fair."[5]

While overt discriminatory practices had declined substantially, the persistence of institutionalized practices left barriers in place. Social values and customs continued to restrict minorities and women to low-level jobs. The informal recruitment methods used by most employers gave notice of job openings primarily to friends, relatives, or peers of the existing work force. Prerequisites that had little correlation with job performance tended to exclude disproportionate numbers of minorities and women. For those of lower socioeconomic status, these headwinds were reinforced by discrimination in education and housing which made progress difficult.

Title VII of the Civil Rights Act proscribed discrimination in employment but failed to give federal agencies any enforcement power. Because some employers were either unaware of the law or unwilling to modify practices that promoted discrimination, voluntary measures were largely ineffective. The federal courts provided the only avenue for redress. The courts expanded the scope and impact of Title VII by focusing on institutional discrimination which remained the most formidable obstacle to expansion of employment opportunities for women and minorities.

In 1971 the Supreme Court ruled that Title VII "proscribes not only overt discrimination but also practices that are fair in form, but discriminatory in operation."[6] Preemployment tests that were not job-related were ruled illegal if they had an adverse impact on the selection of minorities. The use of achievement tests was foreclosed by the courts because they were likely to screen out blacks and other minorities and, in any event, were not especially good predictors of success in blue collar occupations. The Court expanded the adverse impact criterion to include job requirements that were not related to performance, such as the use of arrest records to automatically disqualify applicants. This standard was held to be discriminatory because blacks are statistically more likely to be arrested than whites.[7] The introduction of statistical evidence showing disparities in treatment by race helped the courts to draw inferences of discrimination; this evidence helps the courts resolve the often conflicting subjective testimony of employees and employers.

Congress Follows the Courts

The 1972 amendments to Title VII empowered the EEOC to bring civil actions in federal courts on behalf of those who had suffered from discrimination. The commission's authority to file class action suits raised considerable concern among employers, causing some to become more amenable to conciliation and settlement rather than risk litigation. The 1972 amendments also extended affirmative action requirements to small organizations (15 or more persons), state and local governments, government organizations, and educational institutions.

In 1973 the American Telephone and Telegraph Company signed a consent decree with the Justice Department providing $15 million in restitution and back pay for several classes of female employees and a $23 million promotion package for women and minorities. This agreement set the precedent for settlements reached later with other employers including Uniroyal, Bank of America, United Airlines, and major steel manufacturers. The risk of expensive court decisions led many employers to reevaluate their utilization of minorities and women.

The U.S. Commission on Civil Rights endorsed affirmative action in 1973, including the numerical remedies the courts and the federal government had been implementing. Numerical goals were based on the number of vacancies realistically expected to occur and the number of qualified applicants in the relevant job market. If, through no fault of the employer, the expected number of vacancies did not materialize or qualified applicants were in insufficient supply, the employer was not expected to displace existing workers or hire unnecessary workers to meet his goal, provided a good faith effort could be demonstrated.[8]

Affirmative action was further defined by the Supreme Court in *United Steelworkers of America v. Weber,* decided in 1979. The case arose out of a 1974 agreement between the steelworkers' union and Kaiser Aluminum & Chemical Co. that set up training programs to teach production workers the skills needed for movement into craft jobs at a Louisiana plant. To help overcome the exclusion of black craft workers in that area, Kaiser set aside 50 percent of the training slots for blacks. Admission to the program was by seniority, with separate seniority lists by race. Brian Weber, a white man, sued the union claiming that the plan resulted in his nonselection for training because several blacks with less overall seniority than he were admitted. The Supreme Court upheld the Kaiser plan:

> Congress did not intend to limit traditional business freedom to such a degree as to prohibit all voluntary, race-conscious affirmative action. . . . The Kaiser-USWA plan for the Gramercy plant falls within the area of discretion left by Title VII to the private sector voluntarily to adopt affirmative action plans designed to eliminate conspicuous racial imbalance in traditionally segregated job categories.[9]

It appears from this decision that private parties may act voluntarily upon evidence of discrimination without waiting for government intervention. The remedy, however, should be tailored to the problem, should redress the effects of past discrimination, and should terminate when these effects have faded.

During the 1970s Congress expanded affirmative action to include veterans and handicapped persons. In these cases, affirmative action was advanced as a national policy to address the special needs of defined groups in society, but without the numerical goals and timetables associated with Title VII or Executive Order 11246.

In 1978 responsibility for federal contract programs was transferred to the Department of Labor's Office of Federal Contract Compliance Programs (OFCCP) from eleven other federal agencies. This consolidation was designed to improve coordination and efficiency in monitoring contractor compliance.

Protecting Older Workers

The Age Discrimination in Employment Act (ADEA) of 1967 prohibits discrimination in hiring, retaining, compensating, and promoting older persons. Workers who are at least 40 but less than 70 years of age are protected. The volume of age discrimination cases grew slowly during the first decade following ADEA's passage because efforts to attack age discrimination were subordinated to the civil rights movement of the 1960s and the women's rights movement of the 1970s. Since 1978 age discrimination complaints have increased while race and sex discrimination complaints have declined.

	Sex and Race	*Age*
1978	75,000	5,400
1984	52,130	15,000

Age discrimination claims constituted 22 percent of the EEOC's 1984 caseload; the proportion was still rising in 1985.

Part of this increase is undoubtedly due to the rising attention given to age discrimination by the press and the government in recent years. Public awareness has been increased by the 1978 congressional debate over raising the legal retirement age from 65 to 70, big money awards for a few successful complainants, and EEOC public service announcements. Nevertheless, according to a 1981 national Harris survey, only two in five Americans were aware of the ADEA.[10]

Most age discrimination claims result from economic problems. Mass layoffs and plant closings during the recessionary early 1980s exacerbated the employment problems of older workers—many were offered early retirement, some were forced to retire, and others faced prolonged layoffs. Company attempts to create a leaner work force posed additional problems for older workers. Most age discrimination charges filed with the EEOC in 1981 involved forced termination in the form of discharge, layoff, or involuntary retirement. Typical complainants were middle management, middle-aged, white, and male.[11]

Federal age discrimination legislation is an attempt to balance the interests of older workers with the economic concerns of employers. Older workers tend to earn higher wages and salaries than younger employees, have more accrued benefits, and are typically vested in pensions. As a result of these real costs, as well as perceptions that older workers are less productive, employers tend to identify older workers with higher labor costs.

The evidence is mixed, however, on the productivity of older workers. An older employee's capacity for physical work usually does decline with age but there is considerable variation among individuals. On the other hand, older workers tend to exercise better judgment and have lower absenteeism and turnover rates. Consequently, the advantages and disadvantages to employers in hiring and retaining older workers vary according to the nature of the work to be performed. This fact is taken into account by the ADEA which permits age to be considered as an occupational qualification. Some courts have ruled that in the case of firefighters, police, and airline pilots, the public interest is best protected by establishing an age limit. In two 1985 decisions, however, the Supreme Court narrowly interpreted the use of age as a factor determining capability, and imposed substantial burdens of proof on employers who seek to set generalized age limits.[12]

The right to trial by jury and damage awards provided under the ADEA can make discrimination against older workers costly. Patterned after the Fair Labor Standards Act rather than Title VII, these provisions give plaintiffs in age discrimination suits relatively greater clout than Title VII litigants. Employers complain that because juries are more responsive to emotional appeals than judges, older plaintiffs often receive higher damage awards than other discrimination victims.[13]

The best way to balance the needs of employers and older workers is through the implementation of a fair and objective system of performance evaluation. Generally, the courts require that evaluation criteria relate functionally to the work being done, that procedures be regularly applied to all employees, and that standards be communicated to all workers.[14]

Mandatory retirement is a continuing area of conflict. Legislation has been introduced repeatedly during recent sessions of Congress to remove the upper age limit of 70 years, in the belief that retirement decisions should be made by individuals rather than imposed by an arbitrary federal guideline. Premature labor force withdrawal can have adverse economic consequences for older workers as well as for the nation's productivity. Delaying retirement could also reduce the pressure on an already overburdened social security system.

Reagan Administration Changes

Since 1981 federal equal employment opportunity policies affecting women and minorities have been substantially revised. The Reagan administration, while endorsing a federal role in combating discrimination, has maintained that employment decisions should be based on merit alone and has advocated the substitution of color-blind and gender-blind policies for race- and sex-based approaches. It follows, therefore, that only proven individual victims of discrimination should receive relief because market forces alone provide sufficient incentive for employers to abandon discriminatory practices. Emphasizing and relying on voluntary compliance, the Reagan administration has curtailed federal enforcement. In addition, compliance requirements have been scaled back sharply to reduce paperwork and cut employer costs.

Reagan's Justice Department has vigorously opposed previous equal employment policies. It no longer seeks relief that may benefit individuals who are not "identifiable victims of discrimination"; it believes that the use of race- or sex-based measures constitutes "preferential treatment" in violation of the color-blind mandates of the Constitution and Title VII. The Justice Department has also intervened in litigation urging reconsideration of goals or ratios to which the parties involved and the courts had already agreed.

In *Memphis Fire Department v. Stotts* the Supreme Court ruled that the seniority rights of white firefighters outweighed an existing consent decree designed to increase black representation in the city fire department.[15] The court declared that only individuals personally discriminated against can be granted super-seniority by a court. Relying on this interpretation of Title VII, the Justice Department has increased its intervention in other employment discrimination cases, and has announced that it intends to review antidiscrimination agreements with federal contractors for evidence of unjust quotas.

On the strength of the Supreme Court's decision in the *Stotts* case, the Justice Department urged some 50 state and local government affirmative action program administrators to reopen and reexamine court-approved consent decrees containing goals and timetables. Officials of some cities—including Boston, Chicago, Los Angeles, Miami, Philadelphia, and San Francisco—replied that their programs were working well and federal intervention was, therefore, not warranted. In addition, lower courts have rejected the Justice Department's narrow interpretation of the *Stotts* decision and have been reluctant to throw out existing consent decrees.[16] "By pushing hard to alter the current procedures of affirmative action," *Business Week* editorialized, "Meese has brought conflict where harmony prevailed earlier. Both of the major players in affirmative action, business and civil rights groups, find the present system workable. Only the Attorney General is calling for change."[17]

President Reagan has made effective use of his appointment and budget powers to shape the operations of the federal civil rights agencies. Dramatic changes have taken place at the U.S. Commission on Civil Rights. In existence for two decades as an independent, nonpartisan body, the commission has monitored and studied federal civil rights policy and enforcement. In 1983 a newly constituted commission with a majority of Reagan appointees reversed its long-standing endorsement of race-conscious numerical affirmative action policies. Asked how the body could make such sweeping policy judgments with no study, Commission member Morris A. Abram claimed he did "not need any further study of a principle that comes from the basic bedrock decision of the Constitution . . ., equal means equal."[18]

Similar changes have taken place at the EEOC, where chairman Clarence Thomas has expressed a desire to "get away from the numbers game entirely." He has pledged more vigorous efforts to seek back pay and other compensation for identified individual victims of discrimination. These efforts are at the expense of class action lawsuits that benefit a group—not only those individuals who have been specifically discriminated against. In response to public criticism, however, Thomas and the EEOC have somewhat modified this position. In November 1985 the EEOC, based on statistical evidence of discrimination, filed lawsuits against three companies.[19]

Other factors have affected EEOC operations. Adjusted for inflation, its budget was cut by 20 percent between 1980 and 1985. Authorized full-time, permanent staff positions have been reduced to 3,125 in 1985—a 17 percent cut in five years. The number of discrimination suits brought by the agency was cut by more than half, from 322 in 1980 to 146 in 1984. Policy shifts and funding constraints have reduced the pursuit of Title VII class action suits as well as broad systemic investigations of discrimination.

Similar changes have had an impact on OFCCP activities. Program funding was cut to $47 million in 1985, a real reduction of one-third since 1980, and authorized staff levels were reduced. Fewer complaint investigations have resulted in findings of discrimination, and a higher percentage of cases have been closed without full investigation.

Critics oppose equal employment measures on several grounds. The most familiar criticism is that affirmative action constitutes reverse discrimination against white males. Another charge is that affirmative action undermines individual merit and reduces productivity because protected individuals benefit at the expense of more meritorious candidates. A third charge is that the beneficiaries of affirmative action are stigmatized because their selection was based on policy rather than ability. Last, it is charged that policies which affect groups inevitably will benefit some individuals who have not been victims of discrimination, at the expense of other individuals who have neither practiced discrimination nor benefited from it.

Advocates of preferential hiring argue that discrimination is so systematic and widespread that the remedy should address the problem of the whole group. Justice Thurgood Marshall stated: "It is unnecessary in 20th century America to have individual Negroes demonstrate that they have been victims of racial discrimination. . . ."[20] Despite popular notions that in the past ethnic minorities "pulled themselves up by their own bootstraps," there is no evidence that any minority group overcame discrimination and low skills by openly competing for jobs. White immigrants relied on informal networks along ethnic lines to secure employment in predominantly unskilled occupations. The increasing emphasis on credentials in today's job market bars blacks from following a similar course. Changes in labor market institutions tend to preclude valid comparison with the practices of a century ago. The long fight for social justice and the limited effectiveness of less stringent federal equal employment opportunity laws has shown that minorities and women need the strong and direct federal intervention of affirmative action to help them overcome discrimination. Affirmative action is supported not only by civil rights groups, but also by many businesses as well as state and local governments.

Impact of Federal Intervention

Many factors affect the employment opportunities of minorities, women, and older workers, making the task of isolating the effects directly attributable to federal equal employment activities a normative exercise. Some critics of affirmative action cite findings showing no discernible positive impact of federal programs and call for an end to federal intervention. Other observers extol the progress that has been made since the 1960s and recommend scaling back federal equal employment programs on that basis. The analysis that follows, however, shows that while progress has indeed been made and can be directly linked to federal programs, equity for the protected groups remains a distant and elusive goal.

Econometric Evidence

Analysts have tried to measure the extent to which EEOC and OFCCP have increased the wage and employment levels of protected groups by attempting to control for changing economic conditions, education, and other factors that might influence occupational mobility. These studies suggest that federal programs have achieved positive results, although findings for the earlier program years vary significantly depending on the assumptions, data, and methodology employed.[21]

Econometric studies of employment discrimination rely mainly on two data sources: annual EEO-1 reports submitted to the EEOC by employers with 100 or more employees, and the monthly Current Population Survey (CPS) of households (60,000 in 1985) conducted by the Census Bureau. The EEO-1 reports classify all employees in nine broad occupational categories by race and sex and indicate whether the firm is a federal contractor. The CPS reports include data on earnings by sex and occupation.

Assignment of workers to various categories is left to the respondent firm, which results in considerable lack of uniformity. Even if the reports are accurate and timely—a heroic assumption—their value for assessing the impact of EEO efforts is limited by the aggregate level of occupational classification, which does not measure within-category mobility. Some evidence suggests that employers reclassify employees to enhance their antidiscrimination record. One survey concluded that during the 1970s monitored firms "reclassified jobs in a way that expanded the minority representation in the managerial ranks."[22] Since EEOC lacks sufficient staff and resources to monitor the accuracy of reported classifications by employers, this problem persists.

A major problem for researchers is the lack of information reported to EEOC regarding wages. Attempts to bridge this gap by matching EEO-1 data with CPS earnings and occupational data are beset with methodological problems. An alternative approach is to rely on CPS data alone since it offers information on both occupation and earnings, but it does not differentiate between workers who are covered by federal antidiscrimination laws and those who are not. Conclusions about changes in occupation and earnings as a result of federal programs are, therefore, of limited reliability.

In addition to data problems, investigators are confronted with questions about how to construct their experiment. Identifying the variables and quantifying their impact are subjective decisions which pose measurement problems. The impact of each variable on the dependent variable is measured but because interaction between variables is inevitable and difficult to isolate, the findings may be biased. For example, most comparisons of federal contractors with noncontractors ignore the effect that EEOC's presence has on OFCCP's compliance.

The appealing, but only presumed, objectivity of an econometric approach masks a host of data and experimental design problems. The findings and conclusions depend upon the assumptions and variables selected by the researchers and may reflect their biases and preconceived conclusions. Their efforts, therefore, have been of little value to policymakers.

Aggregate Data

In the absence of reliable data to measure the impact of equal opportunity legislation, it is obviously difficult to isolate changes due to federal intervention from overall variations and shifts in the economy. Nevertheless, a number of studies have concluded that the federal equal opportunity drive has contributed to ameliorating wage and employment discrimination.[23]

Since the early 1960s blacks and women have made substantial gains in the job market, moving into better-paying and higher-status jobs. Because progress is limited by shifting economic currents and time lags in acquiring appropriate education and skills, changes have been slow. But a pattern of sustained improvement is apparent and the labor market position of minorities and women is better now than at any time in the nation's history.

Between 1960 and 1984 the proportion of blacks employed as managers, professionals, and craft workers rose, while the proportion employed in service work, nonfarm, and farm labor fell. The black share of clerical, operative, and sales jobs also increased during this period. However, these broad categories mask the continuing effect of past occupational segregation.[24]

Black workers are still underrepresented in many of the higher paying and more prestigious white and blue collar jobs (Figure 2).

Growth in white collar occupations opened new opportunities for minorities. In 1960 blacks constituted less than 2 percent of all accountants, engineers, lawyers, dentists, and managers. Although black entry into these occupations has risen dramatically, their overall share remains very small and few have penetrated into higher salaried professional and managerial positions. Black craftsmen have made similar progress, increasing their proportion of electricians, machinists, and plumbers, while maintaining their representation level in the trowel trades. Nevertheless, only in two or three

Figure 2. Proportion of black workers in higher-paid occupations has nearly doubled

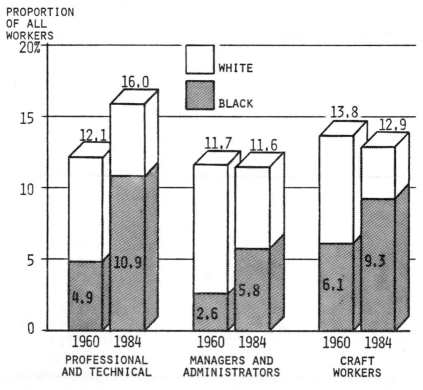

Source: U.S. Bureau of Labor Statistics.

craft occupations does the black share even approach the level of black representation in the work force. Economic conditions have partially controlled the extent and direction of minority occupational advance. During the 1960s minority workers gained greater access to the expanding supply of relatively unskilled blue collar jobs. While the two recessions during the 1970s slowed job creation in this area, minority employment gains continued to follow overall patterns.

Women have also experienced employment gains. Between 1964 and 1984 women made significant inroads in the growing professional and managerial occupations, filling more than half of those new jobs in the 1970s. In 1984 a manager was twice as likely to be a woman as in 1964. Similarly, women's representation among professionals increased from 36 percent in 1964 to 48 percent in 1984, with gains in nearly every occupational subgroup. Women's share of traditional female occupations has remained relatively constant, however, continuing the disproportionate female representation among secretaries and typists, nurses, waitresses, and elementary school teachers (Figure 3).

The improved occupational status of blacks and women has translated into earnings gains for these groups, although the effects have been muted somewhat by other factors. Between 1964 and 1984 the gap between the median wage and salary of full-time, year-round black workers and their white counterparts narrowed perceptibly, as follows:

Black/White Wage and Salary Ratio

	Men	*Women*
1964	0.59	0.62
1984	0.68	0.92

The dramatic improvement in earnings of black women working year-round, full-time relative to those of white women stems from the ease with which employers could substitute black women for white women in traditionally female jobs. (The 1964 Census Bureau figures for blacks include blacks and others.) Women as a whole also increased their earnings relative to men.

**Figure 3. Female employment in higher-paid occupations
has increased more than in traditional occupations**

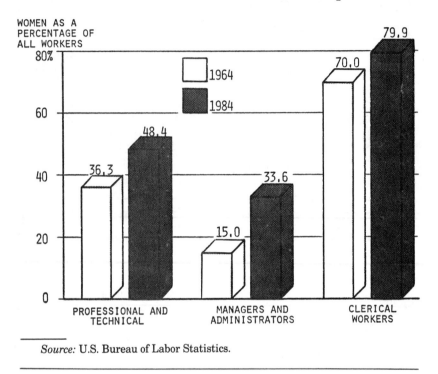

WOMEN AS A
PERCENTAGE OF
ALL WORKERS

Source: U.S. Bureau of Labor Statistics.

Women/Men Wage and Salary Ratio

1964	0.60
1984	0.63

Even when opportunities increase, there is a considerable time
lag in acquiring the necessary education, training, and experience to compete effectively for higher-paying jobs. Older workers, who benefit less from the opening of new opportunities,
remain in traditional occupations, heavily weighting the averages toward the status quo. Because formal seniority and promotion ladders remain in effect in most cases, advancement is
gradual even after barriers are removed. As a result, younger
black workers have benefited more from federal antidiscrimination efforts than their older counterparts. This is
especially true for blacks with a college education. The 1983

gap in the median incomes of year-round, full-time, black and white workers increased with age:[25]

Age	Black/White Median Income Ratio
25 to 34 years	0.79
35 to 44	0.77
45 to 54	0.72
55 to 64	0.63

Finally, as minorities progress to upper-management positions, white males who have traditionally controlled company policy are reluctant to relinquish it and thus slow the pace of change. Because younger workers in protected groups are improving their relative occupational positions, the effect on their earnings over time may be pronounced.

The effects of federal antidiscrimination efforts aimed at older workers cannot be determined from aggregate labor force statistics. The depressing impact of past discrimination on the elderly is generally irreversible because their employment patterns are set. Consequently, progress cannot be measured by employment or occupational distribution. The picture is further complicated by declining labor force participation among male workers aged 45 and over during the past two decades.

Male Labor Force Participation by Age

	45-54	*55-64*	*65+*
1965	95.1	84.6	27.9
1985	90.8	67.4	15.7

On the other hand, labor force participation by women aged 45 to 54 rose.

Female Labor Force Participation by Age

	45-54	*55-64*	*65+*
1965	51.2	41.1	10.0
1985	64.8	42.2	7.3

The most plausible explanations for decreased labor force activity among 45-54 year old males focus on early retirement incentives and stressful jobs. Labor force behavior among the

55-64 year old group is strongly affected by the availability of indexed social security at age 62 which is often combined with private pensions. Taken together, these factors have overwhelmed any effect that age discrimination legislation may have had in prolonging the work life of older workers.

Lasting Effects

Passing a law does not instantly change established institutions and ingrained attitudes. Yet, over a 20-year period, federal equal employment legislation has slowly but significantly altered the personnel policies of employers and unions. Most large companies have institutionalized their equal employment efforts, assembling human resource staffs to comply with affirmative action requirements. Initial business opposition to Title VII and subsequent affirmative action regulations has diminished. For those employers not supportive of federal equal employment goals, the risks of noncompliance bring many in line with social policy and legal requirements.

The Reagan administration's limited commitment to equal employment policies apparently has not dramatically changed employers' practices.[26] Most employers, private and public, instead of supporting an end to goals and timetables, prefer reforms that are specific and involve less paperwork. For example, state and local governments have been reluctant to abandon their affirmative action programs despite suggestions by the Justice Department to review these programs.[27] Even those employers who do not support affirmative action may be concerned about being seen as opposed to civil rights.[28]

Employer attitudes toward older workers appear to be changing.[29] It is likely that substantial monetary awards to proven victims of age discrimination have been partly responsible for this more positive approach, but demographic trends also favor older workers. The increased longevity and overall health gains of the elderly improve the employment outlook for older workers who choose to remain in the work force.

Most unions, particularly at the national level, have responded positively to their responsibility to pursue equal employment opportunities. Unions have aligned themselves with civil rights and women's organizations to push for equal employment opportunity. Union membership among minorities and women has grown significantly in the past two decades. The average earnings of these groups are higher among unionized than among nonunionized workers, indicating that unions have contributed to improving minority and female economic status. In 1984 black union members' weekly paychecks were one and one-half times those of their nonunion counterparts, while women unionists earned nearly one-third more than nonunion women.[30] Traditional union advocacy of uniform wage rates and strict seniority-based promotion systems has worked to the advantage of minority and women union members in terms of compensation, although not necessarily in advancement.

Significant changes have occurred in the building trades where segregation was rampant prior to 1964. The discriminatory practices of some unions provoked a strong challenge from civil rights and community organizations, backed both by federal law and by national union leaders seeking to broaden their union's ranks. Minority participation in apprenticeship programs and membership in referral unions rose significantly during the 1970s. In 1970, only 2.3 percent of all graduates from construction apprenticeship programs were black; by 1979, this number had increased to 9.4 percent. Women made much slower progress because traditions regarding their employment in construction have proved more resistant to change.[31]

The most significant dilemma for unions favoring equal employment opportunity has been in finding the appropriate balance between affirmative action and seniority. Although Congress explicitly exempted bona fide seniority systems from the list of Title VII violations, seniority systems strongly tend to sustain past discrimination. The Supreme Court has consistently upheld valid seniority systems even when they have resulted in a disparate impact on women and minorities.[32] As noted earlier, the Court in 1984 reaffirmed the supremacy of seniority over affirmative action in a layoff situation covering municipal firefighters.

Continued Federal Pressures

Equal employment opportunity had been consistently supported by Congress, the courts, and four successive administrations during the 1960s and 1970s, yet controversy persists. The current debate pits advocates of neutrality against proponents of affirmative action. Attorney General Edwin Meese and other federal officials in charge of civil rights agencies believe that compensating identified individual victims of discrimination is sufficient. They would, therefore, rescind regulations that mandate goals and timetables for federal contractors. They argue that classwide race and sex remedies constitute reverse discrimination and are contrary to American concepts of equal treatment under the law.

In opposition to this view, proponents of affirmative action urge that the federal government play an active role in offsetting and redressing past discriminatory practices. They maintain that the long history and experience of this nation's struggle against injustice demonstrate that without positive programs to correct past wrongs, the goal of guaranteeing women and minorities equal opportunities in the workplace may be further delayed.

Civil rights advocates continue to insist that the federal agencies responsible for enforcement of equal opportunity pursue policies that achieve maximum effectiveness—by actively investigating employer practices and patterns that suggest possible discrimination, then negotiating or filing suit to bring them into conformity with the law. In the view of these advocates, a commitment to nondiscriminatory employment practices on the part of federal contractors should be a necessary condition of securing such contracts.

Advocacy of a more neutral role for the federal government in this area assumes a natural evolution toward equality of opportunity in the labor market. Such a neutral policy would slow the progress achieved in the past two decades. Each step toward greater equality detracts from the urgency of the task, however, dampening the zeal of those who benefited by the equal opportunity efforts and increasing the inertia to be overcome for continued progress. There is a danger that federal efforts will be abandoned altogether and that equal opportunity will remain a distant and elusive goal.

5

The Fair Labor Standards Act

The Fair Labor Standards Act of 1938 established a minimum socially acceptable floor under wages and a standard 40-hour work week. The law has been continually criticized as interference in the operation of the free market, raising the cost of labor and, hence, the level of unemployment. It is nevertheless clear that the law has helped establish reasonable wage and hour conditions and has particularly helped the working poor as well as others with little bargaining power in the labor market.

Minimum Wages—History

Wages have been regulated throughout history either by custom or law. Before the American revolution, several colonies regulated wages by establishing scales or setting maximums. The need for strong governmental wage and hour regulation in the United States became clear at the turn of the 20th century as workers streamed from rural to urban areas to work in the expanding manufacturing sector, while immigrants flocked in from other lands in search of a better life. In the sweatshops, men, women, and children often worked long hours for little pay.

The progressive movement of the early 1900s raised concern for the problems of the working poor and pushed for the establishment of state minimum wage laws. Borrowing from policies used in other countries, early state laws set up wage boards that determined nonmandatory wage levels covering only women and children. Many of these laws were overturned in court on the grounds that they interfered with freedom of contract. Those that survived were not very generous. Walter

Lippmann characterized the minimum wage rates as "not enough to make life rich and a welcome experience, but just enough to secure existence amid drudgery in gray boarding houses and cheap restaurants."[1]

In 1937, in *West Coast Hotel Co. v. Parrish,* the Supreme Court reversed earlier decisions, and ruled that minimum wage laws were constitutional. In November of that year, President Roosevelt called a special session of Congress to pass his fair labor standards bill. Although this special session proved unproductive, nine months later Congress passed the Fair Labor Standards Act of 1938 (FLSA). The Act was passed over the objections of business and despite divided views among labor interests. Some labor leaders were concerned that minimum wage laws might also lead to maximum wage standards.

Although the Act was substantially watered down during the legislative process, it included a number of pathbreaking provisions. It set a national wage standard for the first time in American history and established a standard workweek of 40 hours (with additional hours paid at time-and-a-half). It advanced the principle that work involving excessively low wages and long hours is unacceptable in modern society.

The Minimum Wage Law

The Fair Labor Standards Act of 1938 established a minimum hourly wage rate of 25 cents to be raised in steps to 40 cents seven years later. Since then, Congress has increased the minimum wage level on six occasions, sometimes providing for a series of increases. In the 1950s and 1960s Congress set the minimum at roughly 50 percent of the average hourly wage rate paid in private industry, while in the 1970s the actual level dropped somewhat. The latest round of minimum wage amendments occurred in 1977; after much debate, the level was raised by steps through 1981. In the succeeding five years the minimum wage has remained at $3.35 an hour. As a result, the level of the minimum has slipped below 40 percent of the average hourly wage in private, nonagricultural employment for the first time since 1949 (Figure 4).

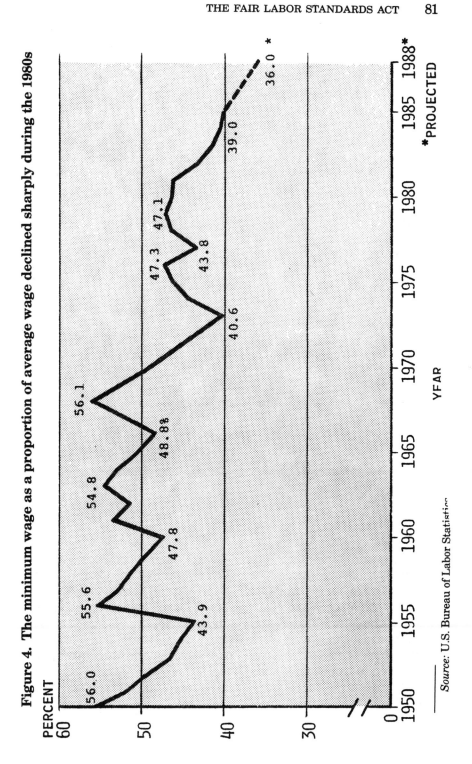

Figure 4. The minimum wage as a proportion of average wage declined sharply during the 1980s

PERCENT

*PROJECTED

YEAR

Source: U.S. Bureau of Labor Statistics

Coverage

The 1938 Act covered only one in every four workers. Opposition to a federal floor on wages was strong, and as a result of the legislative compromise those workers most in need of the Act's protection—retail trade, service, and agricultural laborers—were excluded from coverage. Ensuing amendments to the FLSA have expanded coverage and nearly 90 percent of nonsupervisory employees in the private sector are now subject to minimum wage laws. Still, over 10 million nonsupervisory employees are excluded from the protection of the federal minimum wage law, including 6 million in service and retail trade; 1.2 million in finance, insurance and real estate; and 980,000 in agriculture.[2]

Characteristics of Minimum Wage Workers

In 1984 the earnings of roughly eight million salaried and hourly workers were at or below the minimum wage level. Six million more received wages just above this level.[3]

Hourly Earnings

	Total Workers	Below Minimum	At Minimum	$3.36-3.99
Number (in millions)	92.2	3.8	4.1	6.4
Percent of all workers		4.2	4.5	6.9

The young, women, and blacks are disproportionately represented among minimum wage workers. Roughly 2.4 million of minimum wage workers, or 30 percent, are teenagers; another 22 percent are 20-24 years old; and over three-fifths of minimum wage workers are women. Although the vast majority of minimum wage workers are white, only 8 percent of white workers earn wages at or less than the minimum, as compared to 13 percent of black workers. Twenty-eight percent of all minimum wage workers are heads of households and another 28 percent are spouses.[4] Using 1978 Current Population Survey data, the Minimum Wage Study Commission found that 42.5 percent of workers from impoverished families were employed at or below the minimum wage. However, roughly three-quarters of all minimum wage workers live in families with incomes well above the poverty line.

Family Income	Percent of Employed Workers at or Below Minimum	As percent of All Minimum Wage Workers
Total	13.2	100.0
Below poverty	42.5	10.9
100-124 % of poverty line	32.9	6.4
125-149 % of poverty line	29.3	7.4
150 + % of poverty line	11.0	75.3

Minimum wage workers tend to be concentrated in the service industries, agriculture, and retail trade. Three of every four private household workers earn the minimum or less and one of every three service workers (other than private household) is employed at or below the minimum, as are nearly half of all farm laborers and one in five of all sales workers.[5] It is a curious irony of the free market system that those industries that most often approximate the state of perfect competition also contain high percentages of the working poor.

Impacts

The minimum wage law is a statement by society that certain work conditions are unacceptable. The Act was necessary when sweatshops were commonplace and remains necessary today. Most Americans work in labor markets that offer protection against undesirable work conditions, but millions work in secondary labor markets characterized by unstable, low-wage employment. These workers need the protection of government to bring their work conditions up to socially acceptable minimal standards.

For many individuals and families, the higher wages that result from the mandated minimum are of undeniable benefit. The wage floor has helped some escape poverty and has lessened its severity for others. For those minimum wage earners above the poverty line, the extra income also can be essential. A teenager trying to earn money for school can benefit greatly, as can a multiearner family that may be trying to scrape together enough money to purchase more than bare necessities.

In addition to providing a floor on wages for secondary labor market workers, minimum wages may help employees, as well as employers, less directly. Employers may provide training to employees in an attempt to boost productivity, or they may be "shocked" into organizing the production process more efficiently as a result of higher labor costs.[6]

The minimum wage also reinforces the work ethic by providing an incentive for people to work rather than depend on welfare. Few would disagree that work should pay more than welfare. When individuals earn some income instead of relying entirely on government support, they benefit from the satisfaction of helping themselves, and their possibilities for future advancement are enhanced. Society benefits both from the increase in output and the reduction in welfare costs.

Employment Effects

Over the years the main objection to the minimum wage has been that it reduces employment opportunities. Because the minimum wage is set above the market clearing wage, labor costs rise and employer demand for workers declines. Those who oppose a minimum wage for this reason either implicitly assume or explicitly reason that any job is better than none, ignoring the argument in favor of minimal work conditions.

Economists frequently estimate the effects of minimum wage laws on employment by attempting to measure the responsiveness of labor demand to a change in wages. The complexity of economic interactions precludes consensus on the effects of the minimum wage. Quantitative results from these studies are subject to considerable imprecision, although a few general conclusions can be made.

The minimum wage, not surprisingly, has its largest employment effect on youth and on industries with a high proportion of low wage workers. The 1980 Minimum Wage Study Commission estimated that a 10 percent increase in the minimum wage decreases teenage employment by about 1 percent.[7] The effect of a minimum wage increase on teenage employment would vary, of course, with economic conditions and demographic trends. There is little consensus on the effects of the minimum wage on overall adult employment,[8] although it is clear that the adult labor market is not as sensitive to minimum wage changes as is the youth labor market. This is true both because youth workers are likely to be laid off before adult workers and because a smaller proportion of adults work at the minimum.

Most importantly, the minimum wage has little, if any, perceptible impact on overall economic conditions. The economy has prospered since minimum wage laws were enacted and there has been little noticeable effect on unemployment after specific increases. In the 1950s and 1960s, when the minimum wage rose in both real and relative terms, the unemployment rate remained low. In the 1970s and early 1980s, the wage floor eroded but this has not prevented rising unemployment. Unemployment rate trends reflect factors other than the minimum wage.

Income Effects

The income effects of the minimum wage are as important to consider as the employment effects, yet much less analysis of the former has been undertaken. There is strong evidence, however, that the minimum wage has provided some income support for those at or near the poverty line and for minimum wage workers in general. Since a relatively small number of jobs are lost due to the minimum wage, but a large number of people receive raises, the net income effect is positive. One study found that the gain in income from a minimum wage increase especially overshadows the expected job loss for adult females.[9]

The current minimum wage of $3.35 per hour provides a full-time worker with an annual income of $6,968. Because the official poverty threshold varies according to family size, a single worker with no dependents working at the minimum wage would earn more than the poverty threshold, while a co-worker with two dependents earning the minimum wage would remain substantially below the poverty line. In 1985 the poverty threshold for a family of three was $8,570, requiring full-time/full-year work at an hourly wage of $4.12 to reach this point. For a family of four the threshold was $10,990, equivalent to a full-time/full-year wage of $5.28 an hour. The minimum wage has helped the working poor, but has not been high enough to permit many to escape poverty. Of the 22.2 million people over age 15 counted as poor in 1984, 9.1 million worked, and of those, almost 2.1 million with full-time/full-year jobs were still unable to escape poverty, including 1.4 million who earned less than the minimum wage.[10]

Recent boosts in the minimum wage have raised the income of millions of workers. In 1981, when the hourly minimum wage was raised from $3.10 to $3.35, the Department of Labor estimated that the aggregate increase potentially amounted to $2.2 billion annually, and that 5.5 million workers were eligible to receive increases. Effects in other years were also sizable, involving 4.6 million workers in 1978 and 4.2 million in 1974.[11]

As the minimum wage is raised, the employment loss increases, as does the income effect for those who do keep their jobs. The task for Congress is to strike the right balance between providing a reasonable wage floor and minimizing the disemployment effect. If the minimum is too low, then it loses its effect and does very little to protect the worker. On the other hand, if the minimum is too high, the disemployment effect offsets its positive income effects.

Overhauling the Minimum Wage Law

Indexing

One constructive amendment of the FLSA would automatically adjust the minimum wage to changes in cost of living or in average wages. This approach would prevent the erosion of the wage floor that has occurred during the past five years and which may continue for some years to come. The minimum wage generally rose in real terms until 1968, then stabilized in the 1970s, and has fallen sharply since 1979. The minimum wage level has not been changed since January 1981, although the cost of living rose 25 percent during the ensuing five years (Figure 5).

During the 1977 legislative debate on the minimum wage, the Carter administration favored indexing, but Congress instead adopted a series of increases. In 1981 the Minimum

Figure 5. The real value of the minimum wage has fallen during the 1980s

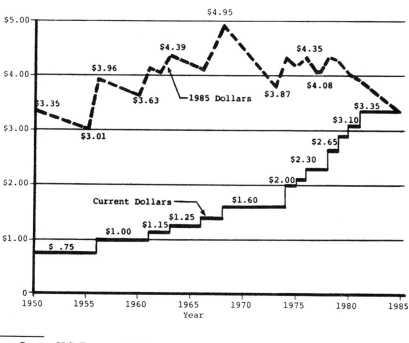

Source: U.S. Bureau of Labor Statistics

Wage Study Commission also recommended indexing the minimum wage. The Commission argued that indexing would not be inflationary and that it would be easier for business to adjust to regular, small increases in the minimum wage.[12] Social Security and other federal programs as well as some union contracts index wages to changes in consumer prices. Similar arrangements would be an appropriate way to trigger changes in the minimum wage.

Indexing would eliminate the erratic changes in the minimum wage level. It is difficult for the working poor to adjust to these abrupt changes and it is also disruptive to business planning, especially in those firms with a large proportion of minimum wage workers. Annual indexing of the minimum wage to a designated economic indicator would ensure small, orderly, incremental increases, thereby smoothing transitions for workers and employers.

Youth Subminimum

In recent years the youth unemployment rate has exceeded the overall unemployment rate by a factor of about two and one-half. In 1985, the teenage unemployment rate averaged 18.6 percent while the overall unemployment rate averaged 7.2 percent. Unemployment among black teenagers is an even more severe problem, it averaged 40.2 percent in 1985.

The Reagan administration has proposed a subminimum wage for youth as a means of reducing high youth unemployment rates, calling it a 'youth opportunity wage.' A subminimum wage is already in effect for some youths. Since 1961, employers have been able to secure Department of Labor certification to hire full-time students at 85 percent of the minimum wage as long as the students work less than 20 hours a week while attending school. In fiscal 1985, an estimated 195,800 students were hired under this program. A difficulty with this program is that it is cheaper to hire full-time students than those who are not in school. The unemployment of out-of-school youth, however, is a graver social problem than that of youths in school.

There have been many efforts to expand subminimum wage eligibility to larger numbers of youth. The Reagan administration would establish a 75 percent subminimum wage for 16- to 19-year-olds that would apply only to summer employment. The proposal is opposed by labor interests, although it has drawn increasing support not only from business but also from some minority groups and big city mayors. The Department of Labor has estimated the proposal would create 400,000 jobs.

There are a number of reasons why a youth subminimum wage should not be adopted. First, the estimates for job increases are based on questionable assumptions about labor market operations. The results of youth wage subsidy programs such as the Targeted Job Tax Credit and the Youth Incentives Entitlement Pilot Projects have not been encouraging. In particular, the subminimum wage may not generate many new jobs if the labor market remains slack. Labor demand is not very responsive to a change in wages under such conditions.

Second, a youth subminimum wage would make it advantageous to hire teenage instead of adult workers. The Minimum Wage Study Commission, which opposed a youth subminimum wage, estimated that a 75 percent minimum would create 400,000 to 450,000 jobs for youth but would displace 50,000 to 150,000 adult workers. The commission noted that its displacement estimate is low because its analysis implicitly examined the possibility of youth replacing average adult workers instead of examining the more likely effect that adult workers earning the minimum wage or slightly higher would be displaced.[13]

Third, youths who need the jobs the most—those who have had trouble breaking into the labor market—are least likely to benefit from a subminimum wage. They lack basic job skills and tend to live in areas with severe job deficits where business expansion is unlikely. They need to master the three R's and require specialized programs, such as the Job Corps, to prepare them for the job market.

Fourth, many teenagers who might have been hired at the established minimum wage would lose income if hired at a subminimum wage. Finally, a subminimum wage departs from the principle of equal pay for equal work. In many cases, teenagers are competing with adults for unskilled jobs. Because their marginal productivity is likely to match that of older workers, their pay should be equal as well.

In short, a subminimum wage would have dubious value for teenagers and its potential effectiveness is likely to be at the expense of adult workers. The current subminimum wage discussion has also preempted discussion of the sharp fall in the real value of the minimum wage since 1981. As long as debate focuses on the subminimum issue, the real value of the minimum wage will continue to erode.

Other Options

One general argument made against the minimum wage is that if its objective is to raise the income of the poor, it would be preferable to use programs more specifically tailored to their needs. A wage floor benefits all covered workers; some beneficiaries are poor but the majority are not. The assumption here is that while only the poor need the help of government regulation, the minimum wage affects both poor and nonpoor.

One alternative approach is to offer employers wage subsidies to hire the poor. The Targeted Job Tax Credit (TJTC),

established under the Revenue Act of 1978 and which expired
in 1985, promoted the employment of targeted groups by lowering the employers' costs of hiring these individuals. TJTC
provided employers with a 50 percent tax credit for the first
$6,000 of wages they pay to targeted employees in the initial
year and 25 percent during the second year. Eligible groups
included the handicapped, disadvantaged youths, Vietnam
veterans, welfare recipients, and former prison inmates.
Almost two-thirds of the 622,000 workers hired in 1985 under
TJTC were disadvantaged youth.[14]

The strength of the TJTC was that it was targeted towards
those most in need of assistance. However, in addition to a loss
in tax revenue, estimated at $440 million in fiscal 1985,[15] the
General Accounting Office has estimated that early in the
program most subsidized employees would have been hired
anyway, indicating a substantial windfall for employers with
few benefits for the targeted populations.[16] Efforts to eliminate
this windfall were not completely effective. Some potential
employees hid their eligibility, fearing, and rightfully so in
some cases, that the stigma attached to the program would
hurt their employment chances.[17] Still some 2.6 million eligible workers were hired under TJTC by the end of 1985. The
number that would have been hired without the tax credit is
unknown.

A demonstration project that offered sizable subsidies to
employers of economically disadvantaged youth suggests that
hard core unemployed youth need more than a wage subsidy to
make them desirable to employers. Some 6,000 businesses
were recruited as work sponsors. The Manpower Development
Research Corporation found that even with a 100 percent wage
subsidy, it was difficult to convince employers to participate in
the program.[18]

Subsidy Level	Company Participation Rate
50%	4.7%
75	10.0
100	18.2

Moreover, the program produced a substantial amount of displacement—about 50 percent of the work done by entitlement
workers replaced work that would have been done by other
workers. Projects that offered preferred jobs experienced

22 percent more displacement than inadequate work sites. Nevertheless, if the objective is to help disadvantaged youth, the role of a targeted subsidy should not be ignored.

Another proposal which seeks to address the needs of the working poor is a guaranteed annual income. This plan would provide low income persons a basic minimum income, with any earnings above that amount subject to a gradual tax. A guaranteed annual income would both bring some consistency to welfare benefits and, if set at the appropriate level, solve some of the poverty problem; the difficulty lies in devising a program that maintains work incentives and is not too costly.

A guaranteed annual income and other income payments to the poor would not, however, make the minimum wage superfluous. The income needs of workers, even if they live in families with total incomes above the poverty line, should not be discounted. Equally important, the minimum wage is necessary to encourage the poor and make it possible for them to work their way out of poverty, achieve self-reliance, and in the process, reduce their dependence on welfare. Finally, if the socially recognized value of work is to have any meaning, the minimum wage is necessary to express and support that value.

Overtime

In addition to establishing a floor on wages, the Fair Labor Standards Act requires the payment of time-and-one-half pay for over 40 hours of work per week. The average workweek declined from over 50 hours in the 1920s to below 40 hours during the Great Depression. Since World War II, the standard workweek for full-time workers has remained at the 40 hour level.

Limiting the workweek serves a dual purpose. It aids employed individuals by allowing them more free time for nonwork activities and by protecting them from the potential safety and health dangers of working excessively long hours. It also promotes work sharing as a way to spread employment. This objective seemed particularly important during the Depression when a quarter of the nation's work force was unemployed.

The proportion of wage and salary workers covered under the FLSA hours standard has risen since 1938 to its current level of roughly 60 percent. Coverage among nonsupervisory employees approaches 100 percent in construction and manufacturing.[19] The Act still excludes executive, administrative, professional employees, outside workers, and agricultural workers. In addition, large gaps in coverage exist in the private household, transportation and public utilities, retail trade and service sectors. State and local government employees were essentially uncovered under the FLSA until the Supreme Court held in 1985 *(Garcia v. San Antonio Metro Transit Authority)* that the FLSA is applicable to these employees. Congress eased the impact of this decision on state and local governments by passing legislation allowing state and local governments to pay for overtime with compensatory time off.

Incentive

A time-and-one-half overtime premium creates an economic incentive for a company to cut down on overtime hours and to hire new employees to work the extra hours at the basic wage instead of having current employees do the work at the time-and-one-half wage. The strength of these incentives depends on the costs of hiring and training a new worker and on the company's fringe benefits.

Fringe benefits have grown significantly; they currently account for almost two-fifths of total manufacturing labor costs as compared to about 20 percent in 1957 (Table 2). For all

---

Table 2. **Increase of Fringe Benefits in Manufacturing as a Proportion of Total Labor Costs**

Year	Employer's Legally Required Payments	Pensions, Insurance	Paid Rest	Pay for Time Not Worked	Other Items	All Fringe Benefits
1957	4.1%	5.8%	2.4%	6.5%	1.5%	20.3%
1967	6.4	7.0	3.0	7.3	1.9	25.6
1977	9.3	12.9	3.6	9.2	2.3	37.3
1983	10.1	14.2	2.4	9.6	2.4	38.7

Source: U.S. Chamber of Commerce, *Employee Benefits 1983*, p. 11; Ronald G. Ehrenberg and Paul L. Schumann, *Longer Hours or More Jobs* (Ithaca: Cornell University Press, 1982), p. 13.

industries, fringe benefits average 37 percent of a worker's pay.

A numerical example illustrates how fringe benefits associated with hiring new workers undermine the effect of the overtime provision. Given the average hourly wage of $8.67 (November 1985), an hour of overtime would cost $13.00 while the total hourly cost of labor was $11.88—$8.67 plus the 37 percent cost of fringe benefits. Even without considering hiring and training costs, there is little incentive to hire a new worker. (This comparison understates the cost of overtime; some fringe benefits fluctuate with hours worked, thus raising the average hourly cost of overtime.)

Fringe benefits serve useful functions for employers and workers. Employers benefit because fringes promote worker efficiency by boosting morale and reducing turnover. Workers gain because health insurance and other fringe benefits, unlike cash compensation, are not taxable and because group plans reduce the costs of benefits, giving workers protection they could not otherwise afford.[20]

Hours Worked

The average workweek for full-time workers has remained remarkably stable since 1950, although the average workweek for all workers has declined due mostly to the large number of part-time workers in the retail and service sectors. Manufacturing industries employ relatively few part-timers, with an average workweek ranging between 38.9 and 41.4 hours since 1947 (Figure 6).

The remarkable stability of average weekly hours worked reflects the broad social acceptance the 40-hour workweek has won, the overtime premium firms must pay, and the increasing percentage of workers covered by the FLSA hourly standard. Longer hours remain common, however—in 1985 some 17 million nonfarm workers labored 49 hours or more a week, including one of every four professional and managerial workers, most of whom are not covered by the FLSA. One of every five craft workers who were not covered by the FLSA overtime provision also labored 49 or more hours a week.[21]

Figure 6. Average weekly work hours have changed little since World War II

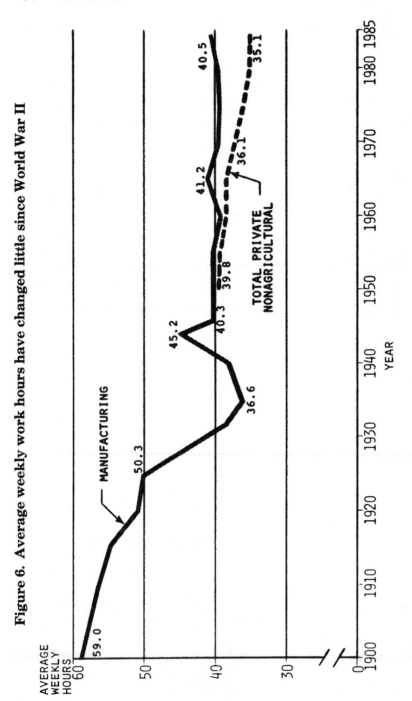

Source: U.S. Bureau of Labor Statistics.

	Number of Workers (in thousands)	Percent of Total in Occupation
Total nonfarm workers	99,064	—
All workers laboring 49 hours or more	17,002	17.2
Managerial and professional speciality	6,558	26.4
Technical, sales, and administrative support	4,345	13.7
Service occupations	1,294	9.5
Precision production, craft, and repair	2,440	19.0
Operators, fabricators, and laborers	2,365	14.8

Employment and Efficiency

The overtime standard creates problems for employers. Workers are not interchangeable parts—one cannot be easily substituted for another. Variations in workers' skills and abilities, as well as the continuity of production processes, often impede employers' ability to reduce the hours of currently employed workers and hire the unemployed.[22] Moreover, occupational shortages may exist even in the midst of high unemployment. In order to maintain work schedules, therefore, employers may require overtime despite the penalty rates.

As a result, average overtime hours rise and fall only slightly with economic fluctuations. When the unemployment rate hit 9.7 percent in 1982—the peak in more than four decades—manufacturing employees worked 2.3 hours of overtime per week compared with 3.4 hours by the end of 1985, three years into the recovery. Reliance on overtime hours, even when the unemployment rate is high, suggests some inflexibility in the labor markets and that overtime pay does not reduce unemployment substantially. Overtime work has remained almost constant since World War II. In the 1960s, manufacturing workers averaged 3.2 hours of overtime each week; in the 1970s, the average was 3.3 hours.

Productivity growth also plays a major role in determining costs associated with the overtime provision. American employees have been able to attain a higher standard of living through productivity gains, particularly in the 1950s and 1960s. High labor costs stimulated employers to push for technological advances and to accelerate the substitution of more efficient machinery for labor. A better educated work force, as well as a reduction in worker fatigue due to shorter hours, also contributed to increased productivity. As industrialization progressed, the productivity increases could have been paid out to the worker in either increased leisure or higher real wages. The stabilization of the workweek around 40 hours indicates that most American workers have chosen higher income over increased leisure.

A Shorter Workweek

Evidently 40 hours has not proven to be an overly burdensome workweek because shorter hours have not been a major bargaining issue in recent years. Collective bargaining agreements show only minor changes in the length of the workweek since the late 1950s. Unions formally favor shorter hours, but reducing weekly hours while maintaining levels of take-home pay without a commensurate rise in productivity has met with strong employer opposition and would inevitably exacerbate inflationary pressures.

In a survey of workers' preferences for various forms of additional compensation, shorter workdays were at the bottom of the list.[23] This study revealed strong desires for extra vacations but little demand for shorter workdays. The order of preference given by the surveyed workers were as follows: 1) extra vacation; 2) pay increases; 3) pension increases; 4) family dental plans; 5) early retirement; 6) a four-day workweek; and 7) shorter workdays. Preferences did vary with age; younger and older workers preferred extra vacation, whereas middle-aged workers preferred extra pay. But, in general, when given the choice between pushing for higher wages or shorter hours, unions and workers have opted for higher wages.

The increasing participation of women in the labor force, however, may shift the trend in the direction of shorter hours of work. Women have traditionally opted for more leisure time because of their commitment to taking care of their homes and families. Also, dual income families are relieved of some of the pressures to work longer hours to increase family income. With two paychecks coming in, each spouse can afford and may prefer to work fewer hours and spend the extra time tending to household responsibilities or enjoying leisure activities. Sharing of provider and parenting roles will require an added measure of flexibility in work hours. These emerging trends in the modern family may well be translated into future demands for paid leisure and shorter or more flexible work schedules.

If there is renewed interest in reducing hours of work, it is likely the change will come about gradually through collective bargaining and the free market. Government intervention is unlikely unless the trend toward job deficits and creeping unemployment continues to plague labor markets. In that case, government intervention may be deemed essential. Consequently, the overtime provision may be raised from time and one-half to double time, or the standard workweek might be reduced.

Raising the overtime provision to double time would counteract the recent rise in the cost of fringe benefits and would restore the impact of the overtime penalty. According to one estimate, increasing the overtime rate to double time would decrease overtime hours by roughly 20 percent. If the reduced hours were converted to hiring new workers, employment could be expected to rise by one to two percent.[24]

Complementing the overtime provisions of the FLSA is the 1936 Walsh-Healey Act, which sets hourly standards for workers producing goods under federal contract and provides for time-and-one-half pay for more than eight hours worked in one day, rather than 40 hours in a week. Congressional proposals to amend the hourly provisions of the Walsh-Healey Public Contracts Act have been frequent in the past decade. Proponents argue that Walsh-Healey should be made consistent with the FLSA. This would facilitate establishing compressed workweeks, which would give employees longer weekends and might also increase productivity. Opponents respond that a compressed workweek is likely to be imposed on employees by management instead of chosen freely, and that working more than eight hours in a day can be excessively strenuous.[25]

FLSA Enforcement

Millions of workers are denied FLSA protection because their employers fail to comply with the law. The Minimum Wage Study Commission estimated that during a two-year investigation period five million employees were underpaid in violation of the FLSA. The retail trade and service sectors, with large numbers of low-wage workers, account for over one-half of all firms violating FLSA provisions and employ over 70 percent of all workers who were illegally paid less than the minimum.[26]

The Department of Labor has a poor record of enforcing wage and hour standards. In 1979, the value of back wages owed to employees from minimum wage violations represented about 8 percent of the total earnings of minimum wage workers. Only about one-fifth of the estimated dollar amount of FLSA violations was detected, and just over half of this amount was then collected. The Labor Department also fails to target enforcement to areas in which it is most needed, specifically retail trade and services. Most wage and hour investigations have been initiated by employee complaints and are ordinarily of repeat offenders.[27] Because of low penalties and slack enforcement, many employers have little economic incentive to comply with the law.

Enforcement has deteriorated even further in recent years. A 1985 study by the General Accounting Office found that most of the problems it identified with FLSA enforcement in 1981 remained in 1985. GAO also found that the numbers of Labor Department staff years spent on FLSA enforcement fell from 558 in fiscal year 1981 to 474 in fiscal year 1984. In the same period, the amount of back wages due that was identified by the Labor Department declined from $127 million to $107 million.[28]

What Has the FLSA Accomplished?

The minimum wage floor and an hourly workweek standard remain of tremendous benefit to major sectors of the American work force. The minimum wage floor raises the income of millions of workers, many of whom are poor. Moreover, it strengthens the work incentive and protects employees from exploitive conditions. The hourly standard protects workers from excessive hours of labor. The value of both standards, particularly the minimum wage, has declined in recent years. Indexing an adequate minimum wage appears necessary, while changing the overtime penalty provision to double time may merit consideration if unemployment creeps upward. These two standards combined have contributed to improving the quality of life in the workplace and their salutary impact needs to be preserved.

6
Securing Safety and Health

The attention and resources a society devotes to job safety and the prevention of health hazards is a measure of its compassion and affluence. Before the era of governmental regulation, insuring a safe and healthy workplace was a private matter between employers and employees, and employees assumed the hazards of the job as a condition of employment. In the absence of government sanctions, firms frequently neglected to provide adequate protection or to assume responsibility for the social and individual costs of workplace injuries and illnesses.

Beginning in the early 1900s, workers received some protection from states—through workers' compensation programs or occasional regulation of workplace conditions—and the courts, but the workplace remained dangerous and pressures mounted for federal intervention. With the passage of the Occupational Safety and Health Act of 1970, the federal government assumed the major responsibility for regulating safety and health in the workplace.

The Need for Federal Intervention

Throughout the industrial age it has been apparent that unchecked market forces create intolerable work conditions. Before the government stepped in, employers often did not adopt measures that would enhance health and safety in the workplace. Employees could expect no relief from the courts because employers relied on three common law defenses—contributory negligence on the part of the worker, negligence on the part of co-workers, or the assumption of risk by the worker in taking the job—to win most cases. During the progressive era, however, courts increasingly ruled in favor of workers in safety and health cases. Progressive politicians also pushed for legislation to aid injured workers and to establish safety standards. By 1920, forty states had enacted workers' compensation laws.[1]

Employers supported the passage of workers' compensation laws because a stable, low-cost system partly of their own design was preferable to the unpredictable and sometimes high costs which resulted from court action. Workers' compensation, even when it provided limited coverage and inadequate income support, offered an alternative to court remedies which few workers could afford. Many workers, therefore, supported workers' compensation because it offered assured, no-fault compensation.[2]

Failure of State Programs

The workers' compensation system failed to provide more than minimal protection to employees and gave employers little incentive to reduce hazards. This is well illustrated by the experience with silicosis during the 1930s. Silicosis is a disease which scars the lungs through inhalation of the silica dust released into the air when rocks are drilled or crushed. This creates severe breathing difficulty and increases susceptibility to tuberculosis. According to one estimate, as many as one million workers had been exposed to harmful amounts of silica dust by 1930; although one in four of these workers could be expected to develop silicosis, only six states had enacted laws making silicosis a compensable disease.

The Gauley Bridge tunnel disaster in Hawks Nest, West Virginia, in the early 1930s focused national attention on the silicosis problem. As a result of dry drilling that failed to meet United States Bureau of Mines standards and that sprinkled mine workers with almost pure silica dust, many workers soon developed acute silicosis, which often leads to death by suffocation. The company responsible for the drilling took a callous attitude towards the plight of the workers. Rush Dew Holt, then Senator from West Virginia, charged that: "The company openly said that if they killed off those men there were plenty of other men to be had."[3]

In the face of widespread public concern and lawsuits for hundreds of millions of dollars worth of damages, 20 states expanded their workers' compensation laws to cover pulmonary dust diseases, of which silicosis is one. These laws, however, primarily served the interests of employers and insurance companies. Most statutes required a worker to file for compensation within a specified time period (usually one to three years) following the last exposure to the hazard that caused the illness or injury. Due to the progressive nature of silicosis, the disease may become serious well after this time period, leaving many workers suffering from the disease unable to file claims. As a result of such restrictions, only a small fraction of the hundreds of thousands of workers disabled by silicosis received any workers' compensation, while workers' compensation laws effectively limited the ability of workers to obtain compensation in the courts.

The silicosis story is only one example of the failure of many employers to establish safe and healthy working conditions and of the failure of state workers' compensation programs to help victims and their families cope with occupational injuries and diseases. It also shows that court suits, even if they do not produce large settlements, do spur some private or governmental action.

Exposure to asbestos, a proven carcinogen, is another notorious example of employer neglect of worker health and safety. While employers have had some knowledge about the effects of asbestos exposure since the 1930s, they took no steps to provide adequate protection and failed to inform employees of the dangers.[4] For the same reasons cited in the silicosis example, employees suffering from asbestos exposure did not receive much assistance from state workers' compensation systems. Not only was the danger to workers ignored, but consumers were also placed in jeopardy when asbestos was installed in countless schools, ships, and commercial as well as residential buildings.

Only after the court cases of the 1960s and 1970s and the active involvement of federal agencies was any progress made to protect workers and the public from asbestos exposure. The nation continues to pay for the earlier neglect. It was estimated in 1985 that exposure to asbestos causes the death of 40 percent of asbestos workers. Most future exposure will occur where asbestos has already been installed; efforts to remove this asbestos or to limit exposure will cost billions of dollars.

From now until the early 21st century, an estimated 220,000 more asbestos related deaths will occur.[5]

Workers' compensation laws failed to provide workers suffering from injuries or illnesses with income commensurate to their losses. Payments during the 1960s averaged 50 to 60 percent of a worker's former wage, and were not adjusted for inflation. No compensation was provided for pain and suffering resulting from injury or illness; the system failed to consider that ruined lives as well as lost wages are involved.

Workers' compensation coverage remained especially spotty in cases of occupational disease. For example, in 1970 three states—Georgia, North Carolina, and South Carolina— accounted for over 50 percent of textile industry employment. Byssinosis, a disease commonly associated with work in textile mills, was not covered by workers' compensation in Georgia and North Carolina. South Carolina did cover byssinosis, but no workers' compensation cases were reported even though an estimated 17,000 textile workers in the state suffered from the disease.[6]

The workers' compensation system also provided inadequate incentives for firms to take preventive measures. Since employers' contributions covered only a portion of pecuniary damages and failed to provide compensation for nonpecuniary damages, employers' outlays accounted for only a fraction of personal and social costs. Moreover, because a firm's contribution to the workers' compensation fund was only marginally related to its accident record, firms with hazardous workplaces were not penalized at a level high enough to provide a sufficient incentive to correct unsafe or unhealthy conditions.

States also attempted to establish and enforce workplace standards, but, with a few exceptions, their regulatory record was abysmal. State regulatory laws were first passed in the latter half of the 19th century. In the early 20th century, states passed the first significant occupational disease laws which regulated worker exposure to lead. By the 1960s, all states had passed legislation dealing with safety hazards but they still offered little protection to workers. Standards relating to occupational health were few and far between—occupational health programs existed in only 20 states—and states conducted very little research on health hazards. The commitment of states to workplace health and safety varied widely, as shown by 1969 state expenditures ranging from $.01 per employee in Wyoming to $2.70 in Oregon. Fragmented and competing administrative jurisdictions within states often prevented the enforcement of occupational health laws[7] and even when laws provided for effective sanctions, officials often chose not to apply them.[8]

A fundamental problem with a state standard approach is that a state establishing stricter standards than exist in other states may forfeit some competitive advantage in attracting business. Another problem is that businesses with plants in more than one state are subject to different standards for different plants, thus reducing efficiency. A federal approach eliminates interstate competition and facilitates the passage and implementation of uniform national standards.

Federal Law

Despite the serious and widespread hazards that plagued the workplace and the failure of existing governmental mechanisms to solve these problems, pressure to adopt federal safety and health laws did not develop until the 1960s. The rise of the environmental movement, which slowly expanded its concern for general community conditions to include the work environment, and heightened union interest in safety and health issues both contributed to the movement for federal regulation. These developments reflected rising educational attainment and improved living standards which affected workers' willingness to shift attention to nonwage objectives.

Although by 1970 nearly two-thirds of all collective bargaining agreements included health and safety clauses, most were boilerplate, and union leaders preferred to achieve safety and health standards by legislation. Lacking health and safety expertise, they felt unable to bargain effectively on these issues. They also believed that many workers would be unwilling to trade wage increases for improved health and safety and that reasonable health and safety standards were a right that should not have to be won at the bargaining table.

Negative trends in worker safety and health also spurred reform. One such trend was a reported 29 percent rise in the industrial accident rate during the 1960s. Another factor was rising concern about occupational diseases, due partly to fear of both new production processes and the products of the technological age. The occupational health and safety problem was of staggering magnitude. In 1969 an estimated 14,500 workers were killed on the job and, by the lowest count, 2.2 million workers were injured. The Public Health Service estimated that some 400,000 persons were affected by occupational diseases and that occupational injuries and diseases combined resulted in the loss of 250 million work days.[9]

Regulation of health and safety factors in the workplace became increasingly popular and had bipartisan support in Congress. After 50 years of ineffective state occupational and health safety programs, the federal government chose to assume center stage in regulating the health and safety of the work environment. The federal government had previously played a minor role in improving working conditions. The Public Health Service, established in 1798, had been intermittently active on health issues, primarily focusing on research and dissemination of information. The Walsh-Healey Public Contracts Act of 1936 directed the federal government to ensure the safety of individuals employed by firms with federal contracts exceeding $10,000, but the federal effort under Walsh-Healey was relatively weak. The federal government also played some role in curbing abusive working conditions in hazardous industries including coal mining and longshore operations.

President Johnson introduced a comprehensive safety and health bill in 1968, but the legislation failed to make it to the floor of either house. A series of coal mining disasters in November 1968, culminating in an explosion which killed 78 miners in Farmington, West Virginia, provided renewed momentum for federal intervention. The public outcry over these disasters led to the passage of the Coal Mine Health and Safety Act of 1969.

President Nixon introduced a comprehensive occupational safety and health bill at the beginning of his first term in 1969, as did Democratic legislators with the active backing of labor unions and other groups. During the legislative debate, discussion of the potential costs of compliance with regulations was somewhat limited. Unions had a direct and obvious interest in avoiding a discussion of costs. Employers' argument that they already did all they could to ensure worker health and safety made it difficult for them to argue that providing a safer and healthier work environment would be costly.[10] Ultimately, rather than requiring that the benefits from standards outweigh their costs, an ambiguous feasibility requirement was established.

The legislative struggle focused on the scope of the bill and the powers of the agency to be entrusted with its administration. President Nixon and management representatives favored the establishment of independent agencies which would set standards but have limited enforcement power. Labor unions and their allies, believing that the Department of Labor would be sympathetic to their concerns, advocated that it be empowered both to set standards and to enforce them. The resulting compromise kept both standard-setting and enforcement in the Department of Labor, subject to review by an independent commission. The Department of Health, Education, and Welfare, however, was to conduct research about standard criteria. Proponents of a strong state role in the new program—state officials, the Nixon administration, and some members of Congress—obtained a provision giving states the option, subject to federal approval and monitoring, to assume administration of the program. States also retained responsibility for workers' compensation, and aggregate 1984 outlays for state workers' compensation programs subsequently rose to $20 billion in 1984.

Senator Jacob Javits characterized the legislative battle preceding passage of the 1970 Occupational Safety and Health Act as "the most bitter labor-management fight in years."[11] President Nixon signed the Act into law on December 29, 1970.

Administration of OSHA

The Occupational Safety and Health Act of 1970 has an ambitious goal: "to assure so far as possible every working man and woman in the nation safe and healthful working conditions." To accomplish this broad mandate, the Act created the Occupational Safety and Health Administration (OSHA), the Occupational Safety and Health Review Commission (OSHRC), and the National Institute for Occupational Safety and Health (NIOSH). Located in the Department of Labor, OSHA sets and enforces workplace safety and health standards. Its primary activities are standard setting, enforcement, overseeing state administration, and education.

OSHRC, an independent three-member panel appointed by the President with the advice and consent of the Senate, reviews and resolves disputes arising out of OSHA enforcement. NIOSH, in the Department of Health and Human Services, is a research agency responsible for conducting the analysis necessary for the development of health and safety standards. This chapter focuses on OSHA, the most important of the three agencies.

Standards

OSHA sets mandatory workplace health and safety standards that preempt any state or local standards. The 1970 law authorized OSHA to adopt existing federal and "national consensus standards" within two years unless the agency could show the standards were unnecessary. "National consensus standards" were defined as those adopted by national groups (such as the American National Standards Institute) through a process that allowed for input from diverse sources and in which interested parties had reached "substantial agreement."[12] OSHA administrators indiscriminately adopted the standards in a few months. This quick action was taken because business representatives had argued during the legislative debate that these consensus standards were already widely accepted and also because quick progress was in accord with congressional intent.

As it turned out, however, many of the consensus standards were outdated, irrelevant, or trivial. One regulation, for example, required that "each water closet shall occupy a separate compartment with a door and walls or partitions between fixtures sufficiently high to assure privacy." Another statute prohibited employers from serving ice water to their employees because years ago when ice was cut in blocks from rivers, it was unsanitary.[13] In 1978 the Carter administration weeded out 900 of these inappropriate standards.

OSHA was also given power to adopt new standards through two rulemaking processes, one for ordinary circumstances and one for emergency circumstances. The standards that have been established by these processes are few in number, although some have greatly affected health and safety conditions in the workplace.

The health standards that OSHA has adopted through rulemaking regulate hazards as important as asbestos, vinyl chloride, and cotton dust exposure. It has also established general procedures for hazard labeling. The Office of Technology Assessment singled out 18 major health standards (Table 3).[14]

Some of the standards listed above are revisions; others—the 1978 benzene standard, and one of the 14 carcinogens—were overturned in court. Some standards are still undergoing judicial review, others are being reconsidered by OSHA, and the application of still others has been deferred by OSHA.

Table 3. OSHA Health Standards
(1972–1984)

OSHA Regulation	Final Standard
1. Asbestos[a,b]	6/07/72
2. Fourteen carcinogens[a]	1/29/74
3. Vinyl chloride[a]	10/04/74
4. Coke oven emissions	10/22/76
5. Benzene[a]	2/10/78
6. DBCP[a,c]	3/17/78
7. Inorganic arsenic	5/05/78
8. Cotton dust/cotton gins	6/23/78
9. Acrylonitrile[a]	10/03/78
10. Lead	11/14/78
11. Cancer policy	1/22/80
12. Access to employee exposure and medical records	5/23/80
13. Occupational noise exposure/hearing conservation	1/16/81
14. Lead—reconsideration of respirator fit-testing requirements	11/12/82
15. Coal tar pitch volatiles—modification of interpretation	1/21/83
16. Hearing conservation—reconsideration	3/08/83
17. Hazard communication (labeling)	1/25/83
18. Ethylene oxide	6/22/84

[a]Subject of an emergency temporary standard.
[b]Emergency standards were issued for asbestos in 1971 and 1983.
[c]1, 2-dibromo-3-chloropropane.

The courts play a key role in the regulatory process. Most health standards have been challenged in court by employers, and some are challenged by employee representatives. Judges must weigh the many controversial and difficult technical issues these standards involve and make the final decision on their legality.

Currently, OSHA uses a four-step process to establish health standards and to consider costs and benefits. It determines if a hazard creates a "significant risk," and then decides if regulation can reduce that risk. The next step involves setting a goal to reduce the risk as much as feasible. Finally, OSHA conducts a cost-effectiveness study to discover the least costly option. Major standards are then subject to OMB review. The agency has issued 26 safety standards through rulemaking, many of which have been revisions of initial standards. On the whole, safety standards have been less wide-ranging than health standards.

OSHA may require the adoption of new technology in order to ensure standard compliance, although consideration must be given to both the economic and technological feasibility of compliance. Performance rather than specification standards have increasingly been used. Performance standards set the level of safety and health the company must achieve, allowing the company to choose the method of control, while specification standards dictate compliance methods to industry.

Enforcement

Inspection is the primary tool used to ensure compliance with OSHA regulations. OSHA inspectors normally enter a workplace without advance notice, although the Supreme Court has ruled that if an employer objects to a voluntary inspection, OSHA must obtain a court-issued warrant. If OSHA anticipates an objection, it can get a warrant in advance. Employee and employer representatives may be present throughout the inspection. The inspector is required to issue a citation if an employer has violated a standard; previously, under state programs, inspectors had more discretion in issuing citations. The citation must be posted near the violation site and follow-up inspections may take place to confirm compliance.

Federal and state OSHA administrators annually inspect fewer than 4 percent of all the nation's workplaces. In 1983, roughly 6.8 million employees were covered by these inspections. The vast majority of inspections, about 82 percent of federal inspections and 90 percent of state inspections, examine safety conditions. Although employees have the right to request inspections if they detect OSHA violations, and inspections may be triggered by reports of hazardous conditions, roughly four-fifths of all inspections are programmed. OSHA programmed inspections have primarily targeted the construction and manufacturing industries.

Civil penalties of up to $10,000 can be issued for each willful or repeated violation of the Act; penalties of up to $1,000 can be levied for any serious violation of the Act; penalties of up to $1,000 per day may be assessed for failure to abate on schedule; and a penalty of up to $10,000 and/or six months imprisonment may be imposed on any employer whose willful violation of any standard resulted in an employee death. A double penalty can be imposed after the first conviction. In practice, fines have been relatively minimal, as figures for the 1983 fiscal year illustrate.[15]

	Federal	State
Total inspections	58,516*	103,879
Total proposed penalties	$6,403,188	$7,033,364
Average proposed penalties		
Serious	$ 177	$ 167
Other	74	139
Willful, repeat	4,555	3,112
Failure to abate	346	191

*Does not include 10,402 "Records Review" inspections. More serious violations are cited than any other category and they account, in dollars, for the majority of penalties.

Employers have the right to contest OSHA citations and penalties, and both employers and employees share the right to contest the length of an abatement period. The first hearing is before an administrative law judge employed by the Occupational Safety and Health Review Commission (OSHRC). All interested parties—OSHA, employees, and employers—can participate in these proceedings. Any decision can be appealed to the Commission and then to the federal court of appeals.

The OSHA enforcement process, as well as its standards setting process, has been hampered by a personnel shortage in the relatively new occupational safety and health field. This shortage includes the personnel needed for ensuring compliance with the rules and standards of the Act, researchers to identify potential occupational safety and health hazards and to assess their effects upon workers, and technicians to help develop and implement techniques, methods, and programs for treating occupational disease and injury.

Early OSHA inspectors, lacking the ability to detect serious health and safety hazards, sometimes focused on trivial violations. These violations, such as the height of a railing, could be easily detected and measured. Over time, as trained professionals began filling inspection and other OSHA positions, inspection quality complaints declined. As more experts are developed in the health and safety field, OSHA's ability to establish and enforce reasonable standards should continue to improve.

State Administration

Section 18 of the OSH Act allows a state to assume administration of health and safety regulations if it provides "for the development and enforcement of safety and health standards . . . which . . . are or will be at least as effective" as federal standards. States assume administration through a step-by-step process involving differing degrees of cooperative administration and federal monitoring. The amount of leeway states have in administering programs, as well as the level of encouragement they have received to assume administrative responsibilities, has varied under different OSHA administrations. As of 1984, 25 states had assumed varying degrees of administrative responsibility for OSHA; by mid-1985 six state programs and the Virgin Islands had received "final approval," allowing for almost complete state administration with minimal federal monitoring.[16]

Public Education

Over the years, OSHA has increasingly turned to education, consultation, and training to help solve health and safety problems. Education is provided through grants to employees, employers, education or nonprofit organizations to establish training programs or develop educational materials. Funding for the program fell from $13.9 million in fiscal 1981 to $5.6 million in fiscal 1985. Another program provides on-site consultations. These consultations are carried out by state officials or private consultants who provide employers with a confidential evaluation of the health and safety of a workplace and other suggestions for abatement. The consultations are financed by OSHA and are provided only on request. Priority is given to small businesses.

OSHA Under Reagan

Recent administration of OSHA has reflected the Reagan administration's fervor for deregulation. As in other policy areas, OSHA deregulation has not occurred through changes in its enabling Act, but through the administration of its mandate. One article on the first four years of OSHA under Reagan summarized: "The Occupational Safety and Health Act has not been amended in four years, but the Reagan administration has relaxed standards and enforcement policies to compensate for what it sees as anti-business excesses of the past."[17]

While nine new and fairly significant health standards were established during the Carter years, in the first Reagan term only five health standards were issued through the standard rulemaking process, and some of these were modifications of earlier standards. The respirator fitting and hearing conservation standards revised earlier rules, and allowed employers more flexibility in compliance.[18] The coal tar pitch volatiles standard modified a previous standard by excluding coverage of petroleum asphalt. OSHA issued the ethylene oxide standard only after an appeals court ordered it to expedite its rulemaking process.[19]

The most important standard issued, hazard communication, provides workers with information about chemical work hazards. It is a far-reaching standard, but one which is weaker than many existing state and local laws and the "hazard identification" standard proposed in the last days of the Carter administration. The hazard communication standard, for instance, fails to cover nonmanufacturing workers, while many state and local laws provide this coverage.[20] An appeals court decision has ordered OSHA to expand the standard to cover those workers unless it can justify not doing so.[21] In contrast to the standard under the Carter administration, the standard under Reagan requires less extensive labeling of containers and pipes holding or transporting toxic substances. The Reagan administration also established an emergency temporary standard for asbestos. While stricter than the 1972 standard, it was overturned by the courts.

Thorne Auchter, Reagan's first assistant secretary of labor for OSHA, emphasized cooperation rather than what he felt was OSHA's adversarial approach.[22] In this spirit, OSHA expanded the use of the "informal settlement" process initiated during the last year of the Carter administration. This process allows OSHA area administrators to informally negotiate citation compliance with employers or employees, although under the Reagan administration employees complain of being shut out of the process. Auchter claimed this approach expedited the prompt abatement of substandard workplace conditions.[23] Contested citations, which postpone abatement until the case is resolved, did drop from 12 percent of all inspections in fiscal 1980 to 2 percent in fiscal 1983. The cooperative approach also led to a 60 percent drop in proposed citation penalties. Since proposed penalties can be bartered down in the informal negotiation process, actual penalties dropped by more than 60 percent. In a similar administrative action, on-site consultations jumped from 22,300 in fiscal 1981 to 28,800 two years later.[24] The use of this voluntary abatement policy was further encouraged by a 1984 OSHA guarantee that if a company agrees to an on-site consultation and commits itself to correct any violations found, then the company will not receive a programmed OSHA inspection in the next year.

In order to improve the targeting of programmed inspections, officials attempted to eliminate inspections of relatively safe workplaces by instituting a "records review" policy that requires an inspector to examine injury records before entering a workplace. If the lost workday rate is less than the national average for manufacturing, then the inspection is terminated. As part of its targeting policy, OSHA also emphasized inspection in the construction industry, which, next to mining, has the highest injury rate of all industries.[25] In fiscal 1983 roughly 58 percent of OSHA's inspections were in this industry. Last, inspections in response to employee complaints were de-emphasized, and dropped by half from the last year of the Carter administration.

The role of states in administering OSHA increased under the Reagan administration. In 1984 OSHA for the first time gave final approval to states to assume essentially complete administration of federal standards. OSHA has also allowed states without final approval substantial discretion in administering the Act.

Reagan's second OSHA administrator, Robert Rowland, assumed office in July 1984, served for one year, and resigned in the wake of charges that he failed to carry out OSHA's mandate. His refusal to issue a field sanitation standard requiring toilets and clean drinking water for farm workers illustrated his lack of concern over unsatisfactory workplace conditions. Also, as a member of the Occupational Safety and Health Review Commission from 1981 to 1984, he voted against upholding OSHA citations 84 percent of the time.[26] The Office of Government Ethics cleared Rowland of conflict of interest charges on the day he resigned.

OSHA's budget was cut from fiscal 1981 to fiscal 1985 by 7 percent in constant dollars, while the number of employees was cut by 25 percent. In the fiscal 1986 budget, the Reagan administration recommended that OSHA's funds be cut by another $7 million from its $220 million appropriation in the preceding year. (State funding of OSHA totaled roughly $53 million.)[27]

The Reagan administration has given the Office of Management and Budget responsibility for overseeing federal regulatory activities. OMB initially directed that OSHA's major standards pass the test of cost-benefit analysis. The Supreme Court invalidated the cost-benefit approach, ruling in *American Textile Manufacturers Institute v. Donovan* that "The Congressional reports and debates certainly confirm that Congress meant 'feasible' and nothing else. . . . Perhaps most telling is the absence of any indication whatsoever that Congress intended OSHA to conduct its own cost-benefit analysis before promulgating a toxic material or harmful physical agent standard."[28] The meaning of "feasible" is ambiguous. Some economic costs are acceptable, but exactly how much of an industry can be shut down before a standard becomes infeasible remains undefined. In accordance with the Supreme Court ruling, OSHA adopted a cost-effectiveness approach to govern its regulations. A cost-benefit test allows adoption of a standard only if it can be shown that the benefits (measured in dollars) exceed the costs of the standard. In contrast, a cost-effectiveness test chooses the least costly method of achieving a standard.

Two concerns have been raised about OMB's increased role in safety and health regulations.[29] One charge raised in Congressional hearings is that because OMB is biased in favor of employers, often meeting with them secretly, OSHA regulations in areas such as hazard communication and commercial diving have been undermined. A second concern is with OMB's focus on the costs of regulation. Despite the Supreme Court ruling in *American Textile*, cost-benefit analysis dominates the thinking of the Reagan administration and such analysis often measures only costs—which are more easily quantified—and ignores benefits.

OSHA's Effectiveness

Passionate opinions about OSHA's effectiveness are the rule. Business representatives have attacked the agency on the grounds of excessive, arbitrary, and irrelevant involvement in the workplace. Labor leaders, for their part, have criticized OSHA for its inactivity, and this criticism has been turned up more than a few decibels since President Reagan took office. Given these contradictory claims, reaching an even-handed and precise assessment of OSHA's effectiveness has not been achieved. It is clear, nonetheless, that an active federal role can produce a healthier and safer workplace and, in its brief history, OSHA has shown some positive results.

Evaluation Difficulties

A basic obstacle to the evaluation of OSHA is that it is a new agency with a broad and complex mandate. It will be years before the impact of the effort to improve safety and remove health hazards in the workplace can be fully assessed. OSHA has had its start-up problems, some of which were avoidable. In particular, the quick adoption of consensus standards proved to be a mistake. Some of the agency's initial problems were less avoidable. It takes time to train the safety and health personnel necessary to establish and enforce standards as well as to educate employers and workers about workplace hazards. Start-up problems are to be expected with any new agency and they should be discounted when judgments are made.

Even under ideal circumstances, it would be difficult to gather the statistics necessary to show that OSHA regulations have cost business X amount of dollars, saved Y lives, and reduced nonfatal occupational injuries and illnesses by Z percent. As in most assessments of social programs, calculations of both costs and benefits are beset with data and causality problems. The government collects no information as to the cost of compliance with OSHA regulations. Some private surveys exist but their samples tend to focus on large companies. Moreover, these cost estimates are based on data supplied by employers who not only are motivated to exaggerate, but who also confront the difficult accounting task of separating the incremental costs related to OSHA from other business costs.

Calculating the benefits that result from regulation presents even greater difficulties. Distinguishing the effects of OSHA regulations from the effects of other changes in the work environment may involve subjective judgments. For example, injury rates are affected by changing economic conditions. Some of the factors causing injury rates to fall during recessions include the laying off of inexperienced workers, less overtime, and the slower pace of production. Fluctuations in injury rates may be due to OSHA, to changing economic conditions, to improved management and technological advancements, or to some combination of these factors. The precise causal relationship is difficult to determine.

Even if the costs and benefits of OSHA regulation could be accurately estimated, a cost-benefit analysis of the law's effectiveness would still involve weighing the two. What value should be attached to preventing the loss of an arm? Of the ability to hear? Of a life? This valuation process necessitates a wide range of normative judgments and economic considerations. Reasonable estimates can be made of expected income loss in such cases but such estimates fail to measure the full cost of the loss, particularly in case of death. Another approach is to estimate how much individuals are willing to pay for their lives by, in part, examining their willingness to risk their lives. Not surprisingly, estimates of the value of a life vary widely.

OSHA is currently considering using a value ranging from $2 to $5 million.[30]

Those who reject this valuation process argue that health and safety is a right, and it is inappropriate to assign a dollar value to a limb or to a life. Although this approach ignores resource limitation questions and the reality that individuals are willing to assume some risks in order to make a living, it does make clear the difficulty of the valuation process. It should be recognized that the exercise of attempting to estimate the value of a human life is of limited value to policymakers who cannot ignore moral and subjective judgments.

The difficulty in using cost-benefit standards to analyze OSHA's effectiveness also applies to the standard-setting process, because both the cost of compliance with a standard and a standard's effect on illnesses or injuries are uncertain. The use of explicit cost considerations in applying cost-benefit analysis has been hotly debated throughout OSHA's history. Confrontations between government agencies, between employers and employee representatives, and between OSHA and employees or employers show no signs of moderating. These disputes are often resolved on a case-by-case basis in controversial court decisions.

A balanced evaluation of OSHA's effect on health conditions is subject to even greater uncertainty. Occupational illnesses are tricky to detect and diagnose. Some diseases have long latency periods (workers may develop the disease long after they have left the hazardous work environment), making the establishment of a causal link between the work environment and the disease difficult. This also means that OSHA's influence on some diseases may not be immediately evident. Establishing a causal link is even more problematic for some occupational illnesses that are clinically indistinguishable from illnesses that do not have an occupational origin. The development of lung cancer, for example, may be due to smoking or to inhalation of a chemical in the workplace.

Not surprisingly, independently compiled data on the incidence of occupational illness or disease vary substantially. A widely cited, but insufficiently documented, 1967 survey by the Surgeon General estimated that 390,000 new cases of occupational disease occur each year. The Bureau of Labor Statistics estimates roughly 100,000 new cases each year.[31] By counting only illnesses which are highly visible—from 1972 through 1978, 44 percent of the occupational illnesses reported by BLS were skin disorders[32]—and which have little or no latency period, the BLS data underestimates the problem. Serious and widespread diseases such as respiratory and neurological disorders and cancer are generally not included in the BLS count. Without an accurate recording of the true incidence of occupational illness and disease, the impact of OSHA in preventing or reducing occupational health hazards remains a subject of controversy. Federal government statistics within this area need to be improved.

The Cost of OSHA Compliance

The most systematic annual survey of capital spending by large companies for employee health and safety has been conducted since 1972 by the Economics Department of the McGraw-Hill Publications Company. Estimated national capital spending, derived from the McGraw-Hill sample, has varied from 1.4 to 2.9 percent of all capital spending. In 1984, the estimated cost was $4.9 billion, or 1.6 percent of total capital spending.[33] The McGraw-Hill estimate covers the cost of all health and safety spending, which is greater than the costs of compliance with OSHA regulations. This estimate must be considered ballpark at best because it does not include operating costs related to health and safety. On the other hand, capital spending to improve working conditions often boosts productivity, thus reducing the net cost of the new investment.

Using a conservative and rough estimate, the aggregate cost of occupational injuries and illnesses dwarfs this ballpark figure for capital expenditures on health and safety. The aggregate cost of work-related injuries, estimated by the National Safety Council at $33.4 billion in 1983, is nearly sevenfold the total capital spending for health and safety.[34] These rough estimates suggest that the benefits from a healthy and safe workplace would significantly outweigh current capital expenditures. The Safety Council figure also does not include an estimate for the cost of pain and suffering. All in all, compared to the magnitude of the workplace health and safety problem, business spends very little on prevention.

Injury Rate Trends

Although the data show conflicting trends, some insights can be gained from an examination of occupational injury statistics. While fatality rates have declined steadily and substantially since OSHA's inception, the number of nonfatal workplace injuries, measured in lost workdays, has increased.

National Safety Council data indicate that annual workplace fatality rates from occupational injuries dropped 35 percent from 1972 to 1984, or from 17 per thousand workers to 11 per thousand workers. Fatality rates for private sector workers, as calculated by the Bureau of Labor Statistics, declined by 43 percent from 1974 to 1983. The recent decline in fatality rates is sharper than the general downward trend since 1937. Using National Safety Council data, from 1960–1970, for example, fatality rates fell by 14 percent. Some of the sharp recent decline can be attributed to slow economic growth and recessions (Figure 7).

Although the lost workday rate due to occupational injuries declined between 1979 and 1983, the rate was still 34 percent higher in 1984 than in 1972, 61.8 lost workdays per year per 100 workers as compared to 46.2 in 1972.[35] In addition to more complete data sources due to OSHA and generally improved workmen's compensation systems that may have led to increased reporting of injuries, a number of factors may have contributed to this overall rise. These factors include an increased recognition that certain injuries are workplace related, which leads to their being reported, and workers' probable tendency to take longer to recover from injuries, because employers and doctors, fearing malpractice suits, recommend that they wait until they are fully recovered before returning to work. Another factor may be related to the decline in fatalities: lives are being saved because of improved workplace conditions and medical practices, but the saved workers may be injured or disabled.

Injury and Illness Rates, a Disaggregated Analysis

Because of the difficulty in sorting out OSHA from non-OSHA influences on aggregate trends, a disaggregated approach sheds more light on the issue of OSHA's effective-

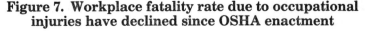

**Figure 7. Workplace fatality rate due to occupational
injuries have declined since OSHA enactment**

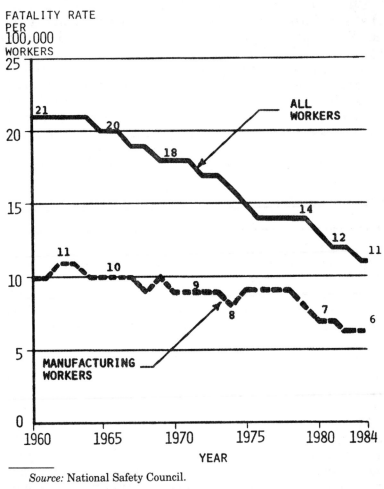

Source: National Safety Council.

ness. Although statistical analyses of OSHA's potential effects
on occupational injuries have had mixed results, one study
found significant decreases in several types of injuries judged
preventable by OSHA activity in California. Two 1985 studies
reinforced this conclusion. One found that the average injury
rate declined in OSHA-inspected companies at more than
twice the average rate of decline for all manufacturing industries in 1981–1983; while the other study found that OSHA

inspections have reduced both the rate of lost workdays and the overall injury and illness rate.[36] Other studies, however, show that OSHA inspections have had limited or no impact on injury rates.[37]

Supporting evidence for the hypothesis that inspections produce results can be found in the two industries subject to the greatest number of OSHA inspections—construction and manufacturing. In the construction industry, occupational injury rates (injury rate data include both injuries that cause lost workdays and those that do not) dropped from a high of 19.4 injuries per 100 full-time workers in 1973 to 15.4 in 1984. Fatalities, in turn, fell from 56 per 100,000 employees in 1973 to 40 in 1982. In manufacturing, occupational injury rates per 100 workers declined relatively steadily from 14.9 in 1972 to 10.2 in 1984, while workplace fatality rates for manufacturing employees were cut from 9 per 100,000 workers in 1973 to 6 per 100,000 workers in 1984.[38]

These improvements can only partially be explained by economic trends. Employment levels were higher in 1984 than in 1972 both in the construction industry and in manufacturing, but injury rates were down sharply.[39] On the other hand, improvements in the injury and fatality rates in the construction industry from 1972–1982 trailed behind the improvement in these rates for all workers.[40] Also, in the recovery year of 1984, injury rates in both construction and manufacturing were higher than in 1983.

A review of the effects of the Mine Safety and Health Act provides more clear-cut evidence that active federal involvement can produce a healthier and safer work environment. A number of studies of federal mine safety regulations concluded that these regulations have had positive effects.[41] In the decade following passage of the Act (1970–79), the fatality rate in the mining industry declined by 44 percent, double the decline in the overall work-related fatality rate of 22 percent. This difference is, in part, attributable to the Mine Safety and Health Administration's devotion of more financial resources and manpower to promoting safety and health in the mines. MSHA's fiscal 1985 budget was roughly 55 percent of federal and state OSHA funding, even though MSHA covers only 1 percent of the workers that OSHA covers. A review of inspection coverage by the two agencies shows the same disparities. MSHA regulations require four mandatory inspections annually of each underground mine and at least two a year of each surface mine. OSHA has no mandatory inspection requirement; in fact, only one in 25 workplaces is inspected each year. The lesson, then, is consistent—focused federal efforts have positive results.

Similarly, case studies of health regulations indicate OSHA effectiveness. Its standards for asbestos, vinyl chloride, cotton dust, and lead all reduced exposure and resulted in a healthier workplace environment. The vinyl chloride standard, for example, which costs far less to implement than industry projected, will save an estimated 2,000 lives by the year 2000.[42]

The cotton dust standard further illustrates OSHA's capability to reduce occupational health hazards in a manner that both enhances the safety of workers and improves productivity. OSHA initially adopted the cotton dust standards established under the Walsh-Healey Act. Under those standards, of an estimated 500,000 or more workers potentially exposed to large amounts of cotton dust, 84,000 workers suffered from acute byssinosis (also known as "brown lung"), and 35,000 employed and retired workers were disabled from dust-related diseases. These findings led to the establishment of stricter standards in 1978. Compliance with the new standards reduced exposure levels considerably. In four years the number of employees exposed to health risks was cut almost in half, from 35 percent in 1978 to 19 percent in 1982.[43] Unfortunately, lax enforcement of cotton dust standards under the Reagan administration may have halted or even turned around this progress.[44]

Cost of compliance with the cotton dust standard was less than expected. In 1978 OSHA estimated the capital cost of compliance would amount to $656 million. Four years later, when most of the controls were in place, the total capital cost was estimated at only $165 million in 1978 dollars. The initial figure underestimated productivity increases that accompanied the installment of the new technology; in fact, during this period, the textile industry led all manufacturing industries in productivity gains.[45] The *Economist* commented: "Tougher government regulations on workers' health have, unexpectedly, given the industry a leg up. Tighter dust control rules for cotton plants caused firms to throw out tons of old

inefficient machinery and to replace it with the latest available from the world's leading textile machinery firms. . . ."[46]
Case studies, MSHA's record, and some evidence of positive trends in the manufacturing and construction industries all suggest that OSHA has played a constructive role in promoting worker safety and health. OSHA's record by area of activity is examined next.

Standards

The federal government can develop basic safety and health standards for the workplace more efficiently than the 50 states, who would in many cases duplicate the same research. Furthermore, private employers may place a low priority on such research, partly because the benefits to the entire economy may exceed a firm's research costs, but the benefits to any particular firm may not exceed its costs. Uniform national standards make it easier for multistate businesses to adapt to regulation and they resolve the problem of states competing for business by establishing weak safety and health standards.
Given this solid justification for a strong federal role, the OSHA standard-setting record has been disappointing. Although some of the initial consensus standards established reasonable regulations, others were a disaster. While many of the worst standards have been eliminated, several of the remaining standards need to be updated because they are based on analyses and judgments that are no longer appropriate. Most of OSHA's health standards, for example, were based on exposure limits published by the American Conference of Governmental Industrial Hygienists in 1968 that have been updated annually, while OSHA's standards have not changed.
Standard setting through the rulemaking process has been criticized for its slowness. Some caution is reasonable in light of both the excessive haste displayed in the adoption of the consensus standards and of the difficult judgments that must be made; at the same time, the "need for more analysis" can be used as a delaying tactic. Many standards are subject to lengthy court battles which further slow the process. These court battles also suggest that the OSHA law should be clarified by Congress; currently, because of the ambiguity regard-

ing OSHA's power and mandate, almost all the difficult decisions are resolved in the courts.

In a more positive vein, OSHA has established necessary health standards regulating exposures to asbestos, cotton dust, vinyl chloride, and lead. The hazards involved are significant and the standards have been somewhat successful in improving health conditions in the workplace. These efforts indicate the beneficial role OSHA can play in occupational safety and health.

Enforcement

Enforcement policies and procedures have been continually adjusted during OSHA's history. At first, employers criticized OSHA for its contentious, adversarial attitude. More recently, OSHA has emphasized a cooperative approach. Throughout, however, there has been little economic incentive to induce preinspection compliance.

The remote possibility of being inspected by OSHA (4 percent), the minimal fines that are initially levied, and the often high cost of meeting OSHA standards all contribute to the lack of incentive for an employer to comply with standards prior to an inspection. Even in manufacturing, which receives a disproportionate number of inspections, the incentive is minimal. In fiscal 1983, when the average proposed penalty per inspection was $83, a manufacturing company had a one in six chance of being inspected, yielding an expected cost for noncompliance of $14. Compliance actions are likely to cost much more than that. Even a manufacturing company that is in serious violation of the law has little incentive for preinspection compliance, as the expected cost for each serious violation in fiscal 1983 was about $29.[47]

A variety of approaches have been used under different OSHA administrations to target which industries to inspect. OSHA's consistent targeting of high hazard industries for inspection has been modified by its adoption of the records review process—targeting companies with lost workday rates higher than the national average. One problem with this approach is that it gives employers an incentive to incompletely report lost workdays due to injuries to avoid inspections.

Furthermore, since health hazards are often more serious than safety problems, it is important to raise the proportion of health inspections from their current level of less than a fifth of all inspections. OSHA's decision to selectively respond to worker's complaints establishes, therefore, a dangerous precedent. Given the gaps in any targeting system and the limited number of workplaces inspected, reports by workers of violations should play an important and necessary role in the enforcement system.

Despite the minimal economic incentive for preinspection compliance, and the need to perfect the targeting system, OSHA enforcement has had beneficial effects on the workplace environment. Abatement of violations is likely where inspections occur and OSHA's very existence has raised the level of occupational safety and health awareness among both employees and employers. Firms may improve working conditions out of the increased concern generated by this awareness or for the less altruistic reason that they want to create a positive public image. Employer response to OSHA regulations has established a cadre of safety and health personnel within large companies with a vested interest in these issues. Last, inspections initiated by workers protected from the threat of employer retribution facilitates the detection of workplace hazards.

State Administration

In the short run, the trend towards expanding the role of states in the administration of OSHA programs will probably continue. More states are likely to assume essentially complete administration of health and safety regulation. State enforcement of OSHA standards has differed from federal enforcement in that states conduct more inspections, yet issue fewer serious violations and impose lower penalties. More inspections should mean more abatement, but the lower penalties suggest that states may be more concerned with business reaction than effective enforcement. States also conduct proportionately half as many health inspections as federally administered programs. This suggests that the lack of focus on health hazards is even a greater problem with state administration than with federal administration.

As a result of increased state responsibility for administration of OSHA standards, the federal government may relax its monitoring role and thereby fail to ensure that these programs are "at least as effective" as federal programs. Were this to occur, minimal standards would not be enforced and the days of states competing for business by not enforcing safety and health standards could return. Some evidence that this is already happening is indicated by the lower penalties that states assess, the withdrawal of on-site federal inspectors from states that have assumed OSHA administration, and the relaxation of required state personnel levels.[48]

At the same time, in the face of OSHA inaction, some states have taken the lead in passing stricter health and safety standards in areas such as hazard communication "right to know" laws.[49] However, an appeals court ruled that in states without approved plans, the federal standard preempts state and local laws, even if they are more stringent.[50] Advocates of an increased state role also argue that states are better able to adapt to local needs.

Education

The federal government is well-suited for the role of collecting and disseminating information about workplace hazards. Centrally collected information can be made available to all concerned. Education can serve a useful purpose, inasmuch as ignorance of workplace hazards is one reason for their widespread existence.

A major criticism of OSHA's on-site consultation process is that it usually leaves out workers by providing information only to employers. If the consultation process is to be optimally effective, it is essential that workers be allowed access to results. A second criticism of the process is that it frees employers from being penalized for past violations. On the other hand, since the likelihood of inspection and penalties is low, it is sensible that employers, particularly small businesses, should not be penalized for voluntarily taking steps to detect and correct hazardous working conditions.

The Reagan Record

Thorne Auchter, the first director of OSHA under President Reagan, claimed that OSHA's new cooperative approach contributed to the recent decline in the rate of lost workdays.[51] The evidence, however, is far from conclusive that the cooperative approach is the cause. An OTA analysis of the decline in the rate of lost workdays found that it was due largely to the mini-recession of 1980 and the prolonged recession of 1981-82, rather than to changes in OSHA policy.[52] The jump in the lost workday rates in the 1984 recovery year supports the OTA analysis, although the 1984 rate is still lower than the 1979 rate.[53]

Occupational Injury Rates, Lost Workdays
(rate per 100 full-time workers)

1972	46.3
1973	51.2
1974	53.1
1975	54.6
1976	57.8
1977	60.0
1978	62.1
1979	66.2
1980	63.7
1981	60.4
1982	57.5
1983	57.2
1984	61.8

There is some validity to Auchter's claim that the cooperative approach has led to faster abatement of hazards because the number of contested citations has dropped sharply. At the same time, since the number of follow-up inspections has also declined, it is difficult to verify whether abatement has indeed occurred. In addition, because penalties have fallen substantially, the economic incentive for compliance in the absence of an inspection has declined to the point of being trivial. Furthermore, a cooperative approach is unjustified when a violation is of a serious nature and the company should be aware of the relevant OSHA standard. In such cases, significant penalties should be applied.

In many respects the performance of OSHA from 1981 to 1984 was inadequate. It issued only two new health standards, withdrew one proposed standard, and weakened still others.

In its attempt to cooperate with employers, OSHA has neglected the workers the agency was established to assist. There has been a decline in inspections in response to worker complaints. There have been repeated charges that employees are excluded from the rulemaking process and that the process is improperly influenced by private meetings between OMB or the Presidential Task Force on Regulatory Relief and employers. There has also been increased use of on-site consultations which do not provide workers with information relating to their health and safety.

Agency morale has also been a problem. For example, a top Reagan OSHA official charged that the language in the preamble to the lead standard was "communistic" and that the supervisor had been "trained in Moscow."[54] Also, staff levels were cut by 25 percent from 1980 to 1984, and the administrator in 1984-85 had a record of disagreeing with OSHA rulings and showed little commitment to the agency's mission.[55]

Even more detrimental to OSHA's effectiveness is the increased role of OMB in all aspects of OSHA decisionmaking. A fundamental danger exists when an agency inclined to ignore benefits but emphasize costs is the final arbiter of health and safety regulations. This concern was heightened in mid-1985 when James Miller, who was known as an avid proponent of deregulation and a critic of OSHA, was placed in charge of OMB.

A series of decisions by the Labor Department in late 1985 does, however, suggest that OSHA has been assuming a more positive role. In November 1985, the administration announced a modification of its record reviews practice in response to criticism that it eliminates the incentive for many employers to comply with health and safety standards.[56] In December 1985 OSHA announced a revised cotton dust standard acceptable to both management and labor officials.[57] In the same month OSHA proposed two new and stricter workplace standards regulating benzene and formaldehyde. These regulations suggest that OSHA may become more active in issuing health standards. At the same time, these signs should not be overinterpreted. The benzene and formaldehyde standards were issued under congressional and court pressure, and it was alleged that OMB pressure was responsible for relaxing the proposals favored by the Labor Department.[58] In addition, it was not until March of 1986, nine months after the resignation of the previous administrator, that a new OSHA director was appointed. This delay prevented needed decisions from being made and showed continuing lack of concern by the administration about a drifting OSHA.

Is the Workplace Better Off

OSHA has had its successes. Although a causal relationship has yet to be established, fatality rates have fallen sharply in the OSHA years. The agency has promulgated necessary and effective health standards. Workplaces have complied with OSHA standards where inspections have occurred. On-site consultations provide thousands of employers each year with needed safety and health information. OSHA's existence has also contributed to enhanced awareness of health and safety issues. The increase in health and safety personnel in both companies and unions is also bound to have a positive effect on workplace health and safety.

To be sure, OSHA has not been a model agency. It had more than its share of start-up problems and it has often devoted too much attention to minor safety problems and not enough attention to major health hazards. If OSHA enforcement is further weakened and if OSHA fails to issue health and safety standards, then its effectiveness will erode and the charges of its detractors will become a self-fulfilling prophecy. The challenge is to build on past experience, correct policy and operational deficiencies, and carry out the mission of the agency by vigorously enforcing its mandate.

Safety and health hazards in the workplace persist. Fifteen years after the passage of OSHA, an estimated 25 workers die daily from workplace injuries and another 2.5 million to 11.3 million workers annually suffer nonfatal occupational injuries. The agenda for the regulation of health hazards includes a need for standards covering workers in hazardous waste sites and hospital standards to protect health care workers and unborn children from agents that are "airborne, colorless, tasteless, and odorless."[59] Altogether, some 60,000 chemical substances are unregulated; not all, but surely some of these chemicals should be the subject of OSHA standards.

As the history of workplace health and safety indicates, the private sector, the courts, and state and local government cannot by themselves solve occupational health and safety problems. The underlying rationale for a centralized agency to pull together research, establish uniform standards, ensure enforcement, and disseminate health and safety information, remains sound. OSHA has not yet filled all these roles equally well, but it has made a start. With appropriate modifications and more vigorous administration, OSHA can play a vital role in establishing healthy and safe workplaces in the years to come.

7
Representation Rights in the Workplace

Since the 1930s federal labor laws have sought to protect individual workers by guaranteeing them the right to freely associate and bargain collectively. Because individual workers lack the power to protect their interests in the workplace and to obtain optimal terms of employment, government intervention has been deemed desirable to help them organize to counteract the superior economic power of employers.

The preamble to the National Labor Relations Act of 1935 (NLRA) declared that national policy will encourage "the practice and procedure of collective bargaining by protecting the exercise of workers of full freedom of association, self-organization and designation of representatives of their own choosing for the purpose of negotiating the terms and conditions of their employment. . . ." To that end, Congress proscribed employers from interfering with employees exercising their right to organize for the purpose of collective bargaining, and required employers to recognize and negotiate with representatives chosen by a majority of their employees. Congress recognized that through organization, workers could draw on their collective economic power to offset the bargaining advantage intrinsic to employers in dealing with individual employees.

Another objective of the NLRA was to introduce a measure of industrial democracy and individual rights into the workplace. The sponsors of the legislation reasoned that allowing workers to organize and bargain collectively would enable them to influence decisions vitally affecting their lives and livelihood.[1]

The Act has served as the foundation of an intricate system of industrial jurisprudence devoid of government control.

The agreement arrived at through negotiations between management and representatives of the workers constitutes the law governing the workplace, and the formal grievance machinery insures due process. The collective bargaining process is decentralized so that agreements can be tailored to fit conditions in specific firms or industries. The federal role is to help create an environment for reaching such an agreement.

Evolving Public Policy Toward Unions

The focus of federal policy affecting labor relations has shifted dramatically over the decades, reflecting changing concepts of social welfare and individual liberty. Pre-New Deal policies were generally hostile to unions and collective bargaining. In the 1930s, the federal government reversed itself, creating a climate of overt support for union activities and concern for workers' institutional rights. As unions became a powerful force in society, federal policy shifted in the 1940s and 1950s to balancing the bargaining power of unions and employers through increased regulation of their activities. Public concern over growing union power also manifested itself in the federal regulation of internal union affairs to guarantee the rights of individual members. Finally, in the 1960s and 1970s, federal attention focused almost exclusively on the individual rights of workers, union and nonunion alike.

Prior to the 1930s, the courts were the dominant force in the determination of labor law. Public policy tolerated the existence of unions, but their activities were subject to varying and substantial degrees of restraint. When workers did band together to form unions, employers in most states were under no legal obligation to recognize or even deal with them. Federal and state courts regularly found basic union activities such as picket lines and strikes to be illegal conspiracies in restraint of trade and frequently issued injunctions against union attempts to exert economic pressure. Some employers even required workers, as a condition of employment, to sign "yellow-dog contracts" promising not to join a union.

The Norris-LaGuardia Act of 1932 provided relief from judicial intervention. The Act deprived the federal courts of the power to enjoin union self-help activities such as strikes, picketing, and peaceful assembly, and made yellow-dog contracts unenforceable in the courts. As a result, the federal government established a laissez-faire policy legalizing labor organizing efforts. The point of the Act was not to encourage unions but to permit workers to organize for mutual self-help without judicial interference.

The Norris-LaGuardia Act removed judicial restraints on union activities, but it did not interfere with the power of employers to prevent unionization and block collective bargaining. Three years later the NLRA (also known as the Wagner Act) not only recognized the legal right of employees to organize into unions for collective bargaining, it also established the machinery to protect their rights. The NLRA established the National Labor Relations Board (NLRB) to settle questions of representation, to conduct elections, and to protect the rights of employees by proscribing employers from engaging in specific unfair labor practices. Challenges by critics that the Wagner Act was unconstitutional and prounion were to no avail. In 1937 the Supreme Court upheld the constitutionality of the Act, finding that it imposed no arbitrary restraints on the employer's ability to conduct business. In response to charges of the Act's one-sided concern for the problems of labor, the court held that ". . . legislative authority, exerted within its proper field, need not embrace all evils in its reach."[2]

During the decade following enactment of the NLRA, the NLRB was charged with promoting unions and collective bargaining as complementary objectives.[3] Union organizing thrived in this new climate of federal protection. Workers' placards in the coal fields proudly proclaimed, "President Roosevelt wants you to join the union." Sparked by this government endorsement, the labor movement enjoyed the most spectacular decade of growth in its history.

The Chamber of Commerce and the National Association of Manufacturers initially avoided endorsing collective bargaining, even after leading employers had negotiated collective agreements, but, in response to public support for unions, these organizations later became resigned to government's involvement in labor relations. The business strategy shifted from outright opposition to limiting the scope of legal union activities, to seeking equalizing amendments to the labor laws, and to reining the allegedly excessive powers of union "bosses."

Following World War II employers seized the opportunity to redress the balance in the laws regulating bargaining power. At the end of the war, uncertainty over production cutbacks and pent-up demands for higher earnings touched off a wave of strikes, demonstrating the impressive strength of the unions. In reaction, the public attitude toward unions shifted, and they came to be widely viewed as having achieved too much power. Opinion polls after the war showed "strikes and labor-management problems" to be "the most important problem" facing the nation.[4]

In 1947 Congress passed the Taft-Hartley Act over President Truman's veto. The main purpose of the Act's advocates was to curb what they perceived as the excessive power granted to unions under the Wagner Act. The new law deprived unions of a principal organizing device, the secondary boycott. Although it continued to guarantee workers the right to organize and bargain collectively, Section 14(b) of the Taft-Hartley Act provided for the right of states to pass laws prohibiting union shop clauses within their jurisdictions. The Act also specified union unfair labor practices, including refusal to bargain with an employer, and reintroduced the injunction in disputes imperiling the nation's health and safety.

The Taft-Hartley Act transformed the federal government from an active promoter of unionism to an impartial referee between labor and management. Although the Act established broad guidelines for achieving a rough bargaining balance between employers and workers—mainly by reducing the arsenal of union weapons—it remained for the courts and the NLRB to determine how best to reconcile competing interests in specific labor disputes. Inevitably, however, the infinite variety of union and employer tactics and the infinite variations in the economic power of the respective parties have made it difficult for the government to determine a proper stance of neutrality.

Federal regulation of union activities, initiated by Taft-Hartley, was expanded a dozen years later by the Labor Management Reporting and Disclosure Act (Landrum-Griffin Act). In Taft-Hartley Congress showed an interest in the rights of individual workers, particularly their right not to join the union. By 1959 Congress was also concerned with two additional problems: the lack of democratic procedures in a number of unions, and corruption and collusion both within the union movement and between management, union officials, and consultants. The timing of the Act and much of its substantive content were heavily influenced by the McClellan Committee's exposure of corruption in a number of national and local unions.

The Landrum-Griffin Act superimposed civil law on union law to establish a scheme of constitutional guarantees for union members.[5] The Act set forth a bill of rights for union members, guaranteeing equal rights in elections, the rights of free speech and assembly, the right to vote on increases in dues and initiation fees, and protection against arbitrary discipline. In addition, Congress required unions to regularly report on their finances and operations and required employers to disclose any payments to union officials or labor relations consultants. Finally, a separate title to the Act amended the Taft-Hartley Act by restricting union recognitional and organizational picketing, tightening loopholes in the secondary boycott provision, and proscribing "hot cargo" agreements whereby an employer refuses to handle the products of another employer.

In the quarter century since the Landrum-Griffin Act, public policies have become increasingly concerned with the rights and protection of individual workers. The Supreme Court established the principle that unions, in exercising their power of exclusive representation, have the obligation to treat every member of the bargaining unit fairly and without discrimination. The Court ruled that although an employee has no absolute right to have a grievance arbitrated, and must pursue all available internal remedies first, the individual employee may sue the employer for breach of contract, and may join the union or sue the employer if its treatment of the employee has been arbitrary, capricious, or in bad faith. The union may not "ignore a meritorious grievance or process it in perfunctory fashion."[6] The Court disregarded an arbitrator's decisions and guaranteed the individual employee's right to sue "if the contractual processes have been seriously flawed by the union's breach of its duty to represent employees honestly and in good faith and without invidious discrimination or arbitrary conduct."[7]

Federal interventions to guarantee equal employment opportunity, occupational health and safety, and private pension receipt represent further intrusions into the substantive domain of collective bargaining. Congress deemed that progress in these areas was too slow and that unions were incapable of adequately protecting the interests of individual workers.

The rights and protections set forth in these statutes have had a significant impact on established bargaining relationships.

NLRB Administration

As the federal referee in labor-management disputes, the National Labor Relations Board has two main roles: to resolve charges that employers or unions have committed unfair labor practices under the law and to conduct and monitor elections to determine whether a majority of workers desire union representation. The NLRB process typically begins when an individual worker, union, or employer contacts one of the Board's 33 regional or 19 subregional offices. In 1984 the NLRB handled some 35,000 unfair labor practice charges and 9,000 representation cases.[8]

In unfair labor practice cases, an investigation is usually conducted within 30 days. In 1984 about two-thirds of the charges were found to be without merit and were either withdrawn by the charging party or dismissed by the Board's regional director. Of the remaining cases, 96 percent were settled without further Board action, leaving less than 2 percent for Board consideration. The latter cases were often the most important, requiring legal interpretation in novel situations. Finally, a small percentage of Board decisions were appealed to the circuit courts for review.[9]

In representation cases, a union typically files a petition with the regional office requesting the Board to conduct an election. If at least 30 percent of the employees express interest in an election, then the regional director attempts to secure agreement between the parties involved concerning the appropriate bargaining unit, when and where the election will be held, and other procedural issues. Such agreement is reached in an overwhelming majority of cases; the remaining one-fifth of cases require a hearing and subsequent resolution of disputed issues by the regional director. In 1981, the last year for which data are available, unions and employers filed post-election objections to campaign conduct or challenged ballots in 17 percent of all elections. Some 83 percent of these objections were later withdrawn or dismissed, leaving the Board to consider objections in less than 3 percent of certification elections.[10]

The law excluded from NLRB coverage state and federal agency personnel, agricultural workers, domestic employees in a private home, independent contractors, and supervisors.

More recent legislation expanded NLRB jurisdiction to include employees of the Postal Service, state colleges and universities, and private nonprofit hospitals.

Another restriction on NLRB jurisdiction concerns the effect of an employer's operations on interstate commerce. Prior to 1950 the Board decided jurisdiction on a case-by-case basis. However, to avoid being overburdened by this process, the Board established monetary standards for specific industries, based either on the amount of sales or on gross revenues. Since these monetary standards have not been adjusted for inflation since 1958, the number of employers covered under the Act has steadily increased.

Decision Backlog

Serious delays and a substantial backlog of cases have plagued the Board since the late 1970s. The number of cases awaiting Board decision was 1,184 in February 1986 compared to a monthly backlog of 535 cases in 1980.[11] This situation has caused lengthy delays in the administration of the NLRA and placed in jeopardy the legal rights of workers covered under the Act.

Several factors have been cited to explain the backlog of cases. One logical cause is the expansion of NLRB jurisdiction during the 1970s. The inclusion of new groups of workers not only raised the number of potential cases but also introduced novel and complex issues for Board interpretation. However, since 1978 the average number of cases received by the Board each month has remained relatively stable while the backlog of cases grew substantially.[12]

Fiscal Year	Cases Received	Case Backlog (at end of fiscal year)
1978	1634	489
1980	1813	535
1981	1824	924
1982	1648	842
1983	1577	1385
1984	1825	1313
1985	1546	1196
1986	NA	1184 (February 1)

Part of the problem has been the failure of the Reagan administration to fill vacancies at the NLRB, leaving the agency operating at less than full strength[13] and the Board sometimes deadlocked at 2-2. Also contributing to delays in decisions have been attempts by Donald Dotson, who assumed the chairmanship in March 1983, to modify or reinterpret earlier decisions. As of early 1986, the Board had a full complement of members.

Politics and Policy

Despite substantial legislative revision and court interpretation, many provisions of the NLRA remain sufficiently vague to yield considerable discretion to the Board. Because balancing the bargaining power of labor and management is largely a subjective procedure, unions and employers have joined in a constant struggle to influence the content of Board decisions. Some of the most important battles have been fought over presidential appointments to the NLRB. Various interest groups, especially employers, unions, and law firms, lobby vigorously for candidates of their choice.

New Board members typically reflect the views and predilections of the administration in power.[14] These swings in NLRB policy "directly determine whether the scope of collective bargaining will expand or contract, alter the relative bargaining power of the parties, and affect the ability of unions to organize and managements to resist unionization."[15] President Reagan's appointee as NLRB chairman, Donald Dotson, has provoked union charges that the Board has become an instrument in the hands of antiunion employers. It is significant, however, that past appointments by Democratic administrations have provoked complaints from employer representatives. As a result of the political process, Board policies in areas such as bargaining unit determination, employer free speech, and the duty to bargain in good faith have tended to oscillate with changing administrations.

Appropriate Bargaining Unit

The determination of the unit appropriate for collective bargaining is central to the success of a labor organization's efforts to achieve a majority vote during an organizing drive. An overly expansive definition of relevant employees can dilute scarce organizing resources and jeopardize a union victory. Similarly, unions organized along narrow occupational lines may be hard-pressed to win majority support from workers outside their traditional jurisdictions. Yet, too narrow a bargaining unit definition could require an employer to negotiate with several different unions, representing differing segments of its work force, thereby risking more frequent work interruptions or jurisdictional disputes between the various unions.

Prior to 1947, the Board mainly relied on the extent of demonstrated union support among employees in defining unit boundaries. The Board certified a single department of a retail firm even though a storewide unit was deemed in the best interest of all workers in the establishment, in order to enable workers in the department to engage in collective bargaining without awaiting "the uncertain date when the employees may be organized in a larger unit."[16] Similarly, bargaining rights were granted to a unit covering one store in a retail chain on the premise that some representation was better than none at all.[17]

The Taft-Hartley Act specifically proscribed this approach to bargaining unit determination. Consequently, the Board focused on employer-related interests such as the degree of centralized administration, uniformity of personnel policies, and whether all stores sold the same kind of merchandise. Geographical separation and the degree of employee support for union organization were explicitly discounted.[18]

During the 1960s Board policy struck a different balance. Finding that previous Board policy overemphasized employer interests and ignored labor interests, the Kennedy Board found a one-store unit was appropriate.[19] The Supreme Court later ratified this policy shift, ruling that the extent of union support among employees was an important consideration in defining proper bargaining units.[20]

The 1974 health care amendments to the NLRA reflected legislative concern that the proliferation of too many units at a health care facility might imperil the public's access to medical treatment, sparking a legal debate that has not yet been resolved. Hospital administrators cite the commonality of interests between broad groups of employees and favor fewer bargaining units. However, unions organized along craft or occupational lines stress the difficulties in attracting a diverse group of workers into their ranks. The Reagan Board's policy is to establish as few units as possible.[21]

Free Speech

The NLRA places constraints on the freedom of speech of employers in combating union organizing drives. The law leaves it to the NLRB and the courts to define the limits of free speech that an employer may exercise without infringing on the rights of workers to join a union. In the early days of the NLRA, the Board ruled that practically any statement made by an employer against the union constituted an unfair labor practice.[22] However, dissatisfaction with the NLRB's limitations on the rights of employers to exercise freedom of speech led the framers of the Taft-Hartley Act to provide for employer free speech as long as such expression contained no threat of reprisal or promise of benefit. Thus, the NLRB must balance the employers' right to free speech against the possibility of interference with, restraint of, or coercion of employees in the exercise of their rights under the Act.

In the 1950s the Board appeared to ignore the context in which the employer speech was delivered and thereby avoided finding such speech to be threatening or coercive. The Board found permissible the employer's declaration that labor trouble might bring financial difficulties, which would in turn result in a loss of jobs to the employees.[23] Similarly, the Board viewed as "merely an expression of the employer's legal position" a statement made to employees that the Board's bargaining unit determination was flawed and that if the union won, the employer would refuse to bargain until the court of appeals could review the unit decision a year or two later.[24]

The Kennedy Board moved back in the direction of restricting employer statements and ruled that statutory employer free speech provisions applied only to unfair labor practice cases and not to representation cases.[25] The Board maintained that, in representation cases, conduct that destroys the "laboratory conditions" necessary for employees to exercise "free and untrammeled choice" of bargaining representatives violates election rules even though it does not constitute an unfair labor practice. In reexamining the permissible scope of employer free speech, the Board rejected a narrow legalistic approach and indicated it would "not only consider the entire situation of both employer and employees, but also the entire context of what has been said."[26]

A study in the mid-1970s challenged the NLRB infringements on employers' exercise of free speech.[27] The study of NLRB elections concluded that voter behavior varied little between "clean" and "dirty" campaigns and recommended that the Board cease to interfere with employers' freedom of speech. A majority of the NLRB adopted this advice the following year, ruling that the Board would no longer set aside elections because of misleading statements.[28]

The Reagan Board further expanded freedom of employer action with respect to employer interrogation of union supporters.[29] Earlier Board decisions had held that probing into employees' union sentiments might affect their future status and ruled that the action was coercive.[30] The Reagan Board seems willing to tolerate employers' freedom of speech even if that action may jeopardize the rights of employees to freely engage in collective bargaining.

A similar tug-of-war has been waged over Board policy governing union access to company premises. Obviously, the employer enjoys a significant advantage in communicating its message to workers if union organizers can be barred from company property. The NLRB under the Truman administration interpreted free speech as requiring the employer who discussed unions on company time and property to make equal time and facilities available to the union. Following the passage of Taft-Hartley, the Board and the Supreme Court restricted union access to its potential constituency. They held, first, that the exercise of property rights permitted employers to prevent entry to company premises by nonemployee union organizers as long as other channels of communication were reasonably available; and, second, that an employer could use its supervisors to conduct an antiunion campaign on company time without allowing similar prounion activity by employees, so long as this did not create an imbalance in the opportunities for organizational communication.[31] The Board has expressly declined to set aside an election because an employer made an antiunion speech on company time shortly before an election and refused the union a chance to reply.[32] Predictably, current Board policies on free speech tilt the scales in favor of the employer, frustrating in practice union opportunities to exercise their theoretical rights.[33]

Duty to Bargain

Another area of controversy in NLRB policymaking has been its statutory responsibility to insure that the parties bargain "in good faith." Initial interpretation of the Act envisioned a scenario in which the mere existence of the NLRB would induce the parties to negotiate an agreement on the issues dividing them without government intervention.[34] However, the Board has increasingly become more involved in the procedure and substance of the behind-the-door negotiations.

Concerned that either party could subvert the bargaining process by refusing to discuss an issue of vital importance to workers or the employer, the Supreme Court in 1958 established a framework of "mandatory" and "permissive" subjects in collective bargaining.[35] Either union or employer may insist on seeking agreement on a given mandatory topic to the point of an impasse or breakdown in negotiations. On the other hand, neither party may demand bargaining on a permissive subject if the other party objects. A strike that results from unlawful employer refusal to bargain on mandatory subjects is considered an unfair-labor-practice strike, and in contrast to economic strikers who may be replaced, the workers are entitled to reinstatement and possibly to back pay. Accordingly, an NLRB decision can substantially alter the balance of power in a strike deemed to have been caused by the employer's posture at the bargaining table.

Determining which subjects are mandatory and which are permissible has engendered considerable debate. During World War II, the War Labor Board recommended the adoption of fringe benefits in lieu of wage increases. Following the war, the NLRB and the Supreme Court ruled that pension plans fall within the scope of collective bargaining.[36] This decision paved the way for mandatory bargaining over other fringe benefits.[37] These extensions of NLRB authority into the substantive terms of collective bargaining have provoked criticism from those who feel the law should limit itself to outlining the broad framework within which bargaining should take place and leave specific contract terms largely to the parties.

Over the past 20 years, the most controversial issue concerning the duty to bargain has been the extent to which employers must negotiate about managerial decisions that result in a shrinkage of job opportunities. Initially, the NLRB did not require employers to bargain over decisions involving subcontracting, relocations, or technological improvements, although they did require bargaining about the effects of such decisions on displaced employees. The Kennedy Board broadened mandatory bargaining subjects to include decisions to terminate a department and subcontract its work, to consolidate operations through automation, and to close one plant of a multiplant enterprise.[38] In a 1964 decision, the Supreme Court gave limited approval to this shift in policy, holding that an employer illegally subcontracted maintenance work for economic reasons without first negotiating with the union.[39]

More recently, the NLRB relaxed the scope of mandatory bargaining, ruling that a company could terminate the manufacturing portion of its operations without bargaining over the question.[40] The Supreme Court again followed the NLRB, concluding that "the harm likely to be done to an employer's need to operate freely in deciding whether to shut down part of its business purely for economic reasons outweighs the incremental benefit that might be gained through the union's participation in making the decision."[41] The Court reasoned that it was unlikely that the union could induce the employer to change its mind, and that delay would harm management's ability to act promptly and secretly. However, the decision left open whether the Court might rule differently if the timing of the decision allowed for bargaining to be conducted.

Thus, the proper balance between an employer's freedom to manage the business and the employees' right to bargain over the terms and conditions of employment remains the subject of much debate. To some, the notion that workers may be deprived of their jobs without the opportunity to negotiate over the terms of employment is antithetical to the fundamental principles of collective bargaining. To others, bargaining is required only when an employer's decisions involving plant relocations, partial closings, work transfers, consolidations, subcontracting, and the introduction of new technologies turn on labor-cost factors. The Reagan Board has adopted the latter approach, thereby substantially limiting the employer's bargaining obligation.[42]

Success or Failure?

Fifty years after the enactment of the NLRA, some 35,000 collective agreements are currently in effect—many of which are decades old—and successful bargaining is conducted in virtually every major industry. Labor relations in the public sector, although not governed by the NLRA, closely follow its basic principles.

Collective bargaining has significantly improved the wages and working conditions of unionized and nonunionized workers. Unions are credited with boosting the wages of organized workers to about 20 to 30 percent above unorganized workers in the 1970s.[43] Other benefits of union representation include increased leisure, better medical coverage, and more secure pensions. Finally, collectively bargained grievance and arbitration practices, found in nearly every union-management agreement, promote the rights of individuals in the workplace.

Although unionized workers comprise less than one-fifth of the work force, all workers enjoy some of the benefits of collective bargaining. In looking for a standard by which to set wages, employers make extensive use of industry or area wage surveys. A Bureau of National Affairs, Inc., report indicated that 96 percent of the manufacturing firms contacted relied on such surveys.[44] Since union-negotiated wage increases boost the average rate of pay reported in those surveys, nonunion workers benefit from their firm's desire to maintain its position in the industry or area wage structure.

Employers practicing positive labor relations also closely follow collectively bargained wage and benefit increases to forestall union organizing drives.[45] Moreover, many such employers have also incorporated work rules and personnel practices resembling those found in union shops, although rarely on a sustained and meaningful basis.[46] Finally, unions have helped nonunion workers by lobbying for legislation that grants all workers such protections as equal employment, safe and healthy workplaces, and secure pensions.

Nevertheless, opinion is divided on whether the NLRA is a success or failure. In 1984 a House subcommittee concluded that "the evidence is clear that the law does not encourage collective bargaining. Rather it has become an impediment."[47] Clearly, dissatisfaction with statutory attempts to balance the interests of labor and management remains widespread.

Central to this debate is the post-World War II decline in union strength. During the first 12 years of the NLRB, favorable economic conditions, a nourishing climate created by the government, especially during World War II, and a friendly

NLRB greatly facilitated the growth of unions. In 1935 union membership stood at 3.6 million, constituting 13 percent of the nonfarm labor force. By 1947 union membership had grown to 14.8 million, more than doubling the union proportion of nonfarm workers. Since 1947 union membership as a proportion of nonfarm employment has declined to 18.0 percent in 1985 (Figure 8).

Union supporters attribute much of this decline to weaknesses in the law and to its administration. Under the law, unions are precluded from bringing "secondary" pressures to bear on employers, who, during a work stoppage, may lock out striking workers or hire permanent replacements and continue operating. The law, according to this view, undermines the leverage of the workers while failing to place limits of any consequence on the economic weapons of management.

Another union complaint focuses on the inadequacy of remedies available to the Board to deter unlawful conduct.

Figure 8. Union membership rates have declined during Post-World War II period

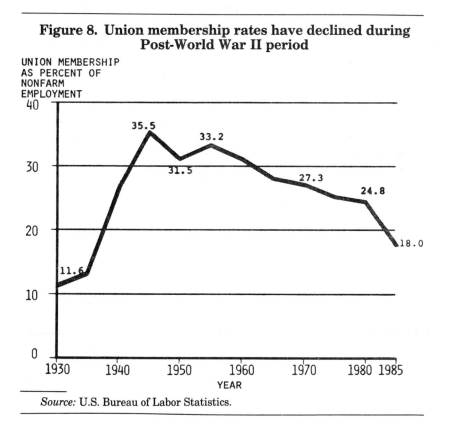

Source: U.S. Bureau of Labor Statistics.

Because the law's remedies are compensatory rather than punitive, the penalty is at worst reinstatement of the employee with lost back pay, less any interim earnings or income garnered by the employee. This remedy fails to adequately compensate the victim, who may be required to wait as long as three years for all appeals to be exhausted. In representation cases, such delays can weight the scales against potential unionization. Unions express similar frustration in cases where employers refuse to bargain in good faith. The NLRB has no authority to impose the terms of a contract on a recalcitrant party or to order a party to concede to a particular point.

To remedy some of these shortcomings, labor's supporters in Congress have made several unsuccessful attempts to amend the law to facilitate unionization. Their most significant effort, the Labor Law Reform Bill of 1977, sought to amend the law by reducing election delays and stiffening sanctions against violators. The business community lobbied vigorously for its defeat, raising the specter of excessive union power, and Congress rejected the proposed legislation. Labor's defeat on labor law reform illustrates the political dilemma facing unions: the law, they claim, renders them too weak to organize, but legislators consider them too powerful to justify statutory enhancement of their bargaining power. The unions' failure to secure a favorable rating from the public also undermines support for labor law reform. The percentage of persons who "approve of labor unions" has dropped from 70 percent in 1965 to 55 percent in 1981, although it rose slightly to 58 percent in 1985.[48]

Other Explanations

While there is little doubt that the legal climate since 1947 has placed some restrictions on new union organizing, many other factors may also be responsible for declining union influence. Industrial shifts have reduced the proportion of the work force employed in highly unionized sectors of the economy, while employment in nonunion industries has expanded. In addition, employment has shifted away from the traditionally heavily unionized North Central and Northeast regions toward the less unionized South. Finally, as foreign competition has intensified over the last two decades, some employment has shifted overseas.

The changing demographics of the work force and occupational shifts have also affected unionization. The growing
numbers of women and youth in the labor force render unionization more difficult since these groups have traditionally
displayed little interest in joining unions. Occupational shifts
toward a higher proportion of white collar workers also constitute an obstacle to union growth. Surveys show that as their
skill level increases, individuals are less likely to join unions.[49]
    The unions themselves have contributed to their declining
fortunes. Union organizing activity, measured by organizing
expenditures and the number of elections held, has diminished
during the past two decades.[50] While the cost of organizing new
members has risen appreciably due to lengthy delays, stem-
ming from legal challenges, union expenditures for organizing
have steadily declined as a proportion of union budgets. With
union membership falling, it is increasingly difficult for union
leaders to justify such expenditures to a membership preoc-
cupied with stagnating, if not declining, real wages and lack of
job security. If union leaders are to maintain their own job
security, they need to respond to the pressing needs of present
members, instead of crafting a future-oriented strategy. In
addition, in 1985 more than half of the AFL-CIO affiliates had
fewer than 50,000 members, often leaving them too weak to
pay organizers or withstand a strike.
    Union opportunities to secure representation through
NLRB elections have declined, and the number of eligible
potential members per election has dropped sharply, so that

Years	Number of NLRB Elections	Eligible Workers	Union Victory Rate
1950	5731	889,848	74%
1960	6617	501,385	58
1970	8074	608,558	55
1980	8198	521,602	46
1981	7512	449,243	43
1982	5116	297,764	40
1983 (preliminary)	4405	209,918	43
1984 (preliminary)	4435	249,497	42

election victories net fewer members. The proportion of representation elections resulting in a union victory has also

fallen—from 74 percent in the early 1950s to less than half in the early 1980s.[51]

Unions may also be concentrating their efforts in the wrong places; as the service sector has grown, union organizing efforts have been slow to shift correspondingly. Furthermore, the union victory rate is much higher in small election units, but union organizing efforts continue to be distributed in the same proportion across units of different size.[52]

Unions have been slow to adapt to a changing economic and labor relations environment. The new techniques and operational modes necessary to keep pace with employer innovations require specialized personnel who must be largely drawn from outside the union ranks. Few unions can afford to hire pollsters, financial analysts, and public relations experts. In addition, the process demands that union leaders act on the findings of the pollsters and relinquish some of their control to the hired experts. Expanding government regulation of the workplace also may have contributed to the decline of unions by reducing worker demand for unionization. Another explanation for the union decline is the rising opposition of employers to union organizing attempts. Before the New Deal, most employers actively opposed unionization. But after passage of the Wagner Act, many large corporations acquiesced to unionization. More recently, many corporate executives have reevaluated their strategy and once again aggressively oppose unionization.

Some analysts attribute this change in employer attitude toward unions to increasing competition and the need for greater management flexibility. Indeed, during the 1970s the gap between union and nonunion wage levels widened considerably as unions successfully negotiated cost-of-living raises for their members in a period of high inflation. Other observers cite the increased professionalism of management and the rise in the use of psychology-based, individual-oriented personnel policies.[53]

Researchers have attempted to measure the relative importance of the various factors affecting unionization. A Bureau of Labor Statistics study estimated that industry and employment shifts accounted for approximately one-third of the decline in the unionized share of the work force since 1961.[54] Other studies have shown that when occupational and demographic changes are also considered, roughly two-fifths of the union decline is accounted for.[55] Another fifth is attributed to union shortcomings, and the remaining two-fifths of the decline in union strength are explained by increased management opposition.[56]

While neat in appearance, this analytical framework treats the political and legal climate as a static force, since changes in this variable do not yield easily to precise empirical measurement. In fact, legal and political factors may heavily influence union decisions concerning the probable outcome of an organizing campaign. Similarly, employers no doubt take such factors into account in gauging how forcefully they will resist union representation and bargaining demands. Debate will likely continue for some time on the relative importance of the various explanations for union decline.

Individual Rights

The success of federal interventions to establish basic safeguards for individual members is subject to less debate. Since the passage of the Landrum-Griffin Act, union constitutions and regulations have been brought into line with congressionally mandated standards, democratic practices have been adopted by most unions, and union corruption has been held in check. Probably the most salutary effect of the law has been the extent to which prescribed union practices have prevented embezzlement and violations of fiduciary responsibilities. The Department of Labor has failed to effectively monitor the reporting provisions of the Act. However, other evidence is available from which some inferences about the law's impact on union democracy can be made.

Survey data indicate that members are free to participate in union activities. Although nearly one in three members mentioned one or more problems with union management, mainly related to the handling of grievances and too much cooperation with company representatives, roughly three-quarters of union members report themselves as somewhat or very satisfied with their union.[57] Moreover, there has been a marked improvement in how union leaders are viewed by their members since the mid-1970s.[58]

Federal regulation of internal union affairs has definite limits. Legal sanctions to help create and maintain an institutional environment conducive to grass roots democracy can only provide the potential for greater membership participation in union affairs. Unions share with other voluntary associations a considerable amount of membership apathy concerning organizational activities. Congress cannot legislate such an interest.

The need to balance membership rights with institutional interests places further limitations on federal involvement. Unions are not merely debating societies. They must act quickly and decisively in times of crisis. Thus, effective union leadership requires the ability to discipline the membership to protect the organization. At the same time, however, the union is supposed to be controlled by its membership and operated for their benefit.

The courts have granted members the right to resign from a union at any time, including during a strike or when a strike is imminent.[59] In the same vein, the individual member's right to sue if unfairly represented by the union places a strain on the collective bargaining process. Union business agents, often acting quickly under pressure, must carefully consider the collective interest while adequately pursuing each individual claim. At times the individual's interests conflict with those of the organization.

The ability of the law to completely eliminate corrupt union practices is also limited. Frequently, problems with racketeering preceded union organization, and new union structures provided convenient vehicles for further pursuing illegal ventures. However, racketeering is mainly concentrated in a few industries, and according to a former attorney general, in 1978 only 300 local unions were "severely influenced by racketeers," implying that less than 1 percent of all local unions face severe problems of corruption.[60]

In short, federal intervention has done much to secure basic rights for individual union members. The federal role, however, is limited. As one study of the Landrum-Griffin Act concluded, "further regulation of the internal affairs of unions will, most likely, produce only diminishing returns in eradicating stubborn areas of union abuse while, at the same time, reducing the democracy inherent in a self-regulating voluntary organization."[61]

Collective Action and Pluralism

Fifty years ago Congress chose to guarantee workers the right to join unions for the purpose of engaging in collective bargaining. Consequently, an intricate system of private and voluntary labor-management relations has evolved. In the past two decades, Congress has increasingly turned toward more direct intervention to protect and advance the interests of specified groups in the labor force. Starting with the single objective of promoting collective bargaining in the workplace, federal intervention expanded into a pluralistic system extending protection in areas such as occupational health and safety to nearly the entire labor force.

The expansion of federal protection, while salutary, is not an effective substitute for workers banding together to advance their interests in the workplace. The federal regulations can establish some guidelines or standards for behavior, but their implementation depends upon constant interaction between management and labor. This calls for self-organization that establishes the necessary institutional arrangements to enable the parties both to monitor the application of the federal regulations and to protect the rights of individuals in the workplace.

The weakened state of the unions reduces the possibility for collective action which is essential for the protection of workers. In the absence of an appropriate balance of bargaining power between employers and employees, worker interests are bound to suffer. As union influence declines, nonunion employers feel less pressure to maintain adequate standards of worker protection.

Advocates of "new industrial relations" suggest that quality of work life programs or similar participative management techniques may render adversarial collective bargaining obsolete. Yet, there is no convincing evidence that employers and workers have found broad new areas of collaboration in the 1980s. With few notable exceptions, workers are allowed to participate in corporate decision making insofar as they do not infringe on management prerogatives. Essentially, the new industrial relations leave corporate power structures unchanged and offer workers no alternative to traditional methods to protect and advance their interests.

Ultimately, some federal intervention is required to adequately balance the interests of workers and employers. Either the federal government must once again tip the scales in favor of labor to encourage collective bargaining or it must increase direct regulation of employers to fill the void left by union ineffectiveness. However, such changes are unlikely under the Reagan administration, whose preference for letting the free market shape the destiny of workers is sharply at odds with either approach. Legislative reform, if it is to be achieved, must await a more sympathetic administration.

Part 3

Beyond Work

8

Helping Workers Forced Into Idleness

The federal-state unemployment insurance system was established under the Social Security Act of 1935 as a "first line of defense" for workers who have involuntarily lost their jobs. Its primary objective is to act as an insurance policy for workers, but the system also acts as a countercyclical program by replacing a portion of lost earnings during a recession. The UI program has been largely successful, providing needed income support to millions of the unemployed each year.

History

Before the enactment of the federal-state unemployment insurance system, only a few groups of workers had protection against unemployment either through their unions or their employers. In 1934 just 100,000 workers were covered by trade union plans, and approximately 65,000 workers, primarily in the garment trades, were covered by joint union-management plans. An additional 70,000 employees were covered by voluntary plans that paid benefits to seasonal workers during the off-season.[1]

In 1931 Wisconsin enacted the first state unemployment insurance law. A major obstacle to state UI legislation was concern that the added taxes to support the unemployed would drive away business. As Franklin Roosevelt said while Governor of New York, "All [states] must act, or there will be no action."[2]

When he entered the White House, President Roosevelt had the chance to push for federal UI legislation, which prior to his election had failed to pass Congress on several occasions. His interest in UI legislation reflected the dire economic conditions prevailing when he assumed office. Existing government aid, private voluntary assistance, and personal savings proved entirely inadequate in the face of mass unemployment. It became increasingly evident that the federal government would have to act if any income was to be provided for workers forced into idleness.

Advocating legislation that would "provide at once security against several of the great disturbing factors in life—especially those which relate to unemployment insurance and old age," Roosevelt appointed a Committee on Economic Security in June 1934 to study the unemployment problem.[3] Given the prevailing support for state rights and the concern that a purely federal system might constitute unlawful federal interference in state regulation of commerce, the committee opted for a tax credit plan with minimal federal standards and substantial state administrative responsibility. Congress accepted this plan and on August 14, 1935 President Roosevelt signed into law the Social Security Act which established the UI system.

Administration

Federal and State Roles

The state, or basic, UI program established in 1935 remains the heart of the current system. Under the basic program, the federal government sets broad standards and monitors and contributes to the financing system. State governments develop the substantive and administrative rules governing the program. The objective of joint federal-state administration is to maintain minimum standards while allowing states to tailor the program to their specific needs. In addition to the basic federal-state system, there are separate programs for railroad workers and veterans. As the system evolved, Congress also provided for supplemental benefits paid out of federal general revenue funds and extended benefits paid with federal and state funds. These programs have provided additional benefits during periods of high unemployment for workers who exhausted their basic state entitlements.

Between 1971 and 1984 the state programs provided 85 percent of UI benefits.[4] There are separate programs for each state, the District of Columbia, the Virgin Islands, and Puerto Rico. Subject to federal minimal standards, states set payroll tax levels, weekly benefits and potential weeks of duration, individual qualification requirements, disqualification provisions, eligibility, and the method of allocating benefit costs among employers. Consequently, provisions for unemployment compensation vary a good deal from state to state. For example, in fiscal 1985 weekly benefits averaged $122 nationally, but ranged from $69 to $153 in individual states.

During the 1958 recession Congress first provided for the temporary extension of benefits to long-term unemployed who had exhausted their state entitlements. Another temporary program was established in 1960, and in 1970 Congress enacted a permanent extended benefits program. This program provides up to 13 weeks of benefits beyond regular UI benefits and is triggered on a state-by-state basis depending on a state's insured unemployment rate (the number of people receiving regular unemployment insurance relative to the total work force covered by it). During the recessions since 1970 the federal government also enacted temporary programs that provided benefits beyond the state and extended benefits programs. In 1983, for example, an unemployed individual from a state with a high insured unemployment rate potentially was eligible to receive 26 weeks of basic state UI benefits, 13 weeks of extended benefits, and up to 16 weeks of federal supplemental compensation benefits.

Financing

State and federal payroll taxes on employers are the main source of UI program funds, with the majority of receipts coming from the state payroll tax. Currently, the Federal Unemployment Tax Act (FUTA) imposes a 6.2 percent gross tax on the first $7,000 of annual wages a covered employer pays to an employee. As long as a state system is in compliance with basic federal UI standards and is not in debt to the federal government, its employers receive 5.4 percent as a tax credit and the balance (0.8 percent) is earmarked for the federal UI trust fund. If a state fund does not meet these conditions, the federal tax credit declines on a sliding scale, thus raising the amount of UI taxes the employers pay to the federal government.

States deposit all UI contributions into the unemployment trust fund of the U.S. Treasury, from which they may withdraw funds to pay regular benefits and the state's share of extended benefits. State UI taxes differ, although the minimum tax base is set by Congress. In 1985 the estimated average state tax base was $7,900, or $900 above the federal minimum, and ranged as high as $21,800 in Alaska, while Puerto Rico taxed all wages.[5] The estimated 1985 average state tax rate as a proportion of taxable wages was 3.1 percent, or an effective tax rate of 1.3 percent of total wages.[6]

Although nine state UI programs originally taxed employees, employee taxes have been repealed over time because employer contributions were adequate to cover outlays. Employers did not press for employee taxes in order to minimize labor influence over the UI system. Taxing employers also gives firms an incentive to keep unemployment low and the costs of the program down. In 1985, employees were sometimes required to pay UI taxes only in four states.[7]

In fiscal 1984, total unemployment insurance revenues amounted to $30.4 billion (Figure 9). Federal revenue finances the administrative costs of the program, one-half of the federal-state extended benefits program, the federal supplemental compensation programs, and a federal loan fund from which states may borrow when their funds are depleted. State revenue finances the entire cost of regular benefits and the other half of the federal-state extended benefits program. Total outlays of all UI programs in fiscal 1984, including both benefits and administrative expenses, amounted to $18.4 billion.[8]

During periods of moderate to low unemployment, UI revenues generally exceed outlays. In high unemployment years, however, the increased number of recipients collecting both regular and extended benefits, together with reduced payroll taxes, puts a drain on the system. Since the 1971 recession, both the federal supplemental benefit programs and the state UI program have continually been plagued by financial problems, which have led both to tax increases and benefit cutbacks. At the beginning of fiscal 1984, following the recession, the states owed the federal government $13.2 billion. By the beginning of fiscal 1986, the states had managed to repay over half of these debts, but 13 states still owed a total of $6.3 billion

**Figure 9. Unemployment insurance revenue exceeded
$30 billion in 1984**

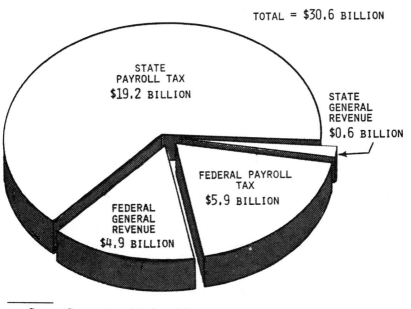

TOTAL = $30.6 BILLION

STATE
PAYROLL TAX
$19.2 BILLION

STATE
GENERAL
REVENUE
$0.6 BILLION

FEDERAL PAYROLL
TAX
$5.9 BILLION

FEDERAL
GENERAL
REVENUE
$4.9 BILLION

Source: Congressional Budget Office.

to the federal government. Four states, Pennsylvania, Michigan, Illinois, and Ohio, accounted for three-quarters of the debt.[9]

Unlike the federal tax, state tax rates are "experience rated," meaning that a firm's payroll tax depends on how much its laid off employees receive in UI funds. The use of experience rating reflects UI's design as an insurance program, in which each firm bears the costs its operations impose on society, as opposed to a welfare program, where society in general would subsidize the costs of unemployment. This principle—that a firm should pay for the financial burdens it places on the UI system—is also consistent with considerations of economic efficiency.[10]

The states have adopted different rules governing experience rating. The most popular plan, currently used by 33 states, is the reserve ratio system. A state keeps a separate account for each employer to which its UI payroll taxes are credited, while UI benefits paid to the firm's former employees are deducted. The ratio of the balance to the employer's taxable payroll provides a basis for setting the employer's tax rate. Another 14 states use the benefit ratio formula, which normally considers only the firm's UI experience during the last three years. The firm's tax rate is determined by the ratio of UI benefits paid to taxable payrolls; the system matches this year's taxes with the previous year's benefits. This method of balancing taxes and benefits over time is less direct than under the reserve ratio system. Puerto Rico is unique in that it charges all companies the same tax rate.

By allocating the costs of unemployment insurance among firms according to the benefits paid to their employees, experience rating influences employment policies. Since a firm's tax liability depends on its layoff history, an employer may be induced to stabilize employment and output (thus decreasing unemployment) or to limit the hiring of workers who might have to be laid off in the future (this incentive would decrease employment). Experience rating may shift business away from firms which tend to lay off workers. When firms have to bear the social costs of their operations, their overall costs rise, and the demand for their product falls. Firms whose operations created limited social costs have a competitive advantage. Experience rating also gives employers a direct interest in limiting unjustified claims and fraud, and in enacting restrictive and disqualifying provisions.[11]

Strict state reliance on experience rating has declined substantially.[12] By not fully matching costs with benefits, the UI system requires some sharing of costs by all employers and partially reflects a social insurance system. Most states have a maximum tax rate, limiting the taxes charged to firms with high layoff rates, and a minimum tax paid by all employers regardless of their layoff rates. A recent Labor Department study of 12 states found that "surplus" firms whose UI costs exceeded their employee's UI benefits paid 70 percent of UI taxes collected in 1983 but received only 36 percent of the benefits.[13] Between 1976 and 1981, employers in wholesale trade, finance, insurance, and real estate paid more than two dollars in taxes for each dollar their workers received in benefits.[14] On the other hand, firms in seasonal industries, such as construction and agriculture, paid slightly more than 50 cents in taxes for each dollar of benefits received by their workers. Within all these industries, employers have sharply different payment-benefit ratios.

Benefits

Coverage under the UI program has expanded considerably since the Act was first passed. Initially, less than half of all wage and salary workers were covered by UI. The 1935 law excluded from coverage businesses with fewer than eight persons, all agricultural enterprises, all government and nonprofit organizations, and domestic workers. A series of amendments, most significantly those in 1966 and 1974, extended coverage so that 97 percent of wage and salary employees are potentially protected by unemployment insurance. Only agricultural workers on small farms and most household workers remain unprotected by the system. Far fewer than 97 percent of the unemployed receive benefits, however, because job leavers, reentrants, and new entrants into the labor force now constitute about half the unemployed and are ineligible, and because of other eligibility restrictions.

To be eligible for unemployment benefits, a claimant must meet the state's employment and earning tests, be available for work, and register with the local employment service office. The worker typically must have been employed during two of the previous four quarters, and annual earnings requirements range from $150 in Hawaii to $3,560 in Oklahoma, with a median of $1,287. In fiscal 1985, 18.7 percent of applicants with sufficient earnings were disqualified, usually due to a claimant's lack of availability for work, voluntary separation without good cause, discharge for cause, refusal of suitable work without good cause, and unemployment resulting from a labor dispute.[15] The goal is to achieve a balance between eligibility criteria to promote the integrity of the UI program and the provision of benefits to deserving recipients.

Several characteristics distinguish UI recipients from unemployed workers in general. Since UI recipients must have had recent work experience and meet earnings requirements, they are more likely to be older, male, and white than all jobless persons. The system thus benefits a category of Americans who are often perceived as being neglected by government welfare programs. In 1983 persons aged 25-54 comprised 72 percent of UI recipients, but only 59 percent of the unemployed. Approximately two-thirds of UI recipients were men, while men were 58 percent of all jobless persons. Only 12 percent of UI recipients were nonwhite, as compared to 17 percent of all the unemployed. Unemployed individuals from low income families are less likely to receive unemployment compensation than middle income families.[16]

	Distribution of	
Annual Family Income	All Unemployed	UI Recipients
less than $10,000	29.0%	19.2%
$10,000–$19,999	26.4	29.9
$20,000–$39,999	31.0	37.4
$40,000 or more	13.5	13.4

The UI system seems of greatest benefit to the traditional blue collar worker. In 1983, two of every three unemployed mine workers and workers in durable goods manufacturing industries received UI benefits, compared with one of every three service and retail trade workers.

Organized labor has favored a permanent federal UI program for the long-term jobless rather than one triggered in and out with recessions. A permanent program would provide a more consistent level of benefits and would protect the long-term unemployed from varying political conditions. Business representatives have argued that states, without federal intervention, have continued to extend benefit duration over the years in line with their special needs and varying employment conditions. Providing extended benefits at all times, business has claimed, would be both costly and subject to abuse, while a standby program can more accurately respond to economic conditions. For the most part, business has won the debate.[17]

The maximum duration of unemployment benefits is now 26 weeks in all but three states, two of which have longer durations. Combining state, extended, and supplemental benefit programs, potential duration of unemployment insurance benefits rose to as long as 65 weeks during the high unemployment period from 1974-1976. During the recession of 1982-1983, maximum duration of benefits reached 55 weeks. The federal supplemental compensation program adopted by Congress in 1982 expired three years later. In January 1986 an extended benefit program was in effect in only two states, limiting to 26 weeks the potential duration of benefits for almost all the unemployed.

Weekly benefits paid to the laid off worker are based on the claimant's earnings, within specified minimum and maximum limits. For more than a decade, average regular UI benefits have replaced slightly more than one-third of a worker's former wage.[18] This figure does not account for an unemployed worker's loss in fringe benefits; on the other hand, it does not reflect the tax-free status of most UI payments. UI benefits were first taxed in 1979; in 1985, benefits paid to individuals with income exceeding $12,000 and to married taxpayers with a joint income above $18,000 were taxable.

Evolution of the Unemployment Insurance System

A combination of insurance principles and welfare considerations have guided the development of the UI system. Although unemployment compensation is not means-tested— it is provided regardless of the recipient's economic condition— UI does differ from a pure insurance program. In 13 states benefits vary with family size. In addition, even though the low tax base causes employers to contribute roughly the same amount in taxes for almost all their workers, benefit amounts vary in proportion to previous earnings. In 1985, full-time workers earning the minimum wage received weekly benefits of $74; workers earning $6 an hour received $126, and workers earning $9 an hour received $165. UI does, however, compensate a greater percentage of the wage loss of low-wage earners than of high-wage workers; for the above categories of workers, UI replaced, respectively, 55, 52, and 46 percent of previous earnings.[19]

Business lobbies have played a major role in maintaining UI's focus on insuring workers with substantial attachment to the labor force against potential wage loss. Throughout the program's existence, business has adhered steadfastly to three guidelines for controlling the costs of UI: limiting the scope of UI assistance to those workers who are forced into idleness, minimizing federal intervention with state programs, and holding each firm responsible for restoring the funds that its unemployed workers have drawn from the system. Pressure by business lobbies to keep costs in check has helped to ensure that the original intentions of the program have been pursued. By preventing Congress from expanding federal standards, business lobbies have also helped keep control of the system in the states where, with few exceptions, organized labor lacks resources and political clout.

Although the scope of UI has remained relatively narrow over the years, the system has proven capable of adapting and changing with the times. Coverage has expanded considerably since the program was first established, while benefit duration has lengthened substantially. In some respects, however, UI has moved in the wrong direction. When the system was established, 98 percent of all wages were subject to the federal UI tax, compared with only 36 percent in 1985.[20] The percentage of the unemployed receiving unemployment insurance has also fallen sharply.

Effects

Income

The UI system provides substantial income support to covered job losers. While some unemployed could draw on savings or other sources of income, for many others UI payments are essential to help combat poverty and meet severe need during periods of economic stress. In fiscal 1985 over 8 million individuals received regular state weekly benefits averaging $122 over 13 weeks.[21]

Although UI often provides necessary benefits, UI income support is less than it should be. First, average benefit levels in some states are inadequate. In 1985 benefits averaged $91 in Mississippi and $98 in Missouri. Across the border from Mississippi, UI payments averaged $151 in Louisiana; in Missouri's neighboring state of Illinois, payments averaged $137.

Second, the historic effectiveness of UI in providing temporary income support to the unemployed eroded in the early 1980s. Support peaked in 1975, when an average of 76 percent of the unemployed received some form of unemployment insurance. The proportion declined to 42 percent in 1979, and subsequently rose to 50 percent during the 1980 recession, then declined again to a historic low of less than 34 percent in 1984 and 1985 (Figure 10).

Figure 10. Percent of unemployed receiving unemployment insurance has declined since 1975

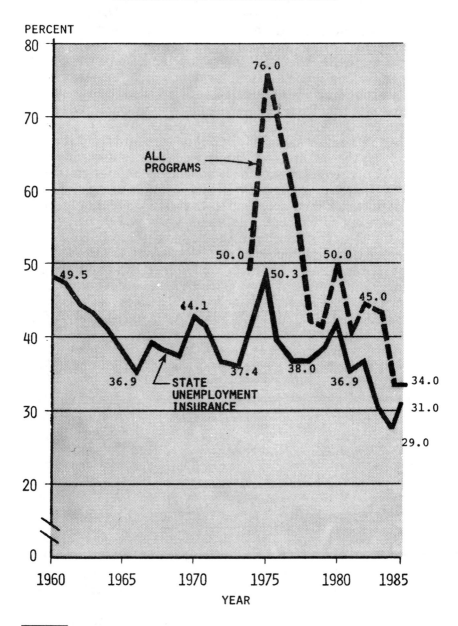

Source: U.S. Department of Labor and House Ways and Means Committee.

One explanation for the drop in the proportion of unemployed receiving UI is the increased number of women in the labor market. Women are less likely to be insured because they have less attachment to the labor force than adult men, and their recent earnings and work experience are frequently inadequate to qualify them for unemployment compensation. A further explanation is that employment has shifted away from goods producing industries to service industries, where because of intermittent employment, fewer unemployed workers receive UI benefits.

Stricter enforcement of eligibility standards and tighter administrative controls—including stronger enforcement of work-search requirements for beneficiaries, tighter state disqualification provisions for quitting a job or being fired for misconduct, and the imposition in 43 states of a minimum one-week waiting period before claimants could receive benefits—contributed to the decline in the percent of the unemployed receiving UI. These actions, partially taken as an effort by states to solve their UI deficits, contributed to a one-third decrease in the number of new job losers receiving regular benefits since 1979.[22] Eligibility for federal benefits has also been restricted; the 1981 Omnibus Reconciliation Act severely tightened the extended benefits trigger.

More evidence of the erosion of the UI system can be found by comparing benefit levels during years of high unemployment: 1975-76 and 1982-83.

			Unemployment Insurance Benefits (in billions, 1983 dollars)		
Year	Unemployed (in millions)	Job Losers	Regular	Extended and Supplementary	Total
1975	7.9	4.4	$21.7	$8.6	$30.3
1976	7.4	3.7	15.7	8.9	24.6
1982	10.7	6.3	20.0	1.9	21.9
1983	10.7	6.3	20.8	8.0	28.8

Even though there were 2.2 million more average monthly job losers in 1982 and 1983 than in 1975 and 1976, the real value of benefits fell by $4.2 billion. Extended and supplementary benefits were cut almost in half. Average benefits per job loser dropped by a third.

For those who do receive benefits, the goal is to set benefits high enough to provide an adequate income cushion, and yet not so high as to prolong their period of job search unnecessarily. The consensus goal has long been to provide a "great majority" (normally 80 percent) of UI claimants with 50 percent of their earnings.[23] The National Commission on Unemployment Compensation found, however, that in none of the states for which information was available did 80 percent of the beneficiaries receive half their weekly wage loss, and in seven states fewer than 50 percent received half their lost earnings. The 1985 average wage replacement rate was 35 percent.

Employment Disincentive

A common criticism of the unemployment insurance system is that it increases measured levels of unemployment. Because unemployment compensation reduces the cost to workers of being unemployed, they are more likely to prolong their period of idleness, particularly in tight labor markets when jobs are relatively easy to obtain. This extended job search period does, however, have a positive aspect: it allows workers more time to look for jobs where their skills can be utilized. UI also increases unemployment because employers, particularly those at the maximum tax rate, are more willing to lay off workers for short periods of time, as the availability of UI benefits reduces the chances that an employee will immediately seek work elsewhere. Finally, UI increases unemployment because the UI payroll tax raises the cost of labor.

Numerical estimates of the work disincentive effects of UI have found that during periods of low unemployment, UI benefits may increase the unemployment rate roughly 10 to 15 percent, as compared to about 5 percent during periods of high unemployment.[24] These estimates necessarily rest on a number of questionable explicit or implicit assumptions and should therefore be used with caution. In particular, since a historically low percentage of the unemployed received benefits in 1984 and 1985, it is not likely that UI could have acted as a significant work disincentive.

As a counterbalance to this increase in unemployment, by replacing a portion of an unemployed worker's earnings, UI benefits have a countercyclical effect helping to stabilize demand and, therefore, output and employment during a recession. Numerically estimating this effect is a difficult proposition, but several studies estimated that recessions from 1948 to 1977 were 10 percent less severe than they would have been without the UI system.[25]

Reforms

As a result of the dynamic nature of the UI program and the significant amount of funds involved, the UI system has often been the subject of analysis and proposed changes. There has been continuing controversy over the appropriate federal role, the level of taxable wages, and the best alternatives to control costs. More recently, reformers have suggested expanding the program to provide more comprehensive support to the unemployed.

The Federal Role

The principle of subsidiarity—the belief that the federal government should undertake no functions that can be performed by lower levels of government—has been used by employers to oppose increased federal intervention in UI. Their position is that employment conditions vary enough among regions to warrant tailor-made state standards. Organized labor, on the other hand, has charged that decentralized authority among competing states is responsible for the inadequacies in unemployment insurance coverage and benefits. Labor has favored a federal UI system or, at the least, stronger minimum federal standards to ensure that all employees, regardless of where they reside, are covered by the same basic rights and protections.

For the most part, there has been a delicate balance between state autonomy and federal intervention in the UI system. States have abided by the basic federal standards and have effectively administered the program. Nevertheless, steps should be taken to establish stricter federal minimum benefit standards so that benefits are not excessively low in some states and to reverse the sharp decline in the percentage of the unemployed receiving compensation.

Unemployment insurance programs that provide benefits beyond the regular state program should be reformulated. The 1981 revision of the extended benefits (EB) trigger undermined this program significantly. In July 1985, the EB program was in effect only in Alaska and Puerto Rico, even though unemployment rates were above 10 percent in Louisiana, Michigan, Mississippi, and West Virginia. The EB trigger is not only too restrictive, but it often fails to reflect the true unemployment situation in a state. Since 1981 the insured unemployment rate trigger does not include individuals receiving either extended benefits or federal supplemental benefits, nor has it ever included individuals who have exhausted UI benefits. During the deep recession of the early 1980s, states with large manufacturing sectors and large numbers of long-term unemployed often had relatively low insured unemployment rates and fell off the EB rolls rather quickly. The EB program failed to adequately help those it is intended to assist: the long-term unemployed in states with severe economic dislocation.

The most recent temporary federal supplemental compensation program was in effect between the fall of 1982 and in the spring of 1985. It provided additional relief to over seven million of the long-term unemployed whose regular and/or extended benefits had expired. However, the confusion and uncertainty caused by three extensions during 1983 and 1984 as well as the program's use of the insured unemployment rate trigger undermined its effectiveness.

In light of the weak EB program and the shakiness of the recent supplemental benefits program, a permanent federal supplemental program is in order. In areas of severe economic dislocation, where job searches may last well beyond 26 weeks, this program would assure job losers additional weeks of compensation. To be effective, the program should either broaden the base of the insured unemployment rate or use the total unemployed rate as an alternative trigger. Finally, because an individual's reemployment possibilities depend heavily on local labor market conditions, substate triggers should be considered.

Wage Base

The federal taxable wage base, which sets a minimum for the state taxable wage base, has been raised only three times from its initial level of $3,000 to $7,000 half a century later. Consequently, the ratio of taxable wages to the total wages of covered employees has declined from 98 percent in 1940 to 36 percent in 1985. The average state base of $7,900 is only slightly higher. In comparison, the social security maximum tax base ($39,600 in 1985) was about five times as high. With a low base, employers pay the same amount of tax for all workers earning at or above the minimum level. This low tax base favors firms with high-wage employees at the expense of low wage firms.

The low tax wage base also acts as an employment disincentive. UI taxes, as a semifixed cost, increase the incentive for firms to lengthen workers' hours at no additional UI expense rather than to hire a new worker and increase costs to a low wage firm by a substantial amount. It also bears repeating that even though contributions per employer vary little with a worker's wages, benefits do vary with earnings; a low wage employer may contribute as much as a high wage firm to the system, but the low wage worker receives substantially less in benefit payments. Raising the UI taxable wage base is worth serious consideration. Further, to prevent future deterioration, the taxable wage should be indexed to the average rise in wages.

Controlling Costs

Despite the recent erosion of UI benefits, some critics believe that benefits should be further reduced. One suggestion is to require a minimum two-week waiting period—as opposed to the current one-week waiting period—before an initial claimant can receive benefits. Although some unemployed could endure a two-week waiting period without much financial strain, others with little or no savings might experience serious deprivation. A second suggestion is to tighten enforcement of job search and other eligibility requirements to ensure that only laid-off employees ready, willing, and able to work receive benefits. This would help cut down on overpayments. The Labor Department estimated that up to 12 percent of UI benefits are overpaid or paid to ineligible claimants each year. The most common reason for these erroneous payments is the failure of UI recipients to meet job search requirements.[26] Although enforcement of existing rules is in order, it would involve increased administrative costs due to added personnel and might delay or prevent deserving recipients from receiving benefits.

Scope

Another perennial issue concerns the scope of the UI system. Several proposals have been introduced in Congress which would expand the role of UI from an income support program to include the promotion of reemployment of benefit recipients. The proposals have included using UI funds for retraining and relocation, for reemployment vouchers, to create individual training accounts, and to stimulate entrepreneurship.[27] These proposals would involve a substantial departure from the program's original role of providing a temporary income cushion for workers forced into idleness through no fault of their own. Reformers argue that it is time to depart from this narrow purpose because the assumption that unemployed workers can quickly find jobs no longer holds true, especially in the case of dislocated workers. Modifying the unemployment insurance system, because of its existing administrative structure and the lack of stigma attached to receiving benefits, is thought to be an excellent vehicle to help these workers.

Proponents of revamping the UI system argue that UI-financed retraining and relocation assistance would help unemployed workers secure employment when they might otherwise have significant difficulty. Either vocational training or on-the-job training could be provided, and UI regulations could be changed to allow individuals to undergo training while they receive benefits. Currently, UI recipients can be certified to receive job training in only 13 states; in other states, an unemployed individual is not eligible for benefits and job training simultaneously.[28]

Another alternative to promote reemployment of long term UI recipients is to allow them the option of using a portion of their benefits as vouchers payable to new employers. This program would have a low added cost compared to some other employment and training programs. However, monitoring such a system to prevent windfalls to employers who, even without subsidies, might have hired the workers, presents serious difficulties.

A third proposal is to finance job training through the use of individual training accounts (ITAs) with administrative ties to the unemployment insurance system. Worker and employer contributions would be collected as a supplement to the federal UI payroll tax. Eligibility to use ITA funds would depend on an individual's UI eligibility. Unused retraining funds would be returned to the worker when he or she retired, with interest. A voluntary system allowing tax deductible contributions would erode the tax base; mandatory contributions would make it necessary to raise the current UI payroll tax.

Some of these proposals merit consideration—most notably, that individuals be allowed to receive UI payments while they participate in training programs. However, fundamental expansion of the system to include reemployment of dislocated and other unemployed workers is beyond the proper scope of UI. Such programs should be financed from general revenue. To turn UI into a comprehensive training or welfare program would interfere with its current limited but effective role of helping workers forced into idleness and would compound the program's financial difficulties. The maxim "when it ain't broke, don't fix it" applies to the well-intentioned proposals to transform the program into a broad welfare system.

The recent sharp decline in the percentage of unemployed who receive UI benefits is a disturbing trend that must be reversed. The system can also be improved by increasing the taxable wage base and by a stronger federal program for unemployed workers who exhaust their regular state benefits. In large part, however, UI has fulfilled its purpose as a non-means-tested social insurance program. By providing an income cushion for workers who have involuntarily lost their jobs, each year it helps millions of Americans cope with the difficulties of unemployment.

9

Social Security for the Working Population

Many older workers lack the physical strength or the good health necessary to continue in productive employment. Other workers become disabled as a result of crippling injuries or disease, robbing them of their ability to support themselves or their families. The federal government has stepped in to provide crucially important income security and health care during old age and protection against income loss due to disability.

Men approaching the end of their working careers in 1985 can expect on the average to spend 13 years in retirement, while women can expect 17 years. Because women tend to outlive their husbands, they often face much of retirement alone; two-thirds of women over age 75 are widows. The elderly receive less than 1 percent of their cash income from their children, and fewer than one in ten live with their children.[1] Federal income support contributes to the economic independence of most elderly persons.

The Social Security System

The social security system is vast. Nearly 37 million persons—15 percent of all Americans—received basic social security payments in 1985 (Figure 11). Old age, survivors, disability, and hospital insurance expenditures totaled $240 billion, accounting for one-fourth of the federal budget. The 1983 amendments to the Social Security Act made social security coverage nearly universal by adding most employees in the public and nonprofit sectors to the system. Only 6 percent of those who reached age 65 in 1984 were not eligible for

173

some benefits; 95 percent of all children and their mothers would receive benefits if the father were to die (Figure 11).

The benefit payable to a retiree is determined by the person's age at retirement and the level of covered earnings. Eligible workers below age 70 who continue to work may lose part or all of their entitlement depending upon their level of earnings. In 1986, persons aged 65 to 69 lost one dollar in benefits for every two dollars earned above $7,800 ($5,760 for beneficiaries aged 62 to 64). Earnings do not affect the benefits

Figure 11. Social security benefits, September 1985

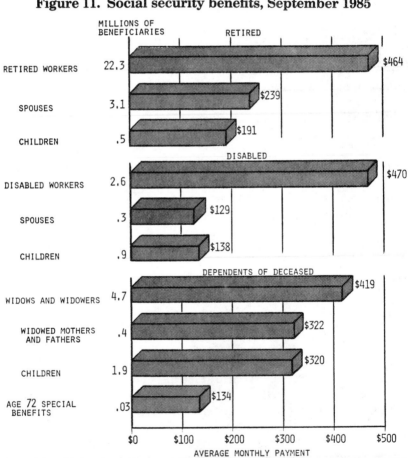

Source: Social Security Administration.

of those aged 70 or older. Defined earnings include income from labor but not rents, royalties, dividends, or pensions.

Survivor benefits are payable to an insured worker's surviving children under 18 years of age, to the dependent parents of the deceased worker, and to dependent widows or widowers. To become permanently insured, individuals must have been covered for 40 quarters while eligibility for disability insurance is contingent on covered employment for at least 20 of the 40 quarters prior to becoming disabled, or at least half of the quarters (but not fewer than six) since turning 21. Disability insurance aids severely disabled adults (aged 18 to 64) and is paid after a five-month waiting period and upon a determination that the impairment rules out gainful employment. One-fifth of the estimated 13 million work-disabled adults receive disability insurance.

The federal government also is the major financial contributor to health care of the aged. Enacted in 1965, medicare is funded from a portion of social security payroll taxes and covers 45 percent of hospital and medical costs both for persons aged 65 or older and for disabled social security beneficiaries. The program is designed to help all the elderly regardless of their income and to prevent, except in extreme cases, wiping out an individual's life savings due to a major illness. The $71.2 billion program (in FY 1985) offers both basic hospital insurance (Part A) and optional supplementary medical insurance (Part B) to cover physicians' fees. Part B is funded through individual monthly contributions, matched by federal general revenues. In July 1984, 26.9 million aged and 2.9 million disabled persons were covered by hospital insurance, including 29.5 million persons enrolled in the optional program.

Principles

Throughout its first half century three basic principles dominated the development of the social security system. The first principle is that a worker's entitlement to benefits is based on past employment, and the level of benefits received is related to earnings in covered work. Work incentives are preserved because the higher an individual's earnings, the higher the benefits received.

The second principle is that benefits are an earned right, paid regardless of income from savings, pensions, investments, or other assets. Consequently, the system encourages workers to provide additional protection for their retirement. Workers at all income levels contribute to and benefit from social security, assuring program support from all sectors of the working population. If the program were not compulsory, its financial soundness would be undermined and its effectiveness lost. On average, social security old age benefits replace 43 percent of a worker's preretirement earnings. In 1986 the benefit formula, weighted in favor of lower-paid workers, replaced 90 percent of the first $297 of average monthly earnings, plus 32 percent of earnings between $298 and $1,790, and 15 percent of the balance (up to $3,500) of covered earnings. A guaranteed minimum benefit for persons who attained age 62 before 1982, means-tested supplemental security benefits, and an upper maximum benefit ($788 in 1986), ensure that lower-income recipients are provided minimal protection, while upper-income beneficiaries do not overburden the system.

The final principle underlying social security is that the system should be completely self-supporting, requiring initially no general revenue appropriations to pay either benefits or administrative expenses. Social security is a "pay-as-you-go" system. The benefits of present retirees are paid out of contributions from those currently in the work force. Separate trust funds are maintained for the old age, disability, and health insurance accounts. Over the first half century of the social security program's existence, Congress made periodic adjustments in the level of covered earnings and payroll tax rates to prevent any shortfall and to guarantee that funds are available to satisfy current obligations.

Structure

The social security system has been molded by longstanding traditions as well as by changing economic and social conditions. Opportunities presented by a rapidly expanding economy, a growing population, an abundance of natural resources, and an open frontier shaped the highly valued model of the "rugged individual." The ideal of individualism in America was reinforced by a predominantly agrarian society in which people depended in large part on their own skill and industry for survival. Family, friends, and neighbors provided assistance when economic disasters and personal catastrophies struck. Public aid in the form of the poor relief system and poorhouses existed as a final safety net, but was meager and often grudgingly given.[2]

The severe depression of the 1930s made it clear that in fact most workers were dependent on factors beyond their control for economic security. Neither the states, local communities, or private charities could muster the financial resources to cope with the growing needs of chronically jobless workers. Of the 7.5 million elderly Americans in 1934, less than 3 percent received old-age benefits from state programs and only 2 percent of retirees received private pensions.[3] The need for federal action was apparent.

The Social Security Act of 1935 established a basic system of contributory social insurance and a supplemental program to fill gaps in the insurance program for the low-income elderly. In 1939, Congress expanded the program to provide benefits to survivors of covered workers as well as to dependents of retirees. This began the transformation of social security into a family insurance program. Over the years Congress expanded and made the program nearly universal and included permanently disabled workers in addition to the aged and their dependents.

Rising productivity and growing affluence in the 1950s and 1960s paved the way for the expansion of the social security system during the Great Society years. The drafters of the 1935 legislation had considered a health insurance program, but abandoned it in the face of strong opposition from organized medical societies and their allies. After three decades of debate over its merits, Congress passed a limited national health insurance program to serve the elderly. Coverage was later extended to the severely disabled. As with the earlier social security legislation, the 1965 legislation established a program, medicare, that covers all elderly citizens, regardless of income, and a means-tested program, medicaid, that provides assistance to the poor. The indexing of benefits in 1972 completed the present structure of the social security system.

A Quarter-Trillion Dollar Program

Over the past five decades the financing of the social security system has been amended repeatedly to keep pace with expanded coverage and liberalized benefits. In 1985 the annual price tag for the three major components of the system—old age and survivors, disability, and health care for the aged—amounted to an estimated $240 billion and rising. The initial tax rate of 2 percent of annual earnings up to $3,000, shared equally by employer and employee, has been periodically increased, as has the taxable earnings base. By 1986 the tax rate was 14.3 percent on the first $42,000 of annual earnings. Until the 1970s, expanding coverage, rising tax rates, and a healthy economy generated sizable surpluses in the social security trust funds. Rising affluence softened public resistance to periodic increases in the tax rate.[4]

In 1972 Congress indexed benefits to safeguard their real purchasing value and adjusted the computation formula so that benefit levels for future retirees would be based on inflation-adjusted preretirement earnings. For instance, if a worker retiring in 1976 had annual earnings of $4,000 in 1960, this figure would have been calculated at $7,689 for benefit-computation purposes to account for the rise in the Consumer Price Index. To help pay for these increases, Congress also boosted and indexed the taxable earnings base. Reasonable as these careful arrangements seemed, economic developments over the succeeding decade threatened to generate deficits in the social security trust fund and provoked a "crisis" in the social security system.

Retirement and Survivors

Because the social security system operates on a pay-as-you-go basis, it is very sensitive to business fluctuations. As long as the economy grew and wages rose faster than prices, sufficient tax revenues were generated to cover increases in social security expenditures triggered by the benefit formula. But in the past decade the sluggish economy and creeping unemployment undercut the tax base while high inflation drove up the level of benefits and the number of retirees continued to rise. Between 1973 and 1985, average weekly real wages declined by 14.5 percent while average monthly social security benefits rose in real terms by 15 percent and the number of persons receiving benefits increased by 44 percent.

The 1977 social security amendments were designed to restore financial health to the ailing system and to rebuild public confidence. The legislation boosted the taxable earnings base as well as the tax rate, and revamped the benefit formula (referred to as "decoupling") to eliminate overcompensation of future retirees. With prices rising faster than wages, it was possible that benefits in the 21st century would be higher than earned wages for many people. Congress responded to this potential problem by indexing past earnings to increases in the average wage, rather than increases in prices. It was estimated that the tax increase would add an estimated $80 billion to the system over five years, while the decoupling provision would save $7.5 billion.[5]

By 1980, however, less than $17 billion in new revenues had been brought into the system. The 1980 social security trustees' report indicated that by late 1981 the retirement trust fund would be completely exhausted. Options for resolving the system's financial dilemma were constrained by increasing public resistance to additional tax increases.

The Reagan administration took its first stab at solving the social security financing problem in its 1981 omnibus budget proposal. Changes included eliminating the "minimum benefit," phasing out student benefits, limiting eligibility for the lump sum death benefit, and tightening eligibility for disability benefits. These provisions were expected to help ease the system's financial problems by saving an estimated $27 billion over the 1981 to 1986 period. Most of these provisions were enacted in 1981, although Congress later restored the minimum benefit for persons who attained age 62 before 1982.

Supply side economic theory colored most of the Reagan administration's social security policy recommendations. The administration ruled out payroll tax increases as inimical to economic growth. Instead it favored private retirement arrangements in the belief that increased savings spurred investment. If government retirement programs could be partially replaced by private saving for retirement, more capital would be available to invest in productive ventures, thus creating the opportunity for even greater private saving. Finally, the administration's supply side economic predictions downplayed the seriousness of social security's financial crisis. The administration expected cuts in the federal personal and corporate income taxes to generate sustained economic growth that would resolve the financial predicament of social security—

payrolls would grow, inflation would recede, and the trust funds would soon be restored to good health. Whatever basis existed for this rosy scenario, the 1981-1982 recession removed any hopes for its realization. The social security system faced a real crisis.

In 1970, the retirement and disability trust funds had reserves amounting to more than 100 percent of that year's expenditures. By 1983, following the severe recession, the trust funds combined had nearly exhausted their reserves (Figure 12). Spurred by a worsening deterioration of the trust funds and frustrated by widespread opposition to further benefit cuts, President Reagan called for the creation of a bipartisan committee to devise solutions to social security's fiscal crisis. Congress and the President adopted the recommendations of the National Commission on Social Security Reform distributing the burden of saving social security fairly evenly.

To resolve the funding crisis, Congress enacted benefit cuts and tax increases, expanded coverage, and added a dose of general revenue financing. The law delayed by six months the annual automatic cost-of-living benefit adjustment to benefits, taxed half the social security benefits of single retirees with an annual income above $25,000 and of retirees filing joint returns with an annual income above $32,000, and advanced the scheduled payroll tax rate increases. The package also broadened the base of social security contributions—principally by bringing all employees of nonprofit organizations and newly hired federal workers into the system, and by prohibiting state and local workers who were in the system when the law was enacted from opting out of it. Finally, the law provided for the transfer of general revenue to the trust funds to cover benefit obligations to World War II and Korean War veterans.

The Social Security Administration estimated that by 1989 these changes would boost social security trust funds by $166 billion, distributed as follows:

Delaying cost-of-living adjustments	$39 billion
Taxing benefits	27 billion
Increasing the payroll tax rate	58 billion
Broadening the tax base	25 billion
Transfers from general revenue	17 billion

**Figure 12. Trust fund contingency levels declined sharply
prior to 1983 amendments**

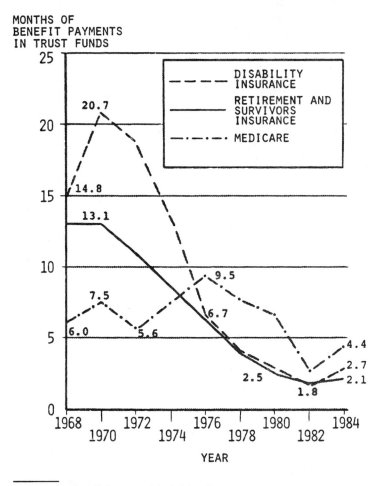

MONTHS OF
BENEFIT PAYMENTS
IN TRUST FUNDS

Source: Social Security Administration.

Barring a deep recession, the changes will enable the system to
meet obligations for the next three decades until the baby boom
children begin to retire after the year 2020. During this time,
people born in the 1930s and early 1940s, low birth rate years,
will retire and draw on payroll taxes contributed by the larger
cohort of workers born during the baby boom. Also, by raising
the age at which full social security benefits can be claimed (to

66 in 2009 and 67 in 2027) and by reducing benefits for early retirees, the 1983 law will generate revenues for the social security system through additional payroll taxes as well as deferred benefit payments. And, no doubt, the 35-year respite will provide ample time for future administrations and Congress to add, as needed, other revisions to guarantee benefits for retirees.

The 1983 law struck a balance between competing interests—future retirees will be denied some benefits, while the working population will shoulder a slightly heavier tax burden. Significantly, no tax rate increase is scheduled after 1990 and benefit growth is expected to slow due to later retirement and taxation of retirement income. The benefits of higher-income retirees will be most affected, but this group also has a larger cushion of private pensions, savings, and other assets to fall back on. The unity of purpose achieved among the National Association of Manufacturers, the Business Roundtable, the AFL-CIO, the National Council of Senior Citizens, and the broad congressional support is testimony to the fairness of the compromise and, above all, to the broad consensus in support of the social security system.

The Burden of Disability

Originally established in 1956, the disability insurance program has also faced fiscal problems due to a combination of relaxed eligibility and the relatively attractive benefits. Although strict medical impairment criteria are emphasized, since 1967 other personal attributes such as age, education, and work experience have been applied to workers not sufficiently impaired to meet the medical standards. By 1975 these other factors accounted for one of every four qualified workers.[6] The subjective nature of these appraisals also opened the door wider to individual appeals. In 1965, 9 percent of all initial disability recipients were awarded benefits after the denial of their initial claims; by 1977 this number had increased to 21 percent.[7]

The financial burden on the system has grown significantly and the number of disabled workers on the rolls peaked at 2.9 million in 1979 and dropped to 2.6 million by mid-1985. However, as a result of inflation, annual benefits paid to the

3.9 million disabled workers, including their spouses and children, continued to rise reaching $19 billion in 1985.

Automatic increases in disability benefits during the 1970s outpaced wage growth and may have made these benefits an attractive alternative for workers facing long-term joblessness, low wages, or intermittent periods of employment in secondary labor markets. In 1979 the average family disability benefit exceeded the full-time year-round pay from a minimum wage job by 20 percent.[8]

The heavy workload of the social security staff also contributed to growth in the disability rolls. In the early 1970s, Congress assigned the agency responsibility for processing black lung claims and shortly thereafter instructed agency personnel to assume administration of the state disability welfare rolls. In addition, budget pressures limited verification of state disability determinations and the public and Congress pressured the staff to expedite the processing of claims. During the 1970s the number of state awards checked by federal personnel prior to approval of benefits declined from 80 percent to 5 percent.[9]

In 1980 Congress attempted to restrain the growth of the disability program. It capped disability benefits so that they would not exceed predisability earnings, increased incentives to encourage disabled workers to return to work, and improved the administration of the program to ensure that benefits go only to those who are eligible. Spurred by reports from the Social Security Administration and the General Accounting Office that as many as 20 to 30 percent of disability recipients may be ineligible, and eager to reduce costs, the Reagan administration also pursued a number of changes in the program, including the decision to accelerate implementation of a 1980 amendment that state agencies reexamine beneficiaries at least every three years, except for those diagnosed as permanently disabled.

Between March 1981 and June 1984, state agencies reviewed 1.2 million disability beneficiaries, and terminated the benefits of 491,000. This action induced a record number of appeals. Between February 1982 and July 1983 administrative law judges heard 126,000 appeals and reversed 61 percent of the termination decisions.[10] A number of court decisions also reversed administrative law judges' rejections of appeals. After the appeals process, some 200,000 persons were removed from the rolls. As the media publicized unjustified terminations that resulted in hardship, 29 states dropped out of the federal-state program and refused to continue the reviews. In 1984 Congress passed a major new disability law making it more difficult to remove persons from the disability rolls unless there is substantial evidence of medical improvement. Another provision requires benefits to be continued in disputed cases until all appeals are exhausted.

The differences between the 1980 and 1984 laws are striking. While the 1980 law reflected a concern over the costs of a rising caseload, many of whom were thought to be ineligible, the 1984 law emphasized the rights of individuals already in the program. Rather than dwelling on presumed abuses of the disability system, the 1984 law reflected concern over the unfair treatment of the disabled.

Inflated Health Care Costs

Rising costs have also been a persistent problem of the medicare program. In the early stages of the program, efforts to improve the quality of medical care for the elderly led to federal requirements that states reimburse hospitals and physicians at prevailing local rates. In order to allay fears of "socialized medicine," however, no provision was made for federal monitoring, and charges of program fraud were common. In the early 1970s, Congress responded by directing federal administrators to spell out standards controlling reimbursements, although it preserved state regulation that precluded stringent monitoring of medicare costs. Limiting federal health care expenditures, which have risen four times as fast as inflation since 1970, continued to be a pressing and urgent challenge. Because the supplementary medical insurance program (Part B) is financed through premiums and general revenues, the burden of rising health care expenditures in this component of medicare has fallen on both participants and the federal government.

The Reagan administration has taken halting steps toward federal control of health care costs by instituting changes in payments for hospital services. Monthly premiums for supplementary medical insurance increased by 41 percent between 1981 and 1986. Congress rejected the administration's proposal in fiscal 1985 to raise participants' contributions further by doubling the monthly premium in a single year. If the Reagan proposals had been accepted by Congress, recipients' out-of-pocket costs under Part B (including deductibles) would have jumped from $250 to $510 per year before medicare reimbursements became available. To preserve the universal nature of the program, Congress also rejected proposals to tax the benefits of higher-income elderly recipients who can presumably afford private medical insurance.

In another cost-cutting effort, Congress placed limits on medicare reimbursements to hospitals with above-average costs in 1982, and during 1983 a more comprehensive system of "prospective reimbursement" was established, setting maximum charges for services to medicare patients. This policy gives hospitals an incentive to hold down medical costs by requiring them to absorb the loss if their costs exceed federally established standards and reimbursement rates, and by allowing them to keep their surplus when covered services cost less than the allowances. In addition, Congress froze the fee schedules paid to physicians in 1984 and 1985, shifting some of the burden to the providers of health care.

The burden of these cost containment measures often shifts to beneficiaries. Evidence is mounting that the new medicare payment system has led hospitals to discharge patients sooner, sometimes prematurely. Between 1983 and 1985 the average length of hospital stays declined by 19 percent, from 9.5 days to 7.7 days. A Senate committee found that some hospitals were pressuring doctors for faster discharges to hold down costs.[11] As hospitals and physicians attempt to recover their costs through reductions in patient care, the conflicts with program advocates determined to resist further retrenchments will intensify.

Social Security Impact

Social security is widely considered the most successful domestic program ever developed in the United States. Thirty years ago, before the system had fully matured, the elderly were a relatively disadvantaged group in the population. Today, that is no longer the case. Since 1950 the percentage of the elderly receiving social security benefits has increased from 16 to 94 percent. Social security benefit increases have outpaced not only inflation but also wages over that period.

	Percent Increase *1950-1985*
Average weekly private nonagricultural earnings	467%
Consumer Price Index	347
Average monthly social security benefits (all beneficiaries)	1039

Since 1960 social security disability benefit increases have also exceeded increases in wages and inflation, rising 52 percent after adjustment for inflation. In 1985, 2.6 million disabled workers received an average monthly benefit of $470 and the average monthly payment to 1.2 million spouses and dependent children of disabled workers was $136.

The median real income of the elderly has more than doubled between 1950 and 1984 primarily as a result of social security. During the 1970s the elderly's income rose faster than that of the working-age population.

	Income (in 1984 dollars) *Age 25-64*	*Age 65 +*	*Elderly/Nonelderly*
1950	$14,888	$ 8,121	54.5
1984	29,716	18,215	61.3

Although a sizable income differential still remains between the elderly and working-age persons, the effective gap is not as large as it appears. Retirees require considerably less than 100 percent of their preretirement income to maintain their standard of living, partially because they have lower average tax rates than the nonelderly and thus have more disposable income. In 1985, persons age 65 years and older were entitled to an additional $1,040 tax exemption. Social security benefits, the main source of income for most elderly, are taxed only at income levels well above the current average for most beneficiaries. In 1984 only 22 percent of all elderly families and 7 percent of elderly individuals had incomes high enough to trigger taxation of benefits.

Because only 16.3 percent of males age 65 and over and 7.5 percent of women in the same age bracket are in the labor force, relatively few have work-related expenses—including transportation and meals purchased away from home. Expenditures are also lower for services—such as cooking, cleaning, or child care—that may have been purchased while working but that retirees perform for themselves. In addition, approximately 60 percent of the elderly own their own homes outright. Taking into account lower taxes, reduced work expenses, and lower household expenditures, retirees require approximately three-quarters of their preretirement earnings to maintain their former standard of living.[12]

The social security system is not the only factor behind rising incomes and declining poverty among the elderly, but it is the most important. Social security benefits constitute more than half the income of two-thirds of all newly retired beneficiaries, and an even greater share for minorities and elderly persons who live alone. Social security accounts for 39 percent of the cash income of the elderly, making it the largest source of income for older Americans.

Percent of Recipients' Income From Social Security

Income Decile	Married Couples	Single Recipients
1st (lowest)	77	87
2nd	67	80
6th	44	52
9th	25	34
10th	13	17

The relative importance to the elderly of income sources other than social security has shifted over the past decade. The most striking change is the sharp decline in earnings income to the elderly because of the reduction in their labor force participation rate. Asset income, however, has assumed much greater importance, particularly for retirees with above-average preretirement earnings whose social security benefits are capped, subject to the formula that is tilted in favor of low earners. There was little overall change in the importance of private pension income to the elderly[13] (Figure 13).

Figure 13. Earnings as a source of income for elderly have declined sharply since 1970

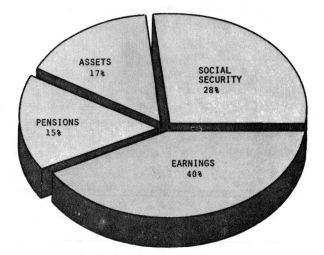

1970

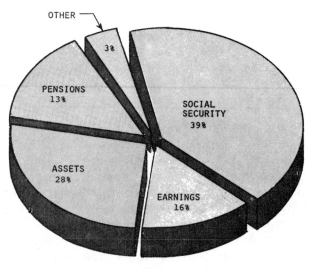

1984

Source: Social Security Administration.

Improved Health

Social security has improved the health of older Americans. When medicare was being debated in Congress, only about 9 million of the 18.7 million Americans 65 years or older had medical insurance. Today, 98 percent of the nation's 28 million elderly are covered by medicare, and more than two-thirds of the elderly have private health insurance to cover expenses not paid by the federal government. The Department of Health and Human Services estimated that medicare pays 45 percent of the costs of health care for the elderly, including 74 percent of their hospital costs and 55 percent of their physician fees.[14] Today, fewer older Americans face the fear that illness will wipe out their savings, eat up their income, and destroy their lifelong dreams of dignity and independence.

Enhanced access to medical care has contributed to significantly improved health and to longer life expectancy among the elderly. From 1965 to 1984 life expectancy at age 65 rose by two years, to 16.8. Although this increase cannot be solely attributed to medicare, the health improvements resulting from medicare expenditures have played a major part.

Labor Force Withdrawal

One direct result of the rise in social security benefits, private pensions, and the availability of medicare has been a decline in the labor force participation rates of older workers.

	55-64 Years		65 Years and Over	
	Men	*Women*	*Men*	*Women*
1970	83.0	43.0	26.8	9.7
1980	72.1	41.3	19.0	8.1
1985	67.4	42.2	15.7	7.3

It is debatable whether the labor force withdrawal of older and disabled workers is in the nation's, or even the worker's, bests interest. The availability of social security makes it socially acceptable to push the elderly out of the work force, causing dependency among workers who could remain productive, thereby reducing the nation's wealth. However, the jobs vacated by older workers frequently open opportunities for advancement for younger workers, who in turn pay a tax to help support the retired workers. Provided that the interests of older workers who leave the labor market voluntarily are well protected through income transfers, intergenerational equity can be preserved.

Effect on Savings

It is often alleged that the social security system reduces incentive for private saving. Arguing that a lower rate of savings reduces capital stock, lowers gross national product, depresses wages, and raises interest rates, critics suggest that social security impairs the economic efficiency of the nation by depriving investors of private savings.[15] The Reagan administration's policies have focused attention on increasing private investment and raised questions about the wisdom of allocating resources to publicly controlled savings.

Social security is thought to reduce private savings because the expectation of a public pension may cause individuals to save less for their retirement. Some analysts have challenged this conclusion, arguing that compulsory saving through social security may cause some individuals to recognize the need to provide for the future and thus to save more.[16] Also, if saving is motivated by the desire to leave a bequest or to provide for contingencies, it is unlikely that it will be affected by social security.

A widely cited 1974 study estimated that in 1971 social security reduced private saving by 50 percent, but these findings were later found to be flawed. Other studies confirmed social security's negative effect on saving, but concluded that it was considerably smaller than suggested in the 1974 study.[17] On balance, support for the claim that social security significantly depresses private saving remains unproven.[18]

Effects on Women

The influx of women into the labor force in recent years has raised the issue of equity within the social security system. Half a century ago, only 15 percent of all married women were in the work force. When the spouse's benefit was introduced in 1939, Congress assumed that the typical family was composed of a life-long male breadwinner and financially dependent wife and children. However, both the absolute and relative number of women workers has grown enormously. Moreover, the amount of time women spend in the labor force has increased with each generation.

As a result of a history of lower earnings, more time spent out of the labor force, and a higher incidence of part-time work, women tend to have lower benefits than men. Changing work roles of women may close this benefit gap substantially.

As it evolved, the social security system expanded its protection of women. Since 1939 wives, widows, and orphans have received benefits, even if they had not contributed to the system. For women with labor force experience, the social security benefit formula, skewed as it is in favor of lower-wage workers, partially compensates women for the low earnings they have received in the labor market. The provision that permits the five years of lowest earnings to be dropped when computing benefits is also of some help to women workers who interrupted their work careers to care for children.

Some apparent inequities persist. Wives with low earnings frequently may have to forego their benefits because the 50 percent added above the primary income amounts paid to retired couples exceeds the entitlement of the wives. For example, a wife entitled to $360 monthly benefits—the average primary insurance amount for women in 1983—would have been better off to claim separate benefits from the husband if he were entitled to the average of $528 monthly benefits paid to men. However, if the husband's monthly benefits exceeded $720, the couple would have been better off by claiming only the husband's entitlement plus 50 percent. But even in such cases there are some compensating factors. A working wife can claim benefits before her husband retires and she also has disability and survivor protection for her children that would not be available if she were not insured in her own right.

The increasing number of divorces has created another potential problem for social security. Under current law, eligibility for retirement or disability benefits based on a spouse's earnings terminates at divorce unless the marriage lasted at least ten years. One of every five retired women in 1982 received a divorced wife's benefits. Since two-thirds of all divorces occur within the first ten years of marriage, however, the majority of divorcees may lose their protection unless they remarry.[19]

Poverty Levels

Finally, an important indicator of the success of social security is the declining percentage of elderly living in poverty. In 1960, one of every three of the nation's older population had incomes below the federal poverty level compared with one of every five in the rest of the population. By 1984 the poverty rate for the elderly had fallen to 12 percent, 14 percent lower than the population as a whole (Figure 14). In 1985 the average annual benefit paid to a retired couple amounted to $8,300, well in excess of the poverty level (Figure 14).

The elderly have also benefited disproportionately from federal provision of noncash benefits, the most important of which is health care.[20] Inclusion of the market value of food stamps and housing subsidies as income reduced the 1984 poverty level of the elderly from 12.4 percent to 10.5 percent. When the cash value of medical benefits is also included, the poverty rate fell further to 2.6 percent. In comparison, the inclusion of all three noncash benefits reduces the poverty rate of the population under 65 by much less—from 14.4 to 10.6 percent—because they are less likely to receive medical benefits.[21] There is continuing debate, however, on the appropriate valuation of noncash benefits. Estimates of the poverty rate for the elderly based on cash income plus noncash benefits range from the aforementioned 2.6 percent to 7.6 percent, depending on the assumed valuation of benefits.

Social security and medicare benefits are not means tested. Only about 10 percent of these outlays specifically benefit the elderly poor; the remainder is expended for universal retirement and health programs. Moreover, only about half of elderly households living in poverty receive any means-tested benefits, either because they have other assets or are reluctant to apply.[22]

Future Choices

Since President Roosevelt signed the Social Security Act into law, Congress has expanded the scope of the legislation to

Figure 14. Poverty is now less common among the elderly than in the general population

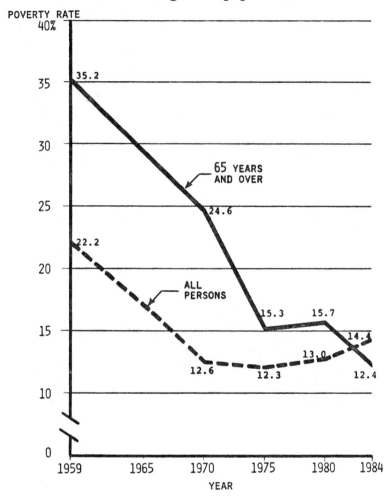

Source: U.S. Bureau of the Census.

provide Americans ever greater protection against the harsh consequences of sickness and loss of earnings during the "golden years." Although the Act has lived up to expectations, the system faces additional challenges if it is to maintain this record of achievement over the next 50 years.

A loss of public confidence in the future of social security continues to plague the program. Seventy percent of Americans between the ages of 18 and 44 have indicated concern about the program's ability to deliver future benefits and more than half of all respondents favored making social security voluntary.[23]

The reforms instituted in 1983 ensure that the system is secure for the foreseeable future, which should help restore public confidence in social security. The social security trust funds now show a surplus for the first time since the mid-1970s. The 1985 trustees' annual report predicts that the combined assets of the retirement and disability trust funds will be sufficient to pay benefits well into the next century, barring a prolonged deep recession.[24]

The recent financial difficulties of the social security system, although resolved, have opened the doors to consideration of numerous alternatives. Critics have argued that individual needs are best met through private arrangements.[25] These proposals take different forms—some would require that a private plan be certified as providing equivalent protection, while others stress individual choice. It must be recognized, however, that few, if any, private plans provide all the protections of social security, especially the guarantee that the full purchasing power of benefits will be maintained.

The primary difficulty in relying on voluntary savings is that too many people will not save or are unable to save because of pressing current needs. Individual savings also lack the element of insurance that is an important aspect of social security. If family savings are spent because of illness or disability, they will not be available in old age. Only about half of the work force is now covered by private group insurance plans, and universal private protection remains unattainable for major sectors of the population.

If individuals were permitted to opt out of social security, certain groups could be expected to leave. Low-income individuals who have difficulty meeting day-to-day expenses may drop out of the system, even though they will ultimately need social security protection the most. Others who might leave the system would be the young, the single, and the high-paid workers who face less risk of death, disability, or retirement, or who have sufficient resources, including private income, to fall back on. Consequently, the costs for those dependent on the system would be spread across fewer taxpayers, raising individual contributions, and potentially driving additional participants to seek private options.

An alternative to the present system is a means-tested program. Aside from the equity problems involved in forcing potential beneficiaries who were self-supporting throughout their lifetime to depend on public assistance, strong economic reasons would argue against such a system. A means-tested program might reduce incentives for private saving since the presence of assets would disqualify retired persons to receive benefits, thus discouraging savings.

Perhaps the most compelling argument against either privatizing or means-testing social security is that in either case public support for the program would be eroded. The universal nature of the current system ensures broad support both from beneficiaries and from the working population who might otherwise bear the financial burden for their parents' support and who expect to receive benefits in the future. If the constituency for social security is narrowed, the guarantees that provide the foundation for the program may be seriously weakened.

The burgeoning federal deficit does present a threat to social security. Although sustained public support has kept the program off limits to federal budget cutters, the program's magnitude presents policymakers with a tempting target for "savings." Under the 1983 reforms, social security will be separate from the federal budget beginning in 1992, a change reflecting the self-financing character of the system. Congress may advance the date of the separation. Mounting pressures to reduce the deficit may lower its resistance to raiding the social security trust fund.

In the expectation that the cost of the retirement and disability programs would rise when the baby boom generation reaches retirement, Congress recommended gradual increases in revenues beginning immediately to prepare for those strains. To lower the tax burden on future generations, the system is expected to accumulate a surplus of more than $1 trillion in the early years of the next century. Pressures to cut payroll taxes or divert the surplus to other uses may prove irresistible if the long-term objectives of the system are forgotten or ignored. Social security will remain sound only if its structure is preserved. The needs of future generations will be met only if the vision of the current generation is as far-reaching as the vision of the New Deal designers half a century ago.

10
Private Pensions

Nearly a third of all retirees supplement their social security checks with a private or government pension.[1] An even greater percentage are likely to enjoy pension benefits in the future since over half of all active workers are covered by a public or private pension plan.[2] Yet, without federal safeguards, many who are covered might never receive expected benefits. Unforeseen events beyond the control of individual workers and their employers can potentially destroy dreams of a comfortable retirement: the pension plan might run out of funds to pay benefits; the employer, and thus the plan, might go out of business; or employees may discover at retirement that breaks in company service render them ineligible for benefits. Since state efforts to regulate private pensions proved inadequate, the federal government has intervened to ensure that employers' pension promises, once made, are ultimately delivered.

Public policy at the federal level has traditionally focused on tax incentives to encourage employers to adopt pension plans and other fringe benefits. As the number of beneficiaries and the size of pension funds have expanded dramatically, the federal government has sought to ensure broad public support for a voluntary pension system by improving its performance and reliability. By guaranteeing the solvency of pension funds and establishing minimum fiduciary and eligibility standards, the federal government protects this important source of retirement income and improves the living standards of older Americans.

The Private Pension System

At present the retirement needs of most Americans are met through two different types of programs. Social security,

197

which is compulsory and almost universal in coverage, provides the basic floor of protection for retired or disabled workers or for the survivors of deceased workers. The other type of retirement program, including private pensions and private savings, is primarily voluntary and seeks to bring retirement income up to levels that more nearly reflect the individual worker's preretirement living standard, building on the floor of protection created by social security.

Pension plans provide either for defined benefits or defined contributions. Three-quarters of pension plan participants are enrolled in defined benefit plans that pay a specified amount on retirement based on years of employment and earnings. A defined contribution plan maintains an individual account for each participant, and the benefit paid to retirees is drawn from the accumulated funds depending on mortality expectations, the contribution rate, and the performance of the plan's investment portfolio. Employees bear the risk in defined contribution plans, while defined benefit plans place the investment risk on the employer. Hourly paid workers are more likely to have defined benefit plans, as are workers in large firms, in public employment, and in unionized firms, while defined contribution plans are more common among professionals and highly paid white collar workers. Employers are responsible for roughly 95 percent of contributions to pension plans, with employees providing the balance.[3]

Not all employees covered by a pension plan will eventually receive benefits. An employee must establish vesting rights based on the age and tenure restrictions specified by the pension plan. Termination of employment before satisfying the minimum vesting conditions results in forfeiture of future benefits in most plans. In some industries collective bargaining agreements provide for portability of pension rights if employees change jobs within the industry. These multiemployer plans are typical in the construction, trucking, and garment industries where small employers predominate and where their employees are members of the same union. Multiemployer plans account for nearly one-quarter of the 36.5 million workers covered by private pension plans.[4] In addition, an estimated 13.1 million government employees are covered by public pension plans.

The federal government encourages individuals to plan for retirement by granting tax-favored status to various savings plans. Eligible persons can invest annually up to $2,000 into an individual retirement account (IRA) and deduct the amount from their taxable income. Self-employed individuals may contribute up to $30,000 annually to a Keogh retirement account with similar tax treatment. Roughly 16 million IRAs have been established, with assets amounting to $32 billion.[5] An increasingly popular alternative to IRAs is the 401(k) salary reduction plan, which allows workers to save up to 25 percent of their wages, to an annual maximum of $30,000. Most employers match workers' tax-deferred contributions, usually at the rate of 50 cents for every dollar saved. Some 80 percent of the Fortune 500 companies offer 401(k) plans, and from one-half to two-thirds of eligible employees contributed about $13 billion in 1985.[6]

Evolving Public Policy Toward Pensions

Pensions provided by employers to take care of workers in their retirement are a relatively recent phenomenon. In fact, few plans were in effect prior to World War II. Early pension plans were designed primarily to reduce turnover among prized employees. In the absence of regulated standards, eligibility restrictions could be manipulated, and even though lower paid employees frequently contributed to the plans, benefits mainly accrued to employees in the upper echelons. Pensions also offered employers a socially acceptable means of easing older, less productive workers out of their jobs.[7] During the 1920s Congress granted tax exemptions to stock-bonus and profit-sharing plans, along with pensions. Although these incentives resulted in significant growth in employer-sponsored pension plans, most failed to survive the Great Depression, inducing unions and employers to turn to the federal government to provide retirement income through the social security system.

In 1942, tax legislation sought to broaden pension participation. These provisions, with successive refinements, still provide the statutory basis for the tax treatment of pension plans. For a pension or profit-sharing plan to qualify for a tax preference, the plan must be for the exclusive benefit of the employees or their beneficiaries, it must be permanent, with the terms spelled out and communicated to employees, its sole purpose must be to either give the employees a share of profits or a retirement income, and it must not discriminate in favor of corporate officers, stockholders, or highly compensated employees.

The most dramatic growth in private pensions has taken place since World War II. Stringent wage-price controls and high corporate tax rates imposed during the war induced both management and labor to trade off wage increases for fringe benefits—mostly paid vacation, paid holidays, and shift differentials.[8] At the end of the war, social security benefits averaged $29 per month, replacing only a fifth of the median wage in the year prior to retirement, prompting union demands to focus on pensions.[9] Bitter strikes in the coal, auto, and steel industries, partially over the establishment and operation of retirement funds, eventually led to a 1949 Supreme Court ruling that pensions are deferred wages and therefore a subject for collective bargaining under the National Labor Relations Act.[10] The 1946 Taft-Hartley Act had established guidelines for private multiemployer pension plans. Thus, the path was cleared for labor unions to press forward with negotiated pensions for their members.

During the next two decades, union interest in pension plans spilled over to nonunion workers, and pension coverage tripled from 9.8 million workers in 1950 to an estimated 29.7 million workers in 1970.[11] The proliferation of new plans after the war prompted congressional action to ensure employee welfare while preventing pension trusts from being used as tax-avoidance schemes.

The rapid growth of pension plans also generated congressional concern that the vast sums being accumulated in pension funds might encourage corrupt practices among plan sponsors. The federal response relied on disclosure of plan provisions to participants to deter abuse, but offered no means of investigation or enforcement.

However, widespread employee complaints that they were unable to qualify for benefits even after long years of service indicated serious weaknesses in pension plans. Frequently, even qualified employees lost all anticipated retirement benefits when their employer's business failed, a situation highlighted by the abrupt termination by Studebaker-Packard Corporation of its pension plan in 1964, leaving approximately 4,400 vested workers with little or no pension.

A cabinet-level committee and subsequent congressional hearings stressed the need for comprehensive federal legislation to improve the soundness of pension plans and to provide a more reliable foundation for their future development. At the hearings a succession of witnesses told of losing their pension rights because of layoffs, plant shutdowns, transfers, and business closings. Many had made regular contributions in expectation of later security and financial protection, only to come up empty upon retirement. Ultimately, the parade of horror stories swayed public opinion in favor of a comprehensive bill.

ERISA

The legislation that ultimately emerged was the outgrowth of considerable debate and compromise. The end product of this long debate, the Employee Retirement Income Security Act (ERISA) of 1974, sets a variety of federal standards safeguarding the pension rights of active workers and retirees and spells out the obligations of plan sponsors and trustees. The Act also regulates the tax status of pension funds. ERISA does not require employers to adopt employee pension plans, but where voluntary plans are established, they must comply with extensive reporting requirements, fiduciary obligations, and minimum standards of coverage, participation, vesting, and benefit funding.

In brief, ERISA establishes rules governing eligibility and vesting rights determined by an employee's age and years of consecutive service with the employer. Workers are vested in a pension (or a portion thereof) whether or not they continue to work for the sponsoring company until retirement. ERISA's provisions (except termination insurance) apply both to defined benefit and defined contribution plans, but do not extend to public employees. The Act also establishes individual retirement accounts (IRAs) offering individuals an incentive to save for their own retirement and providing a vehicle for limited portability of pension benefits when employees change jobs.

A termination insurance program guarantees payments to beneficiaries of defined benefit plans in the event of a fund's termination without sufficient assets to pay promised benefits. Under ERISA, private employer pension plans generally must provide coverage to all employees age 21 or older with one or more years of service. The Act also provides for three vesting options. One requires total vesting after ten years of service, but no partial vesting. The other two options require phased-in vesting after a designated period of service or a specified combination of age and service, with full vesting after 15 years of service.

When first enacted, the ERISA provisions for defined benefit plans potentially involved costs to employers by easing vesting eligibility. Defined contribution plans, on the other hand, were less affected since in most such plans vesting provisions were already more liberal than the Act's requirements. ERISA's funding standards required that employers operating on a "pay-as-you-go" basis or contributing interest-only payments on unfunded benefit liabilities to their pension trusts significantly alter their practices. The law required that current obligations be funded in the year in which they occur, and past-service obligations be amortized over a 30-year period (longer periods were permitted for obligations existing when ERISA became effective). To further guarantee adequate pension funding of defined benefit plans, Congress required employers to pay termination insurance premiums, $.50 per capita in multiemployer plans and $1.00 per capita in single employer plans. The risk pools created by these annual contributions are managed by the Pension Benefit Guaranty Corporation (PBGC), a government agency created by ERISA, and are used to pay benefits to participants in the event their plan terminates without sufficient assets to cover pension obligations.

Multiemployer Amendments

At the time ERISA was passed, single employer pension plans seemed to present greater termination risks than multiemployer pension plans. Presumably, the bankruptcy of a single company could jeopardize a plan's viability, whereas in multiemployer plans there was strength in numbers—if one participating employer could no longer pay, the rest of the employers would pick up the unfunded liabilities. However, this view overlooked the poor health of the construction, apparel, and trucking industries in which multiemployer plans are dominant. In a July 1978 report to Congress, the

PBGC pointed out that termination could present an attractive alternative for about 10 percent of the multiemployer plans experiencing financial difficulties, potentially leaving the PBGC to cover $4.8 billion in unfunded insurance liabilities. To fund such liabilities would have required an increase in annual premium rates of $.50 per participant by a factor of 160.[12]

To avoid this drastic step, which would have led to further terminations and ultimately, the bankruptcy of the PBGC, Congress made it more difficult for employers to withdraw from a multiemployer plan. The Multiemployer Pension Plan Amendments Act of 1980 required that an employer who withdraws from a plan continue to be liable for and pay its portion of the plan's unfunded benefits. In addition, higher premiums were imposed to strengthen the multiemployer risk pool maintained by the PBGC. The annual premium was raised to $1.40 per plan participant for the four years following enactment, and scheduled to increase by $.40 in 1984 and every two years thereafter until it reaches $2.60 in 1988. In exchange for these tougher employer provisions, labor unions agreed to reductions in benefit guarantees to about one-half of that prevailing for participants in single-employer plans. Also, the insurance program no longer automatically incurred a liability for unfunded benefits when an employer terminated a plan, but only when the plan became insolvent. As a result of these changes, studies show that a large majority of multiemployer plans are now in excellent financial condition.[13]

Retirement Equity

Another issue addressed by ERISA but more adequately provided for in later amendments was the equitable treatment of women by pension plans. On average, full-time women workers are paid less than men. Their working careers are often broken by a period of full-time homemaking and child raising. Also, a larger proportion of women than men work in jobs not covered by pension plans. For these reasons, fewer women fully vest in a pension, and the pensions women do earn on the basis of their own work histories tend to be smaller than those of men. The median annual pension received by women is 56 percent less than that received by men.[14]

Before ERISA some pension plans restricted benefit payments to retired workers, with no benefits to a spouse. If the retired worker died first, the surviving spouse frequently had no claim to continued pension income. ERISA required most defined benefit and some defined contribution plans to offer a joint and survivor annuity option, under which a retiring worker could elect to receive a reduced pension, with all or part of the reduced pension continuing to a spouse (or other designated beneficiary) for life if the covered worker died first.

Subsequently, the courts grappled with the issue of whether pension plans may take into account the longer life expectancy of women. Some public plans had determined that because women will, on average, live longer, they will draw benefits for more years than men, and thus women should contribute more than men while working to receive equal pension benefits. In 1978 the Supreme Court ruled this practice illegal under Title VII of the Civil Rights Act of 1964.[15] Other pension plans reduced pension benefits for women so that the total payout for men and women would be approximately equal. However, the Supreme Court ruled in 1983 that if women and men had the same earnings and worked the same number of years, they must get equal pension benefits.[16] Thus, employers and pension plan sponsors must be gender-neutral in determining contributions and benefit levels, even if in the long run women may collect a larger sum.

In most families, the husband is no longer the sole breadwinner, with the wife working at home her entire lifetime. In many families both husband and wife have paid employment, although the wife may withdraw from the paid work force for extended periods to raise children. In addition, many marriages end in divorce, and about one in 20 workers never marry. These significant social developments pose a number of difficult problems for pension laws.

In 1984 Congress acted on some of the pension concerns of women. The Retirement Equity Act of 1984 amended ERISA by lowering the minimum participation age from 25 to 21, and by lowering the minimum vesting age from 22 to 18. This benefits women who might work full time before they are married and have children. The Act also permits maternity and paternity leaves of up to one year without losing work credit for vesting purposes, and workers may take off up to five consecutive years and not lose previously earned credits if they return to the same job. In addition, the law prohibits a worker from forgoing survivor benefits without the spouse's consent, and allows state courts to divide up pension benefits in divorce cases, a growing problem not envisioned by ERISA's drafters. In sum, the amendments are expected to extend pension coverage to more women and younger workers, as well as to guarantee spouses some share of an earned pension. The bill received broad bipartisan support, no doubt fueled to some extent by "gender gap" politics.

The Tax Side

Numerous changes in the tax laws since ERISA have encouraged greater individual private savings. Eligibility for IRAs has been expanded and the limit on annual contributions raised, spurring a significant increase in new accounts. Other employer-sponsored individual savings instruments—such as Keogh plans for the self-employed and section 401(k) plans for wage and salary workers—have also received a boost through changes in the tax code.

Congress has encouraged employee stock ownership plans (ESOPs), a defined contribution plan that invests most or all of its assets in employer securities. Employee benefit plans that provide a favorable tax treatment for employer securities held in trust for eligible employee participants have long been encouraged as a device for giving workers a broader stake in their employer's business. Since 1975 Congress has amended the tax code on several occasions to give greater impetus to the formation and maintenance of ESOPs by firms of all sizes.

ERISA Administration

Three federal agencies are responsible for the administration of ERISA. The Labor Department monitors pension plan reporting and disclosure and pension fund assets. The Internal Revenue Service evaluates pension plans' compliance with participation, vesting, and funding standards specified in the legislation. In addition, the Pension Benefit Guaranty Corporation, established by ERISA, guarantees the receipt of benefits in the event of plan terminations.

The divided authority over ERISA administration was the direct result of competing congressional interests. When the pension legislation was under consideration in Congress, tax and labor committees in both the House and Senate held hearings and sponsored separate pension reform bills. The tax committees favored IRS administration of ERISA, while labor committees supported the Department of Labor. Neither would defer to the other, nor would they accept the creation of an independent agency. The compromise resulted in shared jurisdiction, overlapping responsibilities, and duplicated effort.

Reorganization carried out during the Carter administration divided the overlapping duties between the Treasury and Labor Departments, except in the area of enforcement, which continues to be loosely coordinated. The reorganization produced the strange result of excluding the Labor Department from the primary role of protecting the employee and excluding the IRS from the primary role of dealing with financial transactions. Nevertheless, internal adaptations and cooperative agreements between the agencies have remedied many of the initial implementation problems.

ERISA Impact

In the decade since ERISA's enactment, the number of pension plans has nearly doubled from 423,000 to over 800,000, and plan assets have risen from $250 billion in 1974 to an estimated $1 trillion in 1985 ($458 billion in 1974 dollars). Nearly half of all workers are covered by pension plans and 30 percent of all retired persons now receive pension benefits.[17] Pension receipt among recently retired workers is even greater, and has increased since 1970.[18]

As a result of ERISA's vesting requirements, greater numbers of workers can expect to receive a pension in retirement (Figure 15). In 1972 one-third of all covered nonagricultural workers in private industry were vested in a pension. By 1983 this figure had risen to slightly over one-half.[19] The 1984 amendments to ERISA further broadened pension coverage. By lowering the participation and vesting ages, the 1984 amendments added an estimated 583,000 new participants and 325,000 newly vested workers in 1985[20] (Figure 15).

Figure 15. Private pension vesting rose significantly under ERISA

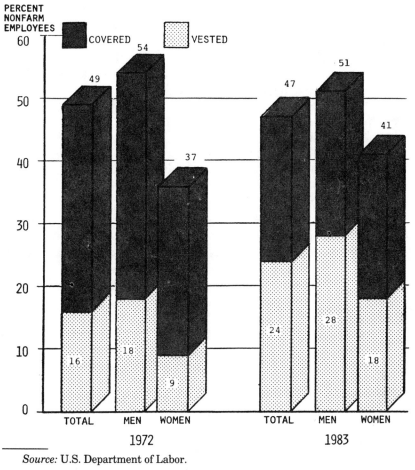

Source: U.S. Department of Labor.

Probably the most important contribution of ERISA is the enhanced financial soundness of qualified pension plans. Workers are far better protected if their plan terminates than they were prior to 1974. Approximately 98 percent of the plans terminated by employers during the past decade have had sufficient assets to cover PBGC-guaranteed benefits. Workers in the remaining plans have received about 85 percent of vested benefits through guarantees extended by the PBGC. In 1984 an estimated 64,700 retirees received benefits under the auspices of the PBGC.[21]

Pension benefits vary widely among individual recipients, depending on years of service and earnings levels, but women generally receive lower benefits than men. A Labor Department survey of workers who retired in 1978 found that the median annual pension paid to women was worth $2,240 in 1984 dollars and replaced 18 percent of preretirement wages.[22] The median for men was worth $5,050 (1984 dollars), replacing on average 22 percent of their preretirement earnings. The lower pension benefits earned by women are the result of lower preretirement earnings and greater job turnover. The Retirement Equity Act may close some of the pension gap by improving women's pension rights, but the earnings gap will not be affected by pension legislation.

Defined Benefit Plans

Although covered workers gain under ERISA's eligibility, vesting, and funding provisions, the effect on coverage is not clear. Prior to ERISA's passage, opponents of the legislation predicted that the law would discourage plan sponsorship, and events in the late 1970s seemed to bear them out. Internal Revenue Service estimates show that defined benefit plan formation fell sharply when ERISA took effect, but regained the 1975 level four years later. Plan terminations also jumped sharply in 1976, exceeding the average number of formations in that year; since that time, annual terminations have averaged about 4,900 per year.

Defined Benefit Pension Plans
(in thousands)

Years	Formations	Terminations
1974	32.6	2.6
1975	15.3	4.6
1976	4.8	9.0
1977	7.0	5.3
1978	9.7	4.6
1979	15.8	3.3
1980	18.8	4.3
1981	23.8	4.5
1982	28.2	5.0
1983	22.1	7.2

Some of the post-ERISA terminations were the result of business conditions. A study by the General Accounting Office found that only 17 percent of the plans were terminated solely because of ERISA, although the new law was partially responsible for the termination of an additional 35 percent.[23] Of the terminated plans, two-fifths were replaced by profit sharing or other alternative coverage. Perhaps the most telling finding was that most of the terminating plans failed to meet ERISA's standards for participation and vesting. These plans represented promises that would probably not have been kept, and it is precisely the role of ERISA to end such practices. Significantly, defined benefit plan terminations increased sharply again after the 1982 recession.

Defined benefit plan formations increased by 44 percent between 1975 and 1983, but their rate of growth is below pre-ERISA levels and the absolute annual level of formations since ERISA's passage has never reached the 1974 level. This slowdown may be partly the result of stringent requirements contained in ERISA for such plans, but other factors are also involved. By the time ERISA was enacted most large employers already had defined benefit plans. Labor Department surveys indicate that throughout the post-ERISA years, pension coverage among employers with more than 250 workers has been nearly universal, with over 90 percent of workers covered by a tax-qualified plan. New plan formation has principally taken place among small employers. Since small firms experience higher employee turnover rates and have a greater need to closely budget expenses, they tend to prefer defined contribution plans.

Another factor contributing to the slower growth in defined benefit plans has been a halt in the growth of multi-employer pension plans. Although the 1980 amendments greatly increased the pension security of existing plan participants, such improvements may be at the expense of plan expansion. The stiff penalties in the law designed to hold employers in the plans provide a strong disincentive to other employers that might be considering establishing a defined benefit plan.[24] Multiemployer pension plans now cover around 9 million workers, virtually the same number covered in 1974.

The decline of unionization in the private sector has also affected defined benefit plan growth. In the past, labor unions, favoring defined plans, provided a prime stimulus to the growth of the pension movement, but their declining strength eases pressures on employers to establish defined benefit plans. In addition, those areas of the economy experiencing the greatest growth tend to be the most difficult to organize, and also tend to be characterized by smaller firms more inclined toward the defined contribution approach. Among public employees, a key area of union growth, pension coverage already runs around 85 percent for state and local workers and is virtually universal among federal employees. Little room remains for expansion.[25]

Defined Contribution Plans

At the time of ERISA's enactment, 55 percent of all private pension plans were defined benefit, while 45 percent were defined contribution. By 1983 the relative positions had more than reversed: 59 percent were defined contribution and 41 percent were defined benefit. During 1983, 67 percent of the newly established plans were defined contribution, indicating that movement continues in the direction of defined contribution.

Growth of Defined Contribution Plans Outpaces Growth of Defined Benefit Plans (in thousands)*

Year	Defined Contribution	Defined Benefit
1974	190.6	232.8
1975	201.8	243.6
1976	216.0	239.4
1977	234.0	241.0
1978	279.3	246.1
1979	312.8	258.6
1980	354.3	273.2
1981	403.2	292.4
1982	450.2	315.6
1983	480.9	330.5

*A new approach to calculating defined benefit and defined contribution statistics found that defined contribution plans in 1984 were 71 percent of all pension plans. This Employee Benefit Research Institute analysis also estimated that defined contribution plans substantially outnumbered defined benefit plans in 1974 as well.

Prior to ERISA most employers viewed defined contribution plans as a "savings" device for their employees, not the main source of retirement income to supplement social security. But as ERISA has increased the costs and burdens of defined benefit plans, surveys indicate that more employers have become interested in defined contribution plans as a primary source of retirement income, frequently reducing or replacing what is provided by defined benefit plans.[26] The defined contribution plan may actually be more expensive in the long run, but will not be greatly affected by future legislation, and can be budgeted because the cost is fixed. Finally, uncertainties related to unfunded liabilities do not apply to defined contribution plans.[27]

Some workers, concerned that their pensions may be forfeited if they leave a defined benefit plan before fully vesting, prefer defined contribution plans. Defined contribution plans appeal to persons who place a premium on keeping track of their entitlement and are interested in having access to their funds. The vast majority of defined contribution plans allow participants access to their funds prior to retirement, a notable exception being the TIAA-CREF plan, which is the largest single retirement plan serving universities and nonprofit research organizations. Under ERISA, defined contribution plans can allow participants to borrow funds from their account under certain circumstances (for example, for a new home, college education, or heavy medical expenses), to withdraw the entire balance under legally defined "hardship" circumstances, or to claim their balance at the termination of employment prior to retirement. In most firms, partial withdrawals of the participant's own contributions can be made without penalties.

The shift toward defined contribution plans merits careful consideration. A 1983 survey indicated that one of ten covered private sector workers and one of five covered public sector workers expected a lump sum payment upon termination of employment. More interesting, though, is what workers do with these funds. Out of the 6.6 million workers who reported receiving a lump-sum distribution in 1983, only one in five reinvested it for retirement income.[28]

Pension plans with such early withdrawal provisions more closely resemble tax-sheltered savings than retirement income programs. The retirement income needs of workers are best served by plans that withhold retirement funds until actual retirement, so that individuals may have economic security in their old age. The shift toward defined contribution plans, as currently structured, seems at odds with the public interest.

Pension Benefit Guaranty Corporation

Intended to be a self-financing system, the Pension Benefit Guaranty Corporation's main source of income is the premiums paid by employers with defined benefit plans. If an employer terminates a defined benefit plan without sufficient funds to pay the full obligated benefits, the PBGC guarantees retiring employees a minimum benefit, which averages about 85 to 90 percent of the benefit due to the retiree. The PBGC absorbs the shortfall from its own revenue. The law requires the agency to insure all pension benefits, including underfunded plans that were in operation when Congress passed the law. But PBGC is authorized to collect only up to 30 percent of an employer's net worth to make up for a shortfall, making the agency liable for any deficits in terminated plans. Since the program's inception, premium income has been inadequate to cover the long-term obligations the corporation has incurred from the termination of poorly funded plans.

Losses to the PBGC fund from underfunded terminations have risen from an estimated $220 million in 1982 to $1.2 billion in mid-1985. A high number of bankruptcies in the early 1980s, particularly some involving larger companies, have substantially contributed to the problem. More than 60 percent of the 1982 losses resulted from the underfunded terminations of just five large pension plans. To shore up the PBGC, the Reagan administration has proposed to increase the annual premium per employee to $7.50, and other bills pending before Congress would raise the ante to $8.50.

Most of the terminations of poorly funded plans have been due to bankruptcy, but a significant number of employers have taken advantage of another provision in the law allowing them to terminate their plans. These companies continue doing business while the PBGC absorbs their inadequately funded pension liabilities. Because PBGC can collect up to 30 percent of the firm's net worth, it is tempting for employers to "dump" their pension liabilities on the PBGC in cases where the long-term pension obligations exceed the amount the agency can recoup. The PBGC estimated that such employer actions have accounted for about a third of its growing deficit.[29]

Some employers have sold off divisions or subsidiaries with poorly funded pension plans. If the new owner terminates the plan and it is still underfunded, the original plan sponsor may be liable to the PBGC to make up the funding shortfall. For example, three years after International Harvester Co. sold its Wisconsin Steel division to Environdyne Industries, Inc., in 1980, the steel company went bankrupt and terminated its pension plan, leaving a shortfall of $57 million for the PBGC to assume. The PBGC alleges that Harvester sold Wisconsin Steel to Environdyne to free itself of its pension liability and has sought payments from both companies. In all, the pension agency estimates that as of 1984 it had lost more than $100 million in such situations.

Another ERISA provision allows employers to receive hardship waivers from the IRS permitting them to skip required annual contributions to their pension plans. These funding waivers can leave shortfalls in pension plans that later become the PBGC's responsibility in the event the plans terminate. The number of waivers the IRS granted more than doubled during the recessionary period from 1980 to 1982, jumping from 173 to 416. The number of requests more than doubled again in 1983.[30]

Legislation pending in Congress is designed to correct these deficiencies by limiting the circumstances under which employers can shed responsibility for a weak pension plan. Under the proposed legislation, employers would be free to terminate their underfunded plans only in cases of demonstrated severe "financial distress." Companies that terminate their plans but remain in business would be required to pay a percentage of future profits to the PBGC for up to ten years. Abuse of waivers granted by the IRS would be restricted.

The looseness of PBGC termination provisions is widely recognized, but reform is not easily achieved. Employer lobbies have generally favored tightening the rules governing terminations since well-established businesses pay most of the PBGC's premiums, and premium rates reflect the PBGC's losses. It makes no sense to rebuild the fund, they argue, as long as some employers are free to dump their underfunded plans, leaving others to pick up the tab. Small employers are divided on amending the PBGC operations. Most small businesses use defined contribution plans and are not affected by the recommended changes, but some are concerned that their pension liabilities might prevent them from selling their businesses.

Labor Force Effects

ERISA may have the unintended effect of reducing labor force participation among older workers. By improving the security of private pensions, the law may have accelerated the retirement decisions of workers nearing retirement age. Not only has pension coverage expanded but greater numbers of pension plans have begun to offer an early retirement option in the past decade, making early retirement affordable. Workers reaching age 62 who are eligible for both social security and pension benefits are twice as likely to retire as those who are eligible for social security alone (Figure 16).[31]

Workers who do not accept early retirement are discouraged from working past normal retirement age by other pension plan provisions. Some defined contribution plans and roughly half of defined benefit plans do not increase monthly pension benefits for additional years of service and compensation beyond normal retirement age. However, this incentive to retire is offset to some extent by inflation, which steadily erodes the buying power of fixed pension benefits. Only around 5 percent of all pension plans regularly adjust retiree benefits to reflect increases in the cost of living, although most large plans grant ad hoc increases to retirees. Continued labor force participation may appear a more attractive alternative than retirement during periods of high inflation.

Early retirement and benefit cutoffs are consistent with the reasons many employers initially establish pension plans. Employers sponsor plans to encourage workers with needed skills to remain on the job for extended periods, but also to ease older employees out of the work force. Older workers are more costly in terms of compensation and accrued benefits, offering incentives to employers to replace them with younger employees often perceived as more productive. Removing older workers also opens up promotional opportunities for younger workers. During the recessionary early 1980s, some employers offered employees substantial bonuses to opt for early retirement as an alternative to layoffs.[32]

Figure 16. Recipients of private pensions have increased under ERISA

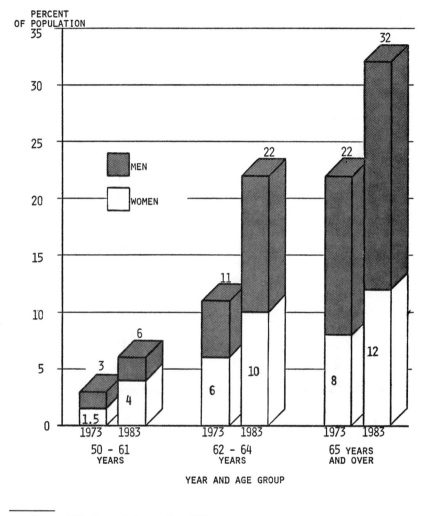

YEAR AND AGE GROUP

Source: U.S. General Accounting Office.

A problem arises, however, in reconciling the early retirement effects of private pensions with other national policy
goals. A person aged 55 to 64 can expect to live on the average
21 more years, and persons aged 65 and over can expect to live
14 years. Current directions in public policy emphasize longer

worklife and later retirement to reduce the burdens upon public and private retirement systems of supporting a growing aged population. A shrinking proportion of younger workers is being forced to shoulder a growing burden of social security taxes, a load that could be lightened considerably if older workers remained on the job. The interests of employers and those of the public at large may diverge on this important issue.

Equity

The special tax treatment of pension plans has had the desired effect of expanding pension coverage, but some equity issues have also arisen. In adopting ERISA, Congress recognized that a large segment of the working population was not eligible for the tax advantages associated with private pension plans. Consequently, ERISA amended the Internal Revenue Code to provide tax incentives for individuals to save for their own retirement through individual retirement accounts (IRAs) as well as liberalized contribution limits on Keogh plans for the self-employed.

The Economic Recovery Tax Act of 1981 expanded IRA eligibility to encompass most workers. However, those already covered by pension plans took disproportionate advantage of IRAs; nearly half of all workers with IRAs in 1982 had vested pension rights, while only 12.1 percent of those without pension coverage had IRAs. Higher-income individuals, those in the best position to save a share of their income, contribute the most to IRAs. Fifty-nine percent of individuals earning over $50,000 contributed to an IRA in 1982, compared to only 10 percent of people earning less than $20,000.[33] Participation in 401(k) plans shows a similar pattern.

Percentage of Eligible Workers With IRAs and 401(k) Plans

Annual Earnings	IRAs	401(k) Plans
$1–9,999	6.9%	NA
10,000–19,999	13.2	31.7%
20,000–29,999	22.3	42.2
30,000–49,999	38.2	51.5
50,000 and over	58.9	62.1

If the main purpose of IRAs is, as the Reagan administration envisions, to increase private savings, the tax incentives may have achieved their desired results. IRAs were intended, however, as an alternative retirement income device for that half of the work force excluded from pension coverage. Since pension plan participants tend to work in higher-paying jobs, most of those without coverage are on the lower rungs of the income ladder. Yet, uncovered and lower-income workers have taken the least advantage of tax-deductible IRAs.

Another equity issue involves the integration of social security payments with private pension benefits. Although private pension plans must be nondiscriminatory to qualify for favorable tax treatment, employers are permitted to consider their contributions to social security as part of the total retirement package. The problem with this provision is that it sanctions the payment of tax-subsidized benefits to higher paid workers, while permitting the denial of benefits to some lower paid ones. Numerous attempts have been made to reform this apparently discriminatory provision. Advocates of the integration concept assert it is essential to maintaining equality in the income replacement rates at all income levels. If private pensions did not consider social security benefits, lower paid workers would receive a higher percentage of their preretirement income—in extreme cases more than 100 percent—while higher paid workers could receive considerably less. Proponents also worry that, because elimination of integration would significantly raise the cost of pension plans to employers, many plans might be terminated as a result of this change in their tax treatment.

Federal Budget

The tax-deferred status of private pensions imposes a substantial hidden cost on the federal budget. The U.S. Department of the Treasury estimates that employer-provided pension plans cost the nation $56 billion in forgone revenue in 1985, while the favorable tax treatment of IRAs reduced IRS collection by another $10 billion.[34] However, an estimated 60 to 80 percent of these losses will be ultimately recouped through taxation of post-retirement income.[35]

Tax expenditures are part of the price of retirement security, but record budget deficits in the 1980s have sparked a growing interest in expanding the tax base. Critics of the tax-exempt status of fringe benefits claim that the erosion of the tax base undermines the ability of the federal government to finance government programs. Another argument against giving tax breaks to employee benefits is that the rewards are not equally distributed. Workers who receive the same total compensation but have a different mix of wages and fringe benefits are subject to unequal tax liability. Since fringe benefits comprise a larger proportion of compensation for higher-paid employees, the benefits of the tax exemption accrue mostly to individuals above the median income. Taxing fringe benefits along with other forms of compensation would eliminate some of the inequity in the tax system by removing this source of disparate treatment. Advocates of preserving the tax-exempt status of fringe benefits, on the other hand, point to the improved living standards of American workers. Tax expenditures have paved the way for better health, longer education, and greater security for workers—commodities for which it is difficult to assign a price.

Tax laws favoring employee retirement, health insurance plans, and other benefits were enacted under the premise that the broad coverage of workers and their dependents under these plans is desirable social policy. Whatever the merits of this argument, repeal will not be easily achieved. Workers and their families have come to depend upon the "free" benefits and expect them. The commitments, once made, are difficult to take away. If these protections are not available through voluntary private channels, then pressure is sure to mount for universal federal provision.

Most proposals to alter the tax treatment of employee benefits have encountered intense opposition from an unusual coalition of labor and business groups. For organized labor, the taxation of fringe benefits represents a threat to the value of benefit packages negotiated for their members. The U.S. Chamber of Commerce and the National Association of Manufacturers oppose the plan since their members would likely face demands for higher wages or more generous benefits if employees had to pay taxes on employer-provided benefits. Moreover, company executives stand to lose cherished privileges. Concerned that its business might suffer, the insurance industry also opposes proposals to tax fringe benefits.

Continued Progress

Since the 1920s the federal government has paved the way for a voluntary system of private pensions. Court decisions in the 1940s made pensions an integral component of collective bargaining. Federal legislation in the 1950s and 1960s sought to curb the abuse of retirement funds by pension managers. And in the 1970s the federal government intervened to guarantee that once employers agree to provide pensions, they make good on their commitments. Progress in improving the income security of retired Americans has continued in the 1980s. Social security has been strengthened so that, barring catastrophic economic downturns, the system may continue to provide an adequate income floor for retired workers into the foreseeable future. And changes in the tax laws have encouraged private savings for retirement. Partly as a result of these efforts, one-third of all workers have some retirement income in addition to their social security checks.

The continued expansion of pension plans, however, is by no means assured. Pension coverage declined from 61 percent of workers in 1979 to 56 percent in 1984. Undoubtedly, much of this drop is due to the adverse economic conditions and record bankruptcies that characterized that period. However, there is no guarantee that coverage will be restored during economic recovery.

A number of pressing concerns have yet to be resolved. The financial solvency of the PBGC is essential to preserving confidence in the pension system. The support of business, labor, and the administration makes it likely that a premium increase is imminent and that faith in the ability of the agency to bail out bankrupt plans will soon be restored.

A more difficult problem arises out of the growing number of employers terminating their defined benefit plans, then plowing excess assets back into their businesses. As a result of high interest rates, higher-than-expected returns on investments, and lower-than-anticipated company payrolls, many employers are finding themselves with overfunded pension plans. Since ERISA prevents companies from removing assets from ongoing pension plans, but does not prevent terminating the plan, companies seeking access to these often sizable pools of pension capital are increasingly terminating existing plans and setting up new fully funded plans, while pocketing the difference. Since 1980 employers have terminated more than 700 pension plans and collected $6.7 billion in excess assets. The $3 billion recovered in 1984 was equal to the total amount of the previous three years, and the 1985 total may have been even higher.[36]

Defenders of this practice claim that excess assets are the property of employers, who contributed the funds initially. Corporate lobbyists argue that since employers assume the risks if investment performance is poor, they should get the windfall if performance is good. Critics, however, charge that such pension "raiding" precludes future benefit increases and may later result in underfunded plans when economic conditions sour. A legislative response, if forthcoming, would have to balance the interests of plan participants, yet avoid disincentives that might significantly deter the establishment or adequate funding of additional defined benefit plans.

Another problem involves how best to guarantee retirement income security to workers currently covered by a pension. Many workers fail to reach the ten year minimum vesting requirement even when covered under a pension plan. Some have advocated that 100 percent vesting be required after five, or even three, years of service. However, the costs to sponsoring employers could be prohibitive. The thrust of these proposals runs directly counter to the interest of employers who establish pension plans. Their vigorous opposition could be expected.

Expanded use of IRAs could solve the problem for some workers, but experience has shown that most workers, especially the young and highly mobile, do not adequately save for the future when left to their own devices. This fact of life underlies most of the federal legislation encouraging group pension plans, as well as the social security system. As an alternative, others advocate reliance on a beefed-up social security system to take up the slack. Since expanding pension coverage would place a greater burden on the federal treasury, greater benefit might be derived from a similar increase in the social security program, which already has the advantage of universal coverage and a proven track record. Private pensions could then be used to meet the early retirement needs of workers in certain occupations and industries.

As the work force grows older but retains better health, pressures on employers to provide a decent pension will build.

In addition, powerful senior citizens organizations will continue to lobby to prevent tampering with retiree benefits. Federal legislation protecting the living standards of retirees will, no doubt, continue to mature.

Part 4

Through the Crystal Ball

11

Prospective Federal Interventions

The preceding chapters examine the web of federal work-place regulations that has developed in response to changing labor market and social needs. These regulations have been of great benefit to workers, but came under increasing attack in the 1970s. While some regulations have been rolled back in the 1980s, new areas that may demand public attention are emerging. The initial enthusiasm for deregulation seems to have run its course, as policymakers seem to have second thoughts about the wisdom of relying upon unfettered free markets to achieve equity in the workplace.

Three emerging policy areas where the federal government might expand its role are employment at will, plant closings, and comparable worth. The issues involved include fairness in the workplace and the basic relationship between the worker and the employer. The courts, employers, unions, and state and local governments have attempted to address these policy areas, but it has become increasingly clear that some form of federal leadership would be of assistance to workers. Although exploration of the appropriate federal role in the three areas is occurring, little concrete action has been taken.

The employment-at-will debate concerns one of the rights that employers in this country have always held: the right to fire an employee without having to supply any justification for the action. The debate's outcome might have far-reaching effects on the relationship between employers and their employees and, if carried to its ultimate conclusion, would parallel employee job security with property rights. The plant closing debate is also concerned with job security but is much more narrow in scope. It centers on the role of the government in encouraging or requiring employers to give advance warn-

225

ing of major shutdowns. Advance warning presumably would help dislocated workers and their communities to adjust to necessary transitions. The comparable worth issue concerns the elimination of gender-based pay differentials. Advocates of comparable worth argue that because discrimination has trapped women in low-paying "female occupations," wages in these occupations should be raised, while their opponents believe free markets will achieve pay equity.

Opposition by the Reagan administration and by business lobbies has not only blocked the expansion of federal intervention in the workplace but has also succeeded in limiting the enforcement of existing regulations. Whether this opposition is only a temporary barrier remains an open question, as does the question of the future direction of existing workplace regulations. Now that some of the excesses of recent regulation have been corrected, the public may demand that the federal government assert a stronger role in regulating the workplace.

Employment At Will

A significant gap in the web of worker protective legislation is the absence of adequate constraints to prevent unjust dismissal. Approximately 80 percent of all private sector wage and salary workers—those not covered by collective bargaining agreements—have virtually no protection against being fired without just cause. Under the reigning common law principle of employment at will, these workers may be discharged for almost any reason or no reason at all, regardless of length of service or the employer's motivation, and without legal recourse.

In recent years, the courts and some state legislatures have demonstrated a willingness to reexamine public policy in this area, modifying the "at-will" doctrine. These developments follow a trend which began in the late 1940s, when American labor law shifted its focus from the protection of collective employee rights to the protection of individual employee rights. Beginning in the 1950s the federal courts began to expand constitutional remedies to afford government employees protection against wrongful dismissal.[1] Particularly influential was a 1972 Supreme Court decision granting public employees a constitutionally protected property right based on expectations of employment tenure.[2]

Most public employees enjoy protection against wrongful dismissal by virtue of civil service statutes. The federal Civil Service Reform Act of 1978 allows the dismissal of a federal employee only "for such cause as will promote the efficiency of the service." The same Act provides federal employees with statutory protection against reprisals for "whistleblowing," and establishes procedural guarantees to ensure due process. State and local civil service statutes provide a similar form of tenure while permitting dismissal only for cause. The burden of proof is on the administrative agency to prove that the employee actually committed the charged infringement and that removal based on the infringement will promote the efficiency of the service. The agency retains substantial discretion in determining what constitutes cause, provided that it articulates a rational basis for its decision.

Private sector workers, however, enjoy little statutory protection against unjust dismissal. Federal legislation provides redress to discharged workers whose termination directly results from discrimination on the basis of race, sex, age, religion, national origin, or physical handicap. In addition, workers discharged for engaging in protected concerted activity or in retaliation for asserting their rights under other labor statutes are guaranteed the right to appeal their employer's decision. Finally, the best protection against unjust discharge is derived from the grievance and arbitration procedures found in nearly every major collective bargaining agreement.

Yet, less than one-fifth of the private sector labor force in the United States is covered by collective bargaining agreements, and other statutory provisions affect relatively few individuals. All other private sector employees, some 66 million, are subject to the employment-at-will doctrine. One industrial relations expert estimated that, of the 3 million private workers discharged annually for noneconomic reasons, about 150,000 would be reinstated if granted the same protections enjoyed by unionized workers.[3]

Judicial Response

The most significant inroads into the employment-at-will doctrine in the past decade have come through the state courts. By 1985 more than half the states had developed judicial exceptions permitting employees who claim to have been fired for refusing to violate a public policy or in violation of an implied employment contract to have their cases heard by a jury.[4]

Under the public policy exception, the courts reinstated a worker who was fired for refusing to commit perjury at his employer's behest.[5] In another instance, the case of an employee fired for refusing to participate in an illegal price-fixing scheme was allowed to go to trial.[6] In a more recent decision, the North Carolina Court of Appeals ruled that a nurse anesthetist was unjustly terminated in retaliation for her refusal to testify falsely or incompletely in a medical malpractice trial.[7]

The courts have given increasing consideration to the implied contract exception. Thirteen states have found an implied promise of job tenure for employees with records of satisfactory performance in employee handbooks, personnel manuals, and oral statements made during employment interviews. The Michigan Supreme Court ruled that employees can use printed company statements and proof of oral assurances of job security to establish a contractual right to be fired only for just cause.[8] In a California case the jury concluded that the company obligated itself to deal with an employee in good faith based on the 32-year duration of his employment, his promotions and commendations, and assurances he had received.[9]

In general, court decisions are moving in the direction of widening the scope of wrongful discharge suits. The volume of cases is also growing. According to one estimate, 5,000 to 10,000 cases are initiated each year.[10] Most cases are dismissed at the lower court level, but employees often win when their cases are decided by juries. Between 1979 and 1983 California employees won 48 of 74 jury verdicts. In the California cases decided in favor of employees in 1983, the average settlement exceeded $500,000.[11]

Even with the most liberal court interpretation of employment at will, however, judicial remedies are inherently limited. The recognized exceptions are much more likely to serve as the basis for a lawsuit by dismissed executive and managerial employees than by hourly workers or low-level salaried employees. The latter groups who make up the overwhelming majority of discharged employees are less likely to afford or consult attorneys, who, in turn, would be quickly discouraged by the small returns from such a case.[12]

Those discharged workers with valid claims also face constraints. The judicial process is painfully slow, no matter how immediate the problem. In addition, finding a new job may reduce the jury appeal of the case. Finally, the employer remains in control of the evidence. These limitations on judicial action have provoked interest in statutory measures.

Legislative Response

While state courts have been gradually modifying the at-will principle on a case-by-case basis, several state legislatures have attempted to write specific remedies into law. Since 1980 legislation granting general protection against wrongful discharge has been introduced in Michigan, New York, Pennsylvania, Wisconsin, and California. Patterned after existing arbitration procedures that resulted from collective bargaining agreements and which permit an employee to appeal a discharge through arbitration, the legislation is intended to extend to nonunion employees statutory protection from unfair dismissal, or would give discharged employees recourse to an impartial panel for remedial actions. No proposed legislation has yet secured passage, but the attempts have clarified many of the thorny issues involved.

The legislative measures would require employers to show just cause for dismissals, thus shifting the balance in the direction of employee interests in defending against unfair and injurious employer actions. Yet, legitimate employer interests must also be considered. Employers should be free to remove an employee guilty of poor performance or misconduct to preserve effective management of their business operations. None of the attempted legislation has grappled with defining exactly what constitutes "just cause" for dismissal, instead leaving the substantive fairness question to be decided by arbitrators on a case-by-case basis.

Some analysts prefer this general approach, claiming that the existing body of arbitral precedent gives the phrase "just cause" workable content, while preserving flexibility.[13] Critics of a general fairness standard, however, warn that the adoption of a vaguely defined "just cause" would lead to deterioration in employment relations.[14] In a collective bargaining context, arbitrators can rely on the existing joint agreement between the parties in deciding specific cases. In the absence of such an agreement, as would be the case under the proposed statutes, the arbitrator would be granted considerable discretion in interpreting "just cause," which would likely result in substantial variation and confusion.

An alternative approach would be to enumerate the reasons why an employee may not be dismissed and to require the employee to prove that one of the prohibited reasons motivated the dismissal. Prohibited grounds might include the various kinds of cases already recognized as violations of public policy, along with dismissal due to whistleblowing, dismissal in contravention of an employer promise, and dismissal for conduct away from the workplace that is not reasonably related to the employee's job performance. Such a limited specific approach might have the additional practical benefit of facilitating the passage of legislation.

Careful balancing of employee and employer interests is also required in constructing an appropriate institutional framework. Proposed legislation has mainly focused on private dispute resolution to avoid the congestion and delays associated with the regular courts and existing or new administrative agencies. A 1983 Michigan bill provided for notifying an employee of the reasons for discharge, for mediation by the State Employment Relations Commission, and if mediation failed, the right to final and binding arbitration. The arbitrator would be selected by both parties, and the costs shared equally.

The bill also contained several measures intended to preserve employer freedom of action. An employer with fewer than ten employees or with a grievance procedure providing for impartial, final, and binding arbitration would be exempt from coverage. Probationary, part-time, confidential, and managerial employees would be excluded from coverage, as would those with written employment contracts covering at least two years.

The original version of a 1984 California bill contained some additional measures to discourage employees from filing frivolous claims. Under the legislation, both employer and employee would be required to deposit $500 with the state mediation and conciliation service to help pay for the costs of administering the act. In addition, if the arbitrator deemed the charge frivolous, attorney fees and costs would be awarded to the employer. If a state legislature were to propose specific standards for employer conduct, those complaints of wrongful discharge not alleging violations of set standards could also be weeded out at the initial administrative stage.

The states are actively groping for a formula that provides adequate protection to private sector employees without infringing too greatly on management prerogatives. So far, the necessary balance to achieve passage remains elusive.

Prospects

Legislative action to protect workers from unjust discharge faces major obstacles. Those who stand to gain the most remain dispersed and have strong economic motives for not advertising their situation. Employers remain determined not to yield further control over their work force and have mobilized opposition in every state in which legislation has been introduced. The unions have yet to commit themselves to the legislative battle in any meaningful way.

Employers faced with unpredictable and often costly jury awards might ultimately prefer legislative action. The remedies available under arbitration would be much more limited than those available through the judicial process. In addition, nonunion employers may find in the legislation a means to neutralize a principal union selling point in organizational campaigns. Currently, however, the growing number of publications and seminars addressing how to avoid legal pitfalls when discharging workers indicates that employers would rather fight than switch.

Unions have not opposed just cause legislation in states where it has been introduced, but neither have they lobbied for its passage. Their primary concern focuses on the added difficulty such legislation might present to union organizing. Nevertheless, there is reason to suspect that this ambivalence may be replaced by more active support. Labor leaders are becoming more aware of their poor public image.[15] By campaigning on behalf of nonunion workers, labor could modify its image as the defender of special interests and enhance its organizational and political influence. Unions have already made halting steps to provide selected services to nonunion workers, and extending a helping hand to discharged workers may gain new friends for labor outside union ranks.

Public support remains strongly in favor of preserving individual rights in the workplace. It is appropriate that efforts at securing statutory relief for unjustly discharged workers are being initiated at the state level. The state legislatures provide the proper forum for the experimentation necessary to refine the various proposals and fashion an effective statute. Most existing federal labor laws followed a similar course. International opinion also weighs in on the side of ultimate passage of federal legislation. The United States remains the last major industrial democracy that has not heeded the call of the International Labor Organization for unjust dismissal legislation.

Recently, the federal courts have begun to grapple with the employment-at-will issue.[16] The Third Circuit found that an insurance company violated public policy by discharging an employee who refused to lobby in favor of no-fault legislation. Public policy exceptions have also been granted to an employee discharged for reporting his employer's intention to deliver adulterated milk and to an employee who refused to fly an aircraft with inoperative items. A Second Circuit decision ruled that an employer cannot terminate an employment contract covering a definite term of one year without just cause, even if the contract itself reserves the employer's right to terminate employment at will. The court allowed exceptions only in the case of confidential employees or in cases where the employer is obligated to compensate the employee. The Supreme Court extended to union members the right to sue in case of a discharge. The Court denied review of an Illinois Supreme Court decision that allowed an employee the right to challenge an at-will discharge. It is important to note, however, that judicial progress is uneven, and there is considerable debate over the extent to which state laws may be preempted by existing federal labor laws.

The only federal statutory attempt to modify employment at will was a measure introduced in the House in 1980. Entitled the Corporate Democracy Act, the bill sought to proscribe dismissal of an employee unless just cause was found to exist.[17] Under the proposed bill, employees would be protected against dismissal resulting from the exercise of their constitutional, civil, or legal rights, the refusal to engage in unlawful conduct, the refusal to submit to a polygraph or other similar tests, and the refusal to submit to an unlawful search. Congress took no formal action on this measure. Federal intervention involving employment at will, if any is to occur, will await the results of experimentation at the state level and in the courts.

Plant Closings

The closing of a large firm can have a devastating effect on the newly unemployed individuals and the local community. The workers often suffer from income losses, even if they find new jobs, and are subject to difficult psychological adjustments that arise during long spells of unemployment. State or local governments and voluntary efforts are frequently inadequate to the task of ameliorating the direct and indirect losses to the unemployed and their families. Moreover, when a large firm shuts down, other businesses lose customers and a town's tax base erodes. A series of closures or mass layoffs can send large cities or entire regions reeling. These individual, community, and sometimes regional difficulties caused by plant shutdowns have led to an interest in public policy remedies.[18]

The Need for Prenotification

Studies of plant closings document a problem that directly affects millions of workers. One study found that from 1978 to 1982, plant closures in manufacturing firms with more than 100 employees caused an estimated annual loss of 900,000 jobs.[19] The Bureau of Labor Statistics estimated that from January 1979 to January 1984 roughly 11.5 million workers aged 20 years or older lost their jobs due to plant closures or employer cutbacks.[20] This group included 5.1 million dislocated workers who had been employed three years or more before losing their jobs. Half of these workers lost their jobs due to plant closures.

Forty percent of the dislocated workers were unable to find new jobs or dropped out of the workplace. The median spell of unemployment for all the dislocated workers was more than six months, but younger workers found new jobs more easily. Of the 2 million workers who were employed full-time in both their old plants and their new positions, 900,000 received pay cuts, including 600,000 workers whose pay cuts exceeded 20 percent. Major earnings losses were most common for workers previously employed in durable goods industries. Of those who lost their jobs because of plant closures, about 60 percent received some advance notice or expected the dismissal. One in ten of these individuals found jobs before their plants closed.

Although concentrated in manufacturing, plant closings occur in all industries and regions. More plants may close during recessions, but many plants close during times of general prosperity. In a dynamic economy constantly adjusting to changing markets and competition, even when the demand for some products rises, demand for other products diminishes, and many plants become obsolete and close down. With the continued explosive growth of technological progress and international trade, the number of plant closings may increase in the future.

Federal plant closing legislation would require businesses to provide advance notification of their intention to shut down a large plant or permanently lay off a substantial number of workers. Proponents claim that early warning of a closure or major permanent layoff would help the workers find jobs more quickly, cut their income loss, trim the costs of unemployment insurance as well as other support programs, and mobilize community resources to make necessary adjustments. Early warning may even help save some plants that may not be profitable enough for the company, but may still be profitable enough to induce employees or other businesses to purchase the plant. Advance notification provides the time to research the feasibility of takeovers and to negotiate a sale.[21]

Plant closing legislation has met fierce opposition. Opponents argue that it would prolong the operation of inefficient plants, that productivity would fall among workers and sales would drop among customers during the period between prenotification and the ultimate closure of the plant, that the necessity to provide advance notification may lock a company into closing a plant it may have been able to save, and that severance or other payments which might be required by plant closing legislation would be too costly. Finally, they note the complexity of designing plant closing legislation. What size layoffs should be affected by the legislation? What if a business is unsure whether a layoff will be permanent or temporary? What sanctions, if any, are appropriate? How far in advance should notice be required?

The magnitude of the dislocated worker problem and the relatively limited scope of current positive adjustment assistance programs points toward the need for plant closing legislation. Experience in other countries, as well as isolated cases in the United States, suggests that opponents overstate the case against a federal plant closing law. Canada's plant closing policy has operated for over 20 years, and the country's experience does not indicate that the dire consequences predicted by United States opponents of such a policy are justified.[22] A streamlined prenotification approach covering only large closures could accomplish much without imposing large new costs on either the private sector or the government.

Current Practice

The closing of plants in America is now subject to few private or public restraints. Collective bargaining agreements generally lack a plant closing process, only a few states and localities have plant closing laws, and federal regulation is nonexistent. Workers cannot obtain protection from the courts. In 1981 the Supreme Court ruled that a company can close a plant without prior discussions with a union, as long as it is only a partial closing (the entire company is not shutting down) and the closure is due to "economic reasons." In *First National Maintenance Corp. v. NLRB* (1981), the Supreme Court overruled a lower court decision that unions always had to receive prior notification.[23]

Some employers, voluntarily or under collective bargaining agreements, inform their workers in advance of an upcoming closure and help them find new jobs. Fifteen percent of collective bargaining agreements covering more than 1,000 employees require prenotification in the case of a closure or relocation.[24] Among recent agreements, a contract between the United Auto Workers and Ford offers a model approach that was first applied in 1982 in the closing of an assembly plant in Milpitas, California. Ford gave six months prenotification and established an on-site UAW-Ford employment and retraining center. The center provided skills assessment, basic education, vocational exploration courses, targeted vocational retraining, job search training, job placement help, and preferential placement at other Ford plants. One and a half years after the plant closed, 83 percent of the 2,400 ex-assembly workers who sought jobs were employed. Worker productivity remained high between prenotification and the firm's closure. Early notification, technical assistance from experienced plant closing sources, the joint labor-management approach, and use of inside resources contributed to the success of this effort.[25] An example of voluntary prenotification was involved in the closing of an Electrolux plant in Old Greenwich, Connecticut. The company provided six months' advance notice and extensive reemployment assistance to the 825 workers who lost their jobs.[26] There has also been some limited experience with employee or community buy-outs of failing operations.

Voluntary approaches by employers as well as negotiated agreements through union contracts have advanced the state of plant closing expertise considerably. Firms, employees, and communities now have a number of plant closing models to draw upon. These new private developments suggest that even absent public policy intervention, some progress will be made toward assisting workers displaced by plant closings. The success of some of these models suggests that public policy measures that would ease adjustment to plant closures can and should be taken.

Some path-breaking plant closing initiatives have recently passed at the state level. By mid-1985, 11 states had some type of plant closing legislation, while another 10 states were considering such legislation.[27] Three states (Massachusetts, Michigan and Wisconsin) encouraged voluntary advance notice and one state (Maine) required advance notice.

Maine requires companies with more than 100 employees to give 60-day notice before closing plants and to provide severance pay to workers with more than three years of experience. Enforcement of the law has been lax. From 1975 to 1981, thirty Maine plants, each with more than 100 workers, were shut down, but only seven provided prenotification. When companies did provide advance warning, the plant closing created less unemployment.[28]

Nonmandatory approaches include the voluntary plant closing code in Massachusetts. The Bay State encourages firms to provide 90-day prenotification and some continued health insurance by making a company's eligibility for various forms of state aid contingent upon compliance. Experience under this law is too limited for any judgment about its effectiveness.

South Carolina uses a different approach. It does not require prenotification, but the state informally collects intelligence about probable plant closings. Based on this information, state officials visit the plant and investigate alternatives either to prevent the closing or to convert the plant to other uses.

Philadelphia is one of the few cities that has passed a plant closing ordinance. It requires 60-day prenotification, but enforcement has been lax and companies have generally ignored the law.[29] An approach used in Jamestown, New York, has proven more successful and has saved thousands of jobs. The city has set up communitywide and in-plant labor-management committees to encourage cooperative solutions to problems that could lead to a plant closing.[30]

One federal government program that provides assistance to workers who lose their jobs due to plant closings is unemployment insurance—the Bureau of Labor Statistics found that two-thirds of dislocated workers received this form of income assistance. Unemployment insurance serves most job losers, while some other federal programs target dislocated workers. The trade adjustment assistance program provides aid to workers who have lost their jobs because of foreign competition, and Title III of the 1982 Job Training Partnership Act established a training program for dislocated workers. But both programs assist only a small percentage of their target populations.

The 1982 Job Training Partnership Act required the Secretary of Labor to develop plant closing data and to publish a report "as soon as practicable." Congress appropriated $6 million to this study, but opposition by the Reagan administration delayed its implementation. By late 1985, however, the study was well off the ground and an annual compilation of plant closing data by the Labor Department may finally occur. The Department of Labor has also established pilot projects to aid workers dislocated by plant closings, including the Downriver Community Conference Economic Readjustment Program in Detroit, Michigan. This program provided job placement and retraining assistance to displaced auto workers.

Plant closing legislation has been repeatedly introduced in Congress since 1974. In November 1985 the House defeated by a narrow margin (208 to 203) a bill requiring employers to provide 90-day prenotification in plant closings involving 50 employees or more. Business groups lobbied against the bill, and the Reagan administration also opposed it. However, to indicate administration concern with the issue, Secretary of Labor William Brock established a task force, headed by former undersecretary of labor Malcolm Lovell, to examine the plant closing issue and policy alternatives. The task force's report is expected in December 1986.

Future Federal Policy

The problems caused by plant closings have been increasingly well-documented in the past few years and will remain a fact of American economic life. The states and some labor-management agreements have taken the lead in exploring policies to solve these problems. A few key lessons emerge from these experiences, including the desirability of prenotification to provide workers and communities time to prepare for transitions and the need for labor-management cooperation. Unless extenuating conditions exist, prenotification of three months with some process for establishing a joint labor-management transition committee is desirable.

Federal intervention is warranted because plant closings are not isolated to a particular region of the country, because a uniform approach would be easier for businesses to comply with, and because a centralized data base would be helpful. Also, a number of plant closings have been the consequence of federal trade policies. In light of Reagan administration opposition there is little likelihood that Congress will soon pass any plant closing legislation. For the next few years, then, we can expect further experimentation at the state and local levels which may provide needed information and help generate future support for federal plant closing legislation.

Comparable Worth*

Although women have advanced in many employment fields in the last decade and a half, on average their pay is still one-third less than that of men. A key reason for this difference

*This section is based on the article "Comparable Worth: In Praise of Muddling Through," Sar A. Levitan and Clifford M. Johnson, *The Journal of the Institute for Socioeconomic Studies*, Summer 1985, pp. 36–52.

is that women still tend to be crowded into traditionally "female occupations" such as secretarial work, nursing or library services, where the pay is significantly less than the pay in "male occupations" such as truckdriving or building trades. Believing occupational segregation and the accompanying pay differential are partially due to discrimination, comparable worth advocates argue that wages in female occupations should be raised to the level of wages in male occupations of equivalent productivity or worth to the employer.

The Gap and Its Causes

For the past thirty years the median annual earnings of women working full time have fluctuated between 57 percent and 64 percent of men. In recent years, however, the ratio has risen to the upper limit of this range. The proportion of women's to men's median weekly earnings has also risen steadily from an average of 62 percent in 1979 to 69 percent in the second quarter of 1985.[31]

The recent decline in the earnings gap is encouraging, but does not mean that the pay equity problem is solved. Even if the trend continues, a substantial gap between women's and men's earnings will remain for some time. Also, the progress of women in the workplace is partially due to a strong government role. Further progress may depend on continued positive action by the government.

What is the cause of the earnings gap? In large part the earnings gap is due to women and men holding different jobs. First, as mentioned, women are concentrated in low-paying occupations. "Women's work" pays much less than "men's work" (Figure 17). Second, women may hold different jobs within the same occupation. For example, women and men accountants at various levels of advancement earn the same, but women accountants on average earn less than men accountants. The explanation is that there are many more women accountants at entry level than at higher levels.[32]

There has been some recent decline in occupational segregation. Using the index of segregation—which measures the proportion of men or women who would have to change jobs for men and women to be in the same proportion in all job categories as they are in the work force—from 1972, the year in which

Figure 17. Annual earnings fall as percentage of female workers in an occupation rises

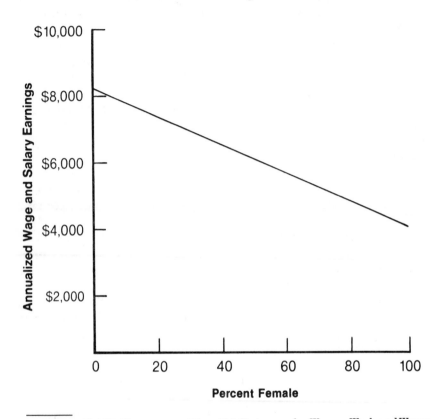

Source: Heidi I. Hartmann and Donald J. Treiman, eds., *Women, Work, and Wages* (Washington, D.C.: National Academy of Science Press, 1981), p. 23.

equal employment opportunity laws were strengthened and in which Title IX education amendments were added, to 1981, occupational segregation dropped from 68 percent to 62 percent. This decline was sharper for women professionals and college graduates, and each cohort entering the labor market has faced less segregation than the previous one.[33]

To explain the concentration of women in low-paying occupations, some analysts note the productivity differences between men and women. But the earnings gap exists among men and women of similar educational levels and estimates of productivity differences generally explain less than 20 percent of the earnings differential.[34] Relatedly, comparable worth opponents claim that women choose occupations which allow them the flexibility to leave the labor market. This free choice model implies that no government intervention should be undertaken.[35] Opponents of intervention also argue that discrimination does not occur in a free market because it would give a nondiscriminating firm a cost advantage, and that the value of a job is best determined by market forces which consider not only the supply of labor but the demand for those labor services. Comparable worth advocates, on the other hand, contend that occupational segregation is due to traditional practices, if not outright discrimination, which relegate women to a few occupations. The crowding of women into these occupations has led to an excess labor supply which drives down wages.

The two theories are not mutually exclusive. Women's earnings are lower because they have a more intermittent commitment to the labor force and because they have a somewhat different preference structure than men in the types of jobs they seek (in part, society's values and laws have dictated these different structures). The difference in preference does not, however, account for the predominance of occupational segregation. Discrimination may be illegal under current law and discriminatory attitudes may be changing, but, as the 1985 National Academy of Sciences study, *Women's Work, Men's Work: Sex Segregation on the Job*, concluded, discrimination still explains much of the current configuration of the work force.[36]

Existing equal opportunity laws can help break down discrimination. They can prevent the exclusion of women from certain occupations and can guarantee equal opportunity for advancement. But even if existing laws are stringently enforced, discrimination will not be rooted out overnight. Also, many women have already invested years in the predominantly female occupations. Starting from scratch in a new occupation is not a viable alternative for these women. They, in particular, deserve comparable worth compensation. Moreover, comparable worth studies can examine the basis for existing pay differentials in gender dominated occupations, and can determine if the gaps are indeed due to discrimination.

Waging Battle in the Courts

Court challenges to pay inequities have provided an impetus for implementation of comparable worth in the early 1980s. Federal courts have not endorsed the concept of comparable worth as an extension of the antidiscrimination provisions of Title VII, but they have considered claims that go beyond the standards of the Equal Pay Act and rely upon cross-occupational pay disparities as evidence of sex-based wage discrimination. In the landmark case of *County of Washington v. Gunther*, the Supreme Court held that Title VII's prohibition against sex-based wage discrimination is not limited to the guarantee of equal pay for equal work, and that women could advance claims of wage discrimination based on pay disparities with their male counterparts even though their work differed substantially.[37]

The Supreme Court, however, confined its ruling to the specific circumstances of that case involving female prison guards employed by the County of Washington. Lacking a definitive ruling on the scope of Title VII, lower courts have attempted to sort out the legality of various comparable worth claims, with some recent cases being decided against the proponents of comparable worth. At present, the willingness of lower courts to require equal pay for work of comparable worth appears to rest heavily on the ability of plantiffs to demonstrate that pay disparities stem from discriminatory intent.

Government Review of Pay Practices

The threat of court challenge, along with political pressure by labor and women's organizations, has prompted most states to address the issue of comparable worth during the 1980s. State pay systems have proven responsive because information regarding their pay-setting mechanisms is readily available and is subject to scrutiny and public pressure. In addition, state employees are often represented by unions or professional organizations that advance comparable worth claims. The resulting state actions have considerably advanced the cause of comparable worth. By mid-1985 most states either had established task forces to study the comparable worth issue or were examining comparable worth as part of overall compensation and classification studies. Seven states had adopted the principle of comparable worth for public sector employees.

The experience of Minnesota provides a valuable model for efforts to eliminate pay inequities. From 1981 to 1982 a task force including state, labor, and public representatives evaluated salary disparities based on the state's job evaluation system, found an unjustifiable wage gap of roughly 20 percent, and recommended adjustments to ensure fair compensation in female-dominated occupations. In 1983 the Minnesota legislature approved an appropriation of $21.7 million for the first half of a four-year wage adjustment scheme to increase annual state payroll costs by roughly four percent. This general approach to public sector pay inequities was extended to Minnesota localities in 1984, and in 1985 the Minnesota legislature allocated another $13 million to complete the pay equity adjustment for state employees.[38]

Broad participation and phased implementation have been central to the success of Minnesota's pay equity program. By involving union representatives and other interested parties in identifying pay inequities, state officials built a consensus in support of subsequent remedies. Furthermore, by closing pay disparities over four years, the program avoided the political resistance engendered by dramatic increases in state personnel costs.[39] Minnesota's employee relations commissioner noted in the fall of 1985 that the program has progressed smoothly and that the concerns of pay equity opponents proved illusory.[40]

Unions have also won gains at the bargaining table for state workers in female-dominated occupations. In 1981 the Connecticut state employees' union won a settlement requiring the state to set up a pay equity fund equal to one percent of its annual payroll to raise the salaries of nearly 7,000 workers in typically female health care occupations.[41] In 1984, after California Governor George Deukmejian vetoed a $77 million bill that would have been used to correct pay inequities, the California State Employees' Association negotiated a one-year contract that included additional pay raises for employees in female-dominated positions.[42] Local bargaining efforts have reinforced this trend toward comparable worth; for example, Los Angeles accepted a union proposal providing special raises to 3,900 clerks and librarians to bring their salaries in line with comparable male-dominated occupations.

In contrast to comparable worth activity at state and local levels, Congress has done little to address the issue. In 1984 the House passed a narrow bill mandating a study of the cause of sex-based disparities in federal employee compensation, but the legislation died in the Senate. In 1985 a similar bill passed in the House, but continued opposition from the Reagan administration and conservatives will probably again block passage in the upper chamber.

Private Sector Responses

A handful of states currently have laws which mandate equal pay for comparable work in private as well as public employment. However, none has established standards for determining the relative worth of dissimilar jobs, and the lack of adequate remedies under such laws has discouraged court challenges to private pay practices.

The likelihood of action by private employers to apply comparable worth standards is decreased by Reagan administration opposition. In April 1985 its Civil Rights Commission explicitly rejected the concept of comparable worth by a 5-2 vote. A majority of the federal Equal Employment Opportunity Commission has expressed similar opposition and the commission has taken no action on its mounting backlog of discrimination charges based on comparable worth.

Given the limited activity of state and federal authorities, the most immediate pressures for reducing the gender-based earnings gap in the private sector are being applied by women's organizations and by unions. Pay inequities can be a powerful organizing issue among relatively low-paid workers in female-dominated occupations. However, the desire of unions to push for pay equity provisions in contract negotiations is limited by competing demands for across-the-board wage gains, improved fringe benefits, and job security protections.

In one of organized labor's earliest attempts to promote pay equity, AT&T established a joint labor-management job evaluation committee in 1980 which examined the Bell System's wage structure.[43] AT&T workers in female-dominated occupations eventually won some salary increases based on the committee's findings, but full-scale implementation of comparable worth pay scales was stymied by the high implementation costs.

Toward Pay Equity

In cases where advocates of comparable worth can identify pay inequities or where unions consider the elimination of sex-based pay differentials as a major issue in contract negotiations, there will be some progress in reducing the female-male earnings gap. Yet the leverage of comparable worth advocates will remain sharply limited until clear standards for establishing claims of sex-based wage discrimination within jobs of comparable worth emerge from job evaluation designs, from the courts, or from state and federal legislatures.

Current arguments against comparable worth echo protestations of the early 1960s when the nation was debating civil rights and equal pay protections. Opponents claimed that it is impossible to legislate human behavior, and that federal intervention would be counterproductive by distorting free labor market forces. The resulting civil rights statutes offered no tidy prescriptions for eradicating discrimination; nonetheless, they yielded substantial political and economic gains among minorities and women. This progress towards equality stemmed from the government's decision to articulate clear equity principles and to raise the stakes for those who would deny access to women and minorities in political and economic arenas. Curiously, some business groups which argued against the reforms of the 1960s now say they favor those reforms but are opposed to comparable worth. For example, Senator Evans of Washington noted that the Chamber of Commerce originally opposed the Equal Pay Act believing it would have disastrous results, yet in 1985 Senate testimony the Chamber expressed support for that Act in lieu of a comparable worth study.[44]

The push toward pay equity is an extension of efforts to define and promote equality of opportunity. The most egregious pay inequities are being challenged and sometimes redressed through case-by-case examinations of sex-based wage discrimination claims by the courts. At the same time, the prospect of litigation is inducing some public and private employers to undertake voluntary reviews of their pay practices and to reduce pay disparities between male- and female-dominated occupations. As more states implement pay equity adjustments in the public sector, increased market, political, and moral pressures will move private employers in the direction of equity. Federal leadership is necessary to establish the principle of pay equity as a goal of public policy, and to provide mechanisms for societal pressure and judicial redress which will move the nation in that direction.

Future Workplace Regulation

Any changes in the political climate and in political leaders will obviously influence the nature of federal workplace regulation both in new policy areas and in existing policy areas. As long as the current political climate prevails, there is little likelihood that the federal government will depart from the deregulatory path it has followed since the late 1970s. Political conditions would have to change sharply for government to alter course and pursue needed and constructive workplace regulation. Whatever course is followed in the short term, the basic need for a strong federal role in regulating the workplace remains; ultimately, then, that will be the crucial factor driving future federal action.

If the Current Path Continues

The lax enforcement of workplace regulations that has so far characterized the terms of President Reagan will probably continue until he leaves office. The new guard in the Department of Labor of the second Reagan term may attempt to halt the erosion of worker protections, but it will probably have difficulty in overcoming the potent forces in the Department of Justice, the Office of Management and Budget, and other parts of the administration that support unbridled free markets and elimination of federal interventions. Most of all, the administration will follow a deregulatory path because President Reagan's faith in free markets remains as strong as ever.

In some areas, deregulation may continue because needed legislation will not be passed. Without statutory action, assuming annual consumer price increases of 3 to 4 percent, the real value of the minimum wage will fall roughly 40 percent during President Reagan's two terms. Without legislation to return the federal commitment to historical levels, the unemployment insurance program will continue to provide benefits to one-third of the unemployed, and job training programs will benefit only a small proportion of the unemployed.

Workplace deregulation may also continue through administrative actions. If so, violations of health and safety standards may go undetected or be subject to puny fines, and new standards regulating health hazards will not be issued. The enforcement of equal employment opportunities will be neglected and the progress of women and minorities in the workplace could be reversed. The National Labor Relations Board will continue siding with employers, further weakening collective bargaining. Federal inaction may also discourage experimentation with workplace regulation at the state or local level.

If the experience of the first five years of the Reagan administration is any guide for the future, basic worker protection programs will probably not be dismantled. The public may accept that these programs need to be modified and sometimes cut back, but it will reject their outright elimination. Congress seems to be sensitive to these sentiments and is likely to retain the existing laws, although it may not prevent workplace deregulation by administrative action. Moreover, even with the changing composition and ideology of the federal courts, workplace regulation laws may be reinterpreted but will not be discarded.

An Alternative Path

Instead of continuing along the deregulatory path, the federal government should reassume its responsibility for regulating the workplace. This would not require a broad expansion of federal powers. Rather, the proper role of the federal government is to repair the recent damage to worker protection programs, to continue modifications where government policy has gone too far or has been misguided, and to reassert the importance of worker rights in the marketplace and of worker income security.

Needed action would include legislation to restore the minimum wage to historical levels and, because the problem of high and long-term unemployment can be expected to continue, legislation to assist workers dislocated by international trade or technological change. Taxes from workers who would find new jobs as well as a decline in welfare and unemployment insurance costs would partially offset the costs of these initiatives. This alternative path would also include stronger administrative actions on behalf of the worker. For example, OSHA would strengthen its enforcement and would issue necessary new health standards, and other appropriate agencies would rededicate themselves to enforcing equal employment opportunity laws. Recognizing the limits of intervention, the federal government would act cautiously in expanding its powers to new areas. It would, however, assert leadership by supporting the objectives of protecting employees from unwarranted firings, of plant closing prenotification, and of equal pay for women in jobs of comparable worth. Accordingly, limited legislation, such as a federal government study of its own as well as private pay practices, would also be considered.

Which Path Will We Follow?

Barring an unexpectedly sharp swing in favor of more activist government in the 1986 congressional elections or an economic recession that fundamentally alters public confidence in the economic policies of the Reagan administration, the direction of workplace regulation in President Reagan's second term will follow that of his first term. Beyond 1988 a more moderate administration is likely to resume the policies followed by Republican and Democratic administrations prior to the 1980s and revive the policies that guided federal regulation of the workplace since the New Deal.

Even another conservative presidential administration is not likely to sustain the rollback of workplace regulations. The market system has been the driving engine that created the highly productive American economy, but, by itself, a free market does not advance all of our society's goals. In particular, it does not provide socially acceptable working conditions and income security for many Americans. As workplace regulations erode, and as the free market exacerbates the problems of many workers, the necessity of government intervention will once again be clear. With government having modified and trimmed back the excesses of earlier regulations, the nation may be ready for the vigorous and fair enforcement of existing statutes and executive orders. An educated and

affluent work force will insist that their elected representatives protect its rights, attend to its interests, and cater to its
needs.

Sooner or later, then, the pendulum will probably swing
back in favor of effective federal regulation of the workplace. In
the hubris of the 1960s, some may have believed the federal
government could quickly solve all social problems; when the
dreams of the Great Society failed to materialize, the pendulum swung to the other extreme, negating the responsibility
of the federal government for the common welfare. The experience of the past two decades has made it clear that social
progress comes slowly, particularly in solving age-old problems such as unemployment, discrimination, and occupational
hazards. But it is equally clear that federal intervention in the
workplace has improved the lives of millions of Americans
when they are unemployed, while they are working, and after
they have retired. In full recognition of these accomplishments, but with deference to the limits of government action,
the federal government should resume its constitutional
responsibility for promoting the general welfare by advancing
the lot of American workers.

Appendix of
Major Legislation
Affecting the Workplace

1917   Smith-Hughes Act, 20 U.S.C. §11

1933   Wagner-Peyser Act, 29 U.S.C §49 et seq.

1935   National Labor Relations Act, 29 U.S.C. §141
       (amended by the Labor Management Relations Act in 1947)

1935   Social Security Act, 42 U.S.C. §301 et seq.

1937   National Apprenticeship Act, 29 U.S.C. §50

1938   Fair Labor Standards Act, 29 U.S.C. §201

1958   Landrum-Griffin Act, 29 U.S.C. §401

1963   Equal Pay Act, 29 U.S.C. §206

1963   Vocational Education Act, 20 U.S.C. §1241 et seq.

1964   Civil Rights Act (Title VII), 42 U.S.C. §2000e

1967   Age Discrimination in Employment Act, 29 U.S.C. §621

1970   Occupational Safety and Health Act, 29 U.S.C. §651

1973   Comprehensive Employment and Training Act, 29 U.S.C. §801

1974   Employee Retirement and Income Security Act, 29 U.S.C. §1000

1982   Job Training Partnership Act, 29 U.S.C. §1501

1984   Carl D. Perkins Vocational Education Act, 20 U.S.C. §2301

Notes

Chapter 1

1. *Adkins v. Children's Hospital,* 261 U.S. 525 (1923).
2. Murray L. Weidenbaum and Robert DeFina, *The Cost of Federal Regulation of Economic Activity* (Washington: American Enterprise Institute, 1978).
3. Everett C. Ladd, "The Reagan Phenomenon and Public Attitudes Toward Goverment," in Lester M. Salamon and Michael S. Lund, eds., *The Reagan Presidency and the Governing of America* (Washington: The Urban Institute Press, 1985), pp. 221–49.

Chapter 2

1. Timothy B. Clark, "OMB to Keep Its Regulatory Powers in Reserve in Case Agencies Lag," *National Journal,* March 14, 1981, p. 428.
2. Richard Corrigan, "Unions Say Labor Board's Hostility Compounds Their Economic Hard Times," *National Journal,* July 23. 1983, p. 1542.
3. Jonathan Rauch, "Stockman's Quiet Revolution at OMB May Leave Indelible Mark on Agency," *National Journal,* May 15, 1985, p. 1216.
4. General Accounting Office, *Improved Quality, Adequate Resources, and Consistent Oversight Needed if Regulatory Analysis Is to Help Control Costs of Regulations,* Report prepared for U.S. Congress, Senate Committee on Governmental Affairs, 97th Cong., 2d Sess., November 2, 1982.
5. Joe Davidson and Linda M. Watkins, "Quotas in Hiring Are Anathema to President Despite Minority Gains," *The Wall Street Journal,* October 24, 1985, p. 1.
6. Chamber of Commerce of the United States, *Congressional Issues 1985* (Washington: Chamber of Commerce of the United States, 1985).
7. Ann Cooper, "Public Policy Focus," *National Journal,* November 30, 1985, p. 2739.
8. Dom Bonafede, "Issue-Oriented Heritage Foundation Hitches Its Wagon to Reagan's Star," *National Journal,* March 20, 1982, p. 503; Sidney Blumenthal, "Heritage Led by a True Believer," *The Washington Post,* September 24, 1985, p. A10.
9. Sidney Blumenthal, "The Conservative Elite," *The Washington Post,* September 22, 1985, p. A1.
10. Stuart M. Butler, Michael Sanera, and W. Bruce Weinrod, *Mandate for Leadership II: Continuing the Conservative Revolution* (Washington: The Heritage Foundation, 1984), Foreword.

11. Blumenthal, *op. cit.* note 9, p. A14.

12. Nadine Cohodas, "Larger and Broader Coalition of Civil Rights Organizations Thrives as White House Foe," *Congressional Quarterly,* September 17, 1983, pp. 1931–36.

13. John L. Palmer and Isabel V. Sawhill, eds., *The Reagan Record* (Washington: The Urban Institute Press, 1984), and related volumes.

14. Office of Technology Assessment, *Preventing Illness and Injury in the Workplace* (Washington: Office of Technology Assessment, April 1985).

15. Steven Pressman, "1984 Races Become Battlefield for Competing Interest Groups," *Congressional Quarterly,* September 1, 1984, p. 2150.

16. *Common Cause News,* Washington, March 14, 1985 and April 12, 1985.

Chapter 3

1. Henry Zagorski *et al.,* "Does Compensatory Education Narrow the Achievement Gap?" *Study of the Sustaining Effects of Compensatory Education on Basic Skills* (Santa Monica: System Development Corp., 1981); Judith Anderson and Robert Stonehill, *A Report to Congress: An Evaluation of the Elementary and Secondary Education Act Title I Program Operations and Educational Effects,* U.S. Department of Education (Washington: Department of Education, 1982).

2. David P. Weikart, "The Cost Effectiveness of High Quality Early Childhood Programs," Testimony Before the U.S. Congress, House Select Committee on Children, Youth, and Families, 98th Cong., 1st Sess., June 30, 1983.

3. Donald A. Gillespie and Lynn Quincy, *Trends in Student Aid: 1980-1984* (Washington: The College Board, 1984).

4. David S. Osman, "Student Financial Aid: FY85 Budget," Library of Congress, Congressional Research Service, September 10, 1984.

5. Roger Thompson, "Colleges in the 1980s," *Editorial Research Reports,* July 27, 1984, p. 562.

6. National Center for Education Statistics, *Two Years After High School: A Capsule Description of 1980 Seniors* (Washington: Government Printing Office, 1984), p. 15.

7. Rupert N. Evans, "Public Secondary and Postsecondary Vocational Education," in Robert E. Taylor *et al.,* eds., *Job Training for Youth* (Columbus: The National Center for Research in Vocational Education, Ohio State University, 1982), p. 257.

8. National Council on Employment Policy, *A Vocational Education Policy for the 1980s* (Washington: National Council on Employment Policy, 1982), p. 17.

9. Office of Management and Budget, *Additional Details on Budget Savings* (Washington: Government Printing Office, 1981), p. 105.

10. Rupert N. Evans and Joel D. Galloway, "Verbal Ability and Socioeconomic Status of Ninth and Twelfth Grade College Preparatory, General, and Vocational Students," *Journal of Human Resources,* Winter 1973, pp. 24–36.

11. National Center for Education Statistics, *The Condition of Education* (Washington: Government Printing Office, 1984), p. 106.

12. Robert H. Meyer, "Job Training in the Schools," in Taylor, *op. cit.* note 7, pp. 307–44.

13. Robert W. Glover, "American Apprenticeship and Disadvantaged Youths," in Taylor, *op. cit.* note 7, p. 183.

14. Ray Marshall and Vernon Briggs, *The Negro and Apprenticeship* (Baltimore: Johns Hopkins University Press, 1967), p. 28; *Employment and Training Report of the President* (Washington: Government Printing Office, 1984), *1983*, p. 41.

15. Herbert Hammerman, *A Decade of New Opportunity: Affirmative Action in the 1970s* (Washington: The Potomac Institute, 1984), p. 52.

16. Department of Defense, *Military Manpower Training Report: FY1986, Volume IV: Force Readiness Report*, March 1985.

17. Carol B. Leon, "Working for Uncle Sam—A Look at Members of the Armed Forces," *Monthly Labor Review*, July 1984, p. 7.

18. Eva Norbloom, *The Return to Military and Civilian Training* (Santa Monica: The Rand Corp., 1976); Richard V.L. Cooper, *Military Retiree's Post-Service Earnings and Employment* (Santa Monica: The Rand Corp., 1981).

19. Dennis DeTray, *Veteran Status as a Screening Device* (Santa Monica: The Rand Corp., 1980).

20. Robert Taggart, *A Fisherman's Guide: An Assessment of Training and Remediation Strategies* (Kalamazoo: The W.E. Upjohn Institute for Employment Research, 1981), pp. 280–94.

21. George Farkas et al., *Impacts From the Youth Incentive Entitlement Pilot Projects: Participation, Work, and Schooling Over the Full Program Period* (New York: Manpower Development Research Corp., 1982).

22. Mathematica, *Evaluation of the Economic Impact of the Job Corps Programs* (Princeton: Mathematica, 1978).

23. Taggart, *op. cit.* note 20, p. 283.

24. Sar A. Levitan and Garth L. Mangum, "A Quarter Century of Employment and Training Policy," in *Jobs for the Future* (Washington: Center for National Policy, 1984), pp. 39–50.

25. Department of Health and Human Services, *1979 AFDC Recipient Characteristics Study—Part 1: Demographic and Program Statistics,* (Washington: Government Printing Office, 1982).

26. Demetra S. Nightingale, *Federal Employment and Training Policy Changes During the Reagan Administration: State and Local Responses* (Washington: The Urban Institute, 1985), p. iv.

27. Peter Kemper, David Long, and Craig Thornton, *The Supported Work Evaluation: Final Benefit-Cost Analysis* (New York: Manpower Development Research Corp., 1980).

28. General Accounting Office, *Information on the Employment Service's Programs, Activities, and Functions,* GAO/HRD-82-71, April 30, 1982.

29. David S. North and Marion F. Houston, *The Characteristics and Role of Illegal Aliens in the U.S. Labor Market: An Exploratory Study* (Washington: Linton & Co., 1976).

30. William Chaze, "Crackdown on Illegal Aliens—The Impact," *U.S. News & World Report*, July 2, 1984, pp. 23–27.

31. Leon F. Bouvier, *Immigration and Its Impact on U.S. Society* (Washington: Population Reference Bureau, 1981), p. i.

32. Vernon M. Briggs, Jr., "Employment Trends and Contemporary Immigration Policy," in Vernon M. Briggs, Jr. and Marta Tienda, eds., *Immigration: Issues & Policies* (Washington: National Council on Employment Policy, 1985), pp. 18–19.

33. Ellen Sehgal, "Foreign Born in the U.S. Labor Market: The Results of a Special Survey," *Monthly Labor Review,* July 1985, pp. 18–24.

34. Joyce C. Vialet, "Refugee Act Reauthorization: Admissions and Resettlement Issues," Library of Congress, Congressional Research Service, August 8, 1984.

35. Michael J. Piore, *Birds of Passage: Migrant Labor and Industrial Societies* (London: Cambridge University Press, 1979).

36. Vernon M. Briggs, Jr., *Immigration Policy and the American Labor Force* (Baltimore: Johns Hopkins University Press, 1984), p. 185.

Chapter 4

1. Milton Friedman, *Capitalism and Freedom* (Chicago: University of Chicago Press, 1962), p. 109.

2. Executive Order 10925.

3. Sar A. Levitan, William B. Johnston, and Robert Taggart, *Still A Dream: The Changing Status of Blacks Since 1960* (Cambridge: Harvard University Press, 1975), p. 269.

4. Executive Order 11246.

5. *Public Papers of the Presidents, 1965* (Washington: Government Printing Office) p. 636.

6. *Griggs v. Duke Power Co.,* 401 U.S. 424, 432 (1971).

7. *Gregory v. Litton Sys.,* 472 F.2d 631 (9th Cir. 1972).

8. "Permissible Goals and Timetables in State and Local Government Employment Practices," Joint Memorandum of Equal Employment Opportunity Commission, Justice Department, and Office of Contract Compliance, March 23, 1973.

9. *United Steelworkers v. Weber,* 440 U.S. 193, 206 (1979).

10. Louis Harris and Associates, "Aging in the Eighties: America in Transition," conducted for the National Council on the Aging, Inc., 1981.

11. Michael Schuster and Christopher S. Miller, "An Empirical Assessment of the Age Discrimination in Employment Act," *Industrial and Labor Relations Review,* October 1984, pp. 64‚ŋ74.

12. "Courts Limit Defense to Age Bias Claims in Two Victories for Older Workers," *BNA's Employee Relations Weekly,* June 24, 1985, p. 772.

13. Mark A. deBernardo, "Forum," *BNA's Employee Relations Weekly,* March 18, 1985, pp. 337–38.

14. *Gill v. Union Carbide, Inc.,* 368 F. Supp. 364 (E.D. Tenn. 1973).

15. *Memphis Fire Dep't v. Stotts,* 104 U.S. 2576 (1984).

16. "13 Months After *Stotts* Decision, Affirmative Action Lives On," *BNA's Employee Relations Weekly,* July 29, 1985, p. 931.

17. "Ed Meese's Right to Be Wrong," *Business Week,* November 4, 1985.

18. U.S. Commission on Civil Rights, *Civil Rights Update,* March 1984, p. 2.

19. Robert Pear, "U.S. Agency Charges 3 Companies With Job Bias," *The New York Times,* November 13, 1985, p. A17. *EEOC v. Citizens Bank*

and Trust Co. of Md. (D. Md. filed Nov. 12, 1985); EEOC v. Panduit Corp. (D. N.Ill. filed Nov. 12, 1985); EEOC v. Peterson, Howell & Heather et al. (D. Md. filed Nov. 12, 1985).

20. Regents of the University of California v. Bakke, 438 U.S. 265, 400 (1978).

21. Charles Brown, "The Federal Attack on Labor Market Discrimination: The Mouse That Roared," in Ronald Ehrenberg, ed., Research in Labor Economics, Volume 5 (Greenwich: Jai Press, 1982), pp. 33–68.

22. James P. Smith and Finis Welch, "Affirmative Action and Labor Markets," unpublished, February 1984, p. 32.

23. Department of Labor, Office of Federal Contract Compliance Programs, Employment Patterns of Minorities and Women in Federal Contractor and Noncontractor Establishments (Washington: Government Printing Office, 1984); Herbert Hammerman, A Decade of New Opportunity: Affirmative Action in the 1970s (Washington: The Potomac Institute, 1985).

24. Bureau of Labor Statistics, Handbook of Labor Statistics, Bulletin 2175, December 1983, Table 16; Employment and Earnings, January 1985, Table 21.

25. Bureau of the Census, Money Income of Households, Families, and Persons, 1983, Current Population Reports Series, P-60, No. 146, Table 46.

26. Anthony Neely, "Government Role in Rooting Out, Remedying Discrimination Is Shifting," National Journal, September 22, 1984, pp. 1772–75.

27. "Affirmative Action Lives On," BNA's Employee Relations Weekly, July 29, 1985, pp. 931–32.

28. Daniel Seligman, "Affirmative Action Is Here to Stay," Fortune, April 19, 1982, p. 158.

29. U.S. Congress, House Select Committee on Aging, New Business Perspectives on Older Workers, 95th Cong., 1st Sess., October 18, 1981.

30. Employment and Earnings, op cit. note 24, Table 54.

31. Hammerman, op cit. note 23, p. 58.

32. Teamsters v. United States, 431 U.S. 324 (1977).

Chapter 5

1. Sar A. Levitan and Richard S. Belous, More Than Subsistence: Minimum Wages for the Working Poor (Baltimore: Johns Hopkins University Press, 1979), p. 35.

2. U.S. Department of Labor, Employment Standards Administration, Minimum Wage and Maximum Hours Standards Under the Fair Labor Standards Act, 1985.

3. Bureau of Labor Statistics, unpublished data derived from Current Population Survey.

4. Report of the Minimum Wage Study Commission, Volume I (Washington: Government Printing Office, 1981), p. 93.

5. Ibid., pp. 19–21.

6. Ibid., p. 32.

7. Ibid., p. 38.

8. Ronald G. Ehrenburg and Robert S. Smith, Modern Labor Economics, 2d ed. (Glenview, Ill.: Scott, Foresman, 1985), p. 78.

9. Edward M. Gramlich, "Impact of Minimum Wage on Other Wages, Employment and Family Incomes," *Brookings Paper on Economic Activity,* 1976:2, pp. 419–52.

10. Bureau of the Census, "Money Income and Poverty States, 1984," *Current Population Reports,* Series P-60, No. 149, p. 27; Bureau of Labor Statistics, *Linking Employment Problems to Economic Status,* Bulletin 2222 (1985), p. 25.

11. Department of Labor, Employment Standards Administration, Division of Employment and Research, unpublished table, February 11, 1982.

12. *Minimum Wage Commission, op. cit.* note 4, p. 84.

13. *Ibid.,* p. 47.

14. Janet Hook, "Tax Credit Could Be Only 'Jobs' Bill in 1984," *Congressional Quarterly,* April 21, 1984, p. 929.

15. *Special Analyses, Budget of the United States Government,* Fiscal Year 1986 (Washington: Government Printing Office, 1985) p. G-45.

16. General Accounting Office, *Targeted Jobs Tax Credit Program Activity,* GAO/PAD-83-44, 1983.

17. Robert Eisner, "Employer Approaches to Reducing Unemployment," Urban Institute Conference Paper, September 5, 1985, pp. 12–13 (in press).

18. Joseph Ball, *The Participation of Private Business as Work Sponsors in the Youth Entitlement Demonstration* (New York: Manpower Development Research Corp., 1981).

19. Ronald G. Ehrenberg and Paul L. Schumann, *Longer Hours or More Jobs* (Ithaca: Cornell University Press, 1982), p. 10.

20. Yung-Ping Chen, "The Growth of Fringe Benefits: Implications for Social Security," *Monthly Labor Review,* November 1981, p. 7.

21. U.S. Bureau of Labor Statistics, *Employment and Earnings,* January 1985, p. 53.

22. Ehrenberg and Schumann, *op. cit.* note 19, p. 131.

23. Levitan and Belous, *op. cit.* note 1, p. 33.

24. Ehrenberg and Schumann, *op. cit.* note 19, p. 131.

25. William Whittaker, "The Walsh-Healey Public Contracts Act and Overtime Pay Requirements," Library of Congress, Congressional Research Service, August 6, 1982, pp. 6–7.

26. *Minimum Wage Commission, op. cit.* note 4, p. 154.

27. *Ibid.,* pp., 152, 157, 161.

28. General Accounting Office, *The Department of Labor's Enforcement of the Fair Labor Standards Act,* GAO/HRD-85-77, September 30, 1985.

Chapter 6

1. Nicholas Ashford, *Crisis in the Workplace: Occupational Disease and Injury* (Cambridge: MIT Press, 1976), p. 48.

2. Marthe B. Kent, "A History of Occupational Safety and Health in the United States," in U.S. Congress, Office of Technology Assessment, *Preventing Illness and Injury in the Workplace,* Volume II-Part A: Working Papers (Washington: Government Printing Office, 1985), pp. 4, 5.

3. Paul Brodeur, "Annals of Law: The Asbestos Industry on Trial," *The New Yorker*, June 10, 1985, p. 64.

4. *Ibid.*, pp. 61, 67.

5. Carolyn Adellate, "Compensation for Asbestos Victims Poses Problems," *Occupational Health and Safety*, February 1985, pp. 62, 64.

6. John Mendeloff, *Regulating Safety: An Economic and Political Analysis of Occupational Safety and Health Policy* (Cambridge: MIT Press, 1979), p. 12.

7. U.S. Congress, Office of Technology Assessment, *Preventing Illness and Injury in the Workplace* (Washington: Government Printing Office, 1985), p. 209.

8. Mendeloff, *op. cit.* note 6, p. 153.

9. U.S. Congress, Senate Committee on Labor and Public Welfare, 91st Cong., 2nd Sess., *Occupational Safety and Health Act of 1970*, Report No. 1282 (1970).

10. Mendeloff, *op. cit.* note 6, p. 21.

11. Bureau of National Affairs, Inc., *The Job Safety and Health Act of 1970*, (Washington: BNA Books, 1971).

12. Benjamin W. Mintz, *OSHA: History, Law, and Policy* (Washington: BNA Books, 1984), p. 40.

13. James Ledvinka, *Federal Regulation of Personnel and Human Resource Management* (Boston: Kent Publishing Co., 1982), p. 183.

14. *Preventing Illness, op. cit.* note 7, p. 228.

15. *Ibid.*, pp. 366, 373, 374.

16. *BNA's Employee Relations Weekly*, July 8, 1985, p. 861.

17. Janet Hook, "Organized Labor Braces for 'Four More Years,'" *Congressional Quarterly*, December 29, 1984, p. 3168.

18. Bureau of National Affairs, Inc., *Occupational Safety and Health Reporter*, Vol. 12, No. 25, November 18, 1982, p. 484 and "OSHA Issues Hearing Conservation Rules, Sees Savings Through Performance Approach," Vol. 12, No. 40, March 10, 1983, p. 827.

19. *Preventing Illness, op. cit.* note 7, p. 363.

20. Julius C. McElveen, Jr., "Despite Pre-Emption Threat, Local Right-to-Know Laws Increase," *Occupational Health and Safety*, January 1985, p. 20.

21. "Unions Hail Order to Revise OSHA Rules," *The Washington Post*, May 30, 1985, p. A17. *United Steelworkers v. Auchter*, 763 F.2d 728 (3d Cir. 1985).

22. "Auchter Expresses Satisfaction With Performance, State of OSHA," *Occupational Health and Safety*, May 1984, p. 25.

23. Statement of Thorne Auchter, U.S. Congress, Hearings Before House Committee on Government Operations, 98th Cong., 1st Sess., November 9, 1983, p. 17.

24. *Preventing Illness, op. cit.* note 7, pp. 236–38.

25. Mary Jane Bolle, "Effectiveness of the Occupational Safety and Health Act: Data and Measurement Problems," Library of Congress, Congressional Research Service, June 20, 1984, p. 27.

26. Peter Perl, "Rowland Quits as OSHA Chief," *The Washington Post*, May 25, 1985.

27. Office of Management and Budget, *Appendix, Budget of the U.S. Government, Fiscal Year 1986* (Washington: Government Printing Office, 1985), p. I-018.

28. Susan J. and Martin Tolchin, *Dismantling America: The Rush to Deregulate* (Boston: Houghton Mifflin, 1983), p. 122.

29. *Ibid.*, pp. 122–126; U.S. Congress, House Committee on Governmental Operations, *OMB Interference With OSHA Rulemaking*, Report No. 853, 98th Cong., 1st Sess. (1983); and U.S. Congress, Hearings Before the House Committee on Government Operations, Subcommittee on Manpower and Housing, 97th Cong., 2d Sess., March 11, 18, and 19, 1982, cited in *Preventing Illness, op. cit.* note 7, p. 287.

30. "DOL's Price Tag for Human Life: $2–$5 Million (Depending)," *BNA's Employee Relations Weekly*, July 29, 1985, p. 934.

31. Harvey J. Hilaski, "Understanding Occupational Illness Statistics," *Monthly Labor Review*, March 1981, p. 29.

32. Bolle, op. cit. note 25, pp. 6–7.

33. *Preventing Illness, op. cit.* note 7, p. 263.

34. National Safety Council, *Accident Facts*, 1984 ed.

35. Karl Kronebusch, "Data on Occupational Injuries and Illness," in U.S. Congress, Office of Technology Assessment, *Preventing Illness and Injury in the Workplace*, Vol II-Part A: Working Papers (Washington: Government Printing Office, 1985), Tables, 1, 2, 19; U.S. Department of Labor, Bureau of Labor Statistics, *Occupational Injuries and Illnesses in 1984*, USDL 85-483 (1985).

36. Centaur Associates, "The Impact of OSHA's Recent Enforcement Activities," submitted to the U.S. Department of Labor, Occupational Safety and Health Administration, January 16, 1985, p. x; W. Kip Viscusi, "Estimates of the Effects of Occupational Safety and Health Regulation, 1973-1983," submitted to the U.S. Department of Labor, Occupational Safety and Health Administration, August 1985.

37. *Preventing Illness, op. cit.* note 7, p. 265.

38. Bolle, *op. cit.* note 25, pp. 31–32.

39. *Economic Report of the President, 1985* (Washington: Government Printing Office, 1985) p. 275.

40. Kronebusch, *op. cit.* note 35, Table 1, Table 19.

41. *Preventing Illness, op. cit.* note 7, pp. 266–67.

42. *Preventing Illness, op. cit.* note 7, pp. 231, 268; N. Ashford, C. Hill, M. Mendez *et al.*, *Benefits of Environmental, Health, and Safety Regulation*, Study prepared by the Center for Policy Alternatives, Massachusetts Institute of Technology, for the U.S. Congress, Senate Committee on Governmental Affairs, 96th Cong., 2d Sess. (Committee print, 1980).

43. Ruth Ruttenburg, "Compliance With the OSHA Cotton Dust Rule: The Role of Productivity Improving Technology," in U.S. Congress, Office of Technology Assessment, *Preventing Illness and Injury in the Workplace*, Volume II—Part C: Working Papers (Washington: Government Printing Office, 1985), pp. 32, 50.

44. Michael Wines, "Auchter's Record at OSHA Leaves Labor Outraged, Business Satisfied," *National Journal*, October 1, 1983, p. 2010.

45. Ruttenberg, *op. cit.* note 43, pp. 49, 99.

46. Cited in *Ibid.*, p. 103.

47. Calculated from *Preventing Illness, op cit.* note 7, pp. 231, 366, 373.
48. Wines, *op. cit.* note 44, p. 2009.
49. McElven, Jr., *op. cit.* note 20, p. 20.
50. "All Sides See Victory in Court Order Requiring Review of Right-to-Know Rule," *BNA's Employee Relations Weekly,* June 3, 1985, p. 674.
51. "Auchter Expresses Satisfaction With Performance, State of OSHA," *op. cit.* note 22, p. 65.
52. *Preventing Illness, op. cit.* note 7, p. 34.
53. Kronebusch, *op. cit.* note 35, Table 19.
54. Kenneth B. Noble, "Panel Is Told of Poor Morale in Agency for Safety on Job," *New York Times,* May 9, 1985, p. D22, and "Job Safety Agencies Accused of Laxity," *New York Times,* May 24, 1985, p. A26.
55. Perl, *op. cit.* note 26, and "OSHA Office Clouded by Threats, House Told," *The Washington Post,* May 10, 1985, p. A4.
56. "OSHA Will Begin Inspecting Firms in Industries With Low Injury Rates," *BNA's Employee Relations Weekly,* November 25, 1985, p. 1447.
57. "Revised Cotton Dust Standard Announced by OSH Administration," *BNA's Employee Relations Weekly,* December 9, 1985, p. 1511.
58. Peter Perl, "OSHA Offers New Rules on Workers' Exposure to Benzene, Formaldehyde," *The Washington Post,* December 4, 1985, p. A25.
59. Jerry Mosser, "Monitoring Employment Exposures Limits Liability, Morale Problems," *Occupational Health and Safety,* May 1985, p. 30.

Chapter 7

1. Clyde Summers, "Past Premises, Present Failures, and Future Needs in Labor Legislation," *Buffalo Law Review,* Winter 1982, p. 12.
2. *NLRB v. Jones & Laughlin Steel Corp.,* 301 U.S. 1, 46 (1937).
3. Frank McCulloch and Tim Bornstein, *The National Labor Relations Board* (New York: Praeger, 1974), p. 57.
4. Derek C. Bok and John T. Dunlop, *Labor and the American Community* (New York: Simon & Schuster, 1970), p. 17.
5. Jack Barbash, *American Unions: Structure, Government and Politics* (New York: Random House, 1967), pp. 148–49.
6. *Vaca v. Sipes,* 386 U.S. 171, 191 (1967).
7. *Hines v. Anchor Motor Freight, Inc.,* 424 U.S. 554, 570 (1976).
8. "ULP Charges Received by NLRB Decline Sharply in Fiscal 1984," *BNA's Employee Relations Weekly,* February 18, 1985, p. 207.
9. National Labor Relations Board, unpublished data on file at the NLRB.
10. *Annual Report of the NLRB, 1981* (Washington: Government Printing Office, 1983), Table 13.
11. National Labor Relations Board, phone communication, February 27, 1986; U.S. Congress, House Committee on Government Operations, Manpower and Housing Subcommittee, 99th Cong., 1st Sess., *National Labor Relations Board Case Backlog,* November 2, 1983, p. 50.
12. Report by House Education and Labor Committee, Labor-Management Relations Subcommittee on "Failure of Labor Law—A Betrayal of American Workers," reprinted in *Daily Labor Report,* No. 193, October 4,

1984, p. D-5; "NLRB Chairman Dotson Cites Progress in Easing Agency's Backlog of Cases," *BNA's Employee Relations Weekly,* April 15, 1985, p. 465.

13. "In Brief," *BNA's Employee Relations Weekly,* May 27, 1985, p. 650.

14. William N. Cooke and Frederick H. Gautschi, III, "Political Bias in NLRB Unfair Labor Practice Decisions," *Industrial and Labor Relations Review,* July 1982, pp. 539–49.

15. James A. Gross, "Conflicting Statutory Purposes: Another Look at Fifty Years of NLRB Lawmaking," *Industrial and Labor Relations Review,* October 1985, p. 18.

16. *May Department Stores Co.,* 59 NLRB 669, 672 (1943).

17. *First National Stores, Inc.,* 55 NLRB 1346 (1944).

18. *Robert Hall Clothes, Inc.,* 118 NLRB 1096 (1957).

19. *Sav-on-Drugs, Inc.,* 137 NLRB 1032 (1962).

20. *NLRB v. Metropolitan Life Ins. Co.,* 330 U.S. 438 (1964).

21. *St. Francis Hosp. II,* 271 NLRB 160 (1984).

22. *The Federbush Co., Inc.,* 24 NLRB 829 (1940).

23. *Silverknit Hosiery Mills, Inc.,* 99 NLRB 422 (1952).

24. *Esquire, Inc.,* 107 NLRB 1238, 1239 (1954).

25. *Hollywood Ceramics Co.,* 140 NLRB 221 (1962); *Dal-Tex Optical Co.,* 137 NLRB 274 (1962).

26. *Annual Report of the NLRB, 1962–63* (Washington: Government Printing Office), p. 60.

27. Julius G. Getman, Stephen B. Goldberg, and Jeanne B. Herman, *Union Representation Elections: Law and Reality* (New York: Russell Sage, 1976).

28. *Shopping Kart Food Mkt,* 228 NLRB 1311 (1977).

29. *Rossmore House,* 269 NLRB 198 (1984).

30. *PPG Indus.,* 251 NLRB 1146 (1980).

31. *NLRB v. Babcock & Wilcox Co.,* 351 U.S. 105 (1956); *NLRB v. United Steelworkers* (Nutone), 357 U.S. 357 (1958).

32. *General Electric Co. and McCulloch Corp.,* 156 NLRB 1247 (1966).

33. Richard B. Freeman, "Why Are Unions Faring Poorly in NLRB Representation Elections," in Thomas A. Kochan, ed., *Challenges and Choices Facing American Labor* (Cambridge: MIT Press, 1985), pp. 54–61.

34. William B. Gould, *A Primer on American Labor Law* (Cambridge: MIT Press, 1982), p. 109.

35. *NLRB v. Wooster Div. of Borg Warner Corp.,* 356 U.S. 342 (1958).

36. *Inland Steel Co. v. NLRB,* 366 U.S. 960 (1949).

37. *NLRB v. Niles-Bement-Pond Co.,* 199 F.2d 713 (2d Cir. 1952); *NLRB v. Bemis Bros. Bag Co.,* 206 F.2d 33 (5th Cir. 1953); *Weyerhauser Timber Co.,* 87 NLRB 672 (1949); *Fleming Mfg. Co.,* 119 NLRB 452 (1957).

38. *Town and Country Mfg. Co.,* 136 NLRB 1022 (1962); *Trenton News Record,* 136 NLRB 1294 (1962); *Ozark Trailers, Inc.,* 161 NLRB 1294 (1966).

39. *Fibreboard Paper Prods. Corp. v. NLRB,* 379 U.S. 203 (1964).

40. *Summit Tooling Co.,* 195 NLRB 479 (1972).

41. *First Nat'l Maintenance Corp. v. NLRB,* 452 U.S. 666, 686 (1981).

42. *Otis Elevator Co.,* 269 NLRB 162 (1984); *Milwaukee Spring Div. of Illinois Coil Spring Co.,* 268 NLRB 87 (1984).

43. Richard B. Freeman and James L. Medoff, *What Do Unions Do?* (New York: Basic Books, 1984), p. 46.

44. Bureau of National Affairs, Inc., "Wage and Salary Administration," *Personnel Policy Forum Survey* No. 131, July 1981, p. 3.
45. Fred K. Foulkes, *Personnel Practices in Large Nonunion Companies* (Englewood Cliffs, NJ: Prentice-Hall, 1980).
46. Bureau of National Affairs, Inc., "Policies for Unorganized Employees," *Personnel Policies Forum Survey* No. 125, April 1979, pp. 1, 12.
47. "Failure of Labor Law—A Betrayal of American Workers," *op. cit.* note 12, p. D–1.
48. "Opinion Outlook," *National Journal*, June 1, 1985, p. 1322.
49. Thomas A. Kochan, "How American Workers View Labor Unions," *Monthly Labor Review*, April 1979, pp. 23–31.
50. Paula Voos, "Labor Union Organizing Programs, 1954–1977," Ph.D. Dissertation, Harvard University, 1982.
51. National Labor Relations Board, Data Systems Branch, phone conversation, March 5, 1986.
52. James L. Medoff, "Study for AFL-CIO on Public's Image of Unions," *Daily Labor Report*, No. 247, December 24, 1984, p. D–1.
53. Thomas M. Kochan and Peter Cappelli, "The Transformation of the Industrial Relations and Personnel Function," in Paul Osterman, ed., *Internal Labor Markets* (Cambridge: MIT Press, 1984).
54. Philip M. Doyle, "Area Wage Surveys Shed Light on Declines in Unionization," *Monthly Labor Review*, September 1985, pp. 13–20.
55. Henry S. Farber, "The Extent of Unionization in the United States," in Kochan, ed., *Challenges and Choices Facing American Labor op. cit.* note 33, pp. 15–43; Freeman, "Why are Unions Faring Poorly in NLRB Representation Elections," *op. cit.* note 33, pp. 45–64; William T. Dickens and Jonathan S. Leonard, "Accounting for the Decline in Union Membership, 1950–1980," *Industrial and Labor Relations Review*, April 1985, pp. 323–34.
56. Freeman, "Why are Unions Faring Poorly," *op. cit.* note 33, p. 62.
57. Survey Research Center, *Quality of Employment Survey* (Ann Arbor: University of Michigan, Institute for Social Research, 1969–70, 1972–73, 1977.)
58. Medoff, "Study for the AFL-CIO on the Public's Image of Unions," *op. cit.* note 52, p. D–10.
59. *Pattern Makers v. NLRB*, 473 U.S. ___, 53 U.S.L.W. 4928 (1985).
60. Freeman and Medoff, *What Do Unions Do?* *op. cit.* note 43, pp. 214–15.
61. Janice D. Bellace and Alan D. Berkowitz, *The Landrum-Griffin Act: Twenty Years of Federal Protection of Union Members' Rights* (Philadelphia: University of Pennsylvania, The Wharton School, 1979), p. 317.

Chapter 8

1. National Commission on Employment Compensation, *Unemployment Compensation: Final Report* (Washington: National Commission on Employment Compensation, 1980), p. 8.
2. Raymond Munts, *Policy Development in Unemployment Insurance* (Madison: University of Wisconsin, Institute for Research on Poverty, 1977), p. 75.

3. National Commission, *op. cit.* note 1, p. 8.
4. Richard A. Hobbie, "Unemployment Insurance: Financial Problems in the Trust Fund," Library of Congress, Congressional Research Service, June 5, 1985, p. 3.
5. Congressional Budget Office, *Promoting Employment and Maintaining Incomes with Unemployment Insurance*, March 1985, p. 9.
6. U.S. Congress, House Committee on Ways and Means, 96th Cong., 2d Sess., *Background Material and Data on Programs Within the Jurisdiction of the Committee on Ways and Means* (Committee Print 14, 1986), p. 323.
7. Congressional Budget Office, *op. cit.* note 5, p. 23.
8. Executive Office of the President, Office of Management and Budget, *Budget of the U.S. Government*, Fiscal Year 1986, p. 5–116.
9. Committee on Ways and Means, *op. cit.* note 6, pp. 301–303.
10. Joseph M. Becker, S.J., *Experience Rating in Unemployment Insurance: Virtue or Vice* (Kalamazoo: The W.E. Upjohn Institute for Employment Research, 1972), p. 10.
11. William Haber and Merrill Murray, *Unemployment Insurance in the American Economy* (Homewood, Ill.: Richard Irwin, Inc., 1966), p. 446.
12. *Strategy for U.S. Industrial Competitiveness* (Washington: The Committee for Economic Development, 1984), p. 63.
13. National Foundation for Unemployment Compensation & Worker's Compensation, "Experience Rating—New Evidence," Bulletin No. 146 U.C., *The Bulletin*, Washington, September 23, 1985.
14. Congressional Budget Office, *op. cit.* note 5, p. 36.
15. Committee on Ways and Means, *op. cit.* note 6, pp. 305–307, 309.
16. Congressional Budget Office, *op. cit.* note 5, pp. 7–8.
17. Sar A. Levitan and Martha R. Cooper, *Business Lobbies* (Baltimore: Johns Hopkins University Press, 1984), pp. 99–100.
18. Ways and Means Committee, *op. cit.* note 6, pp. 346–47.
19. Unweighted state averages calculated from Ways and Means Committee, *op. cit.* note 6, pp. 316–17.
20. The Center for the Study of Social Policy, *Restructuring Unemployment Insurance* (Washington: The Center for the Study of Social Policy, 1985), p. 34.
21. Committee on Ways and Means *op. cit.* note 6, pp. 300, 312.
22. Gary Burtless and Wayne Vroman, "Unemployment Insurance Program Solvency in the 1980s," *Monthly Labor Review*, May 1985, p. 27.
23. Joseph M. Becker, *Unemployment Benefits* (Washington: American Enterprise Institute for Public Policy Research, 1980), p. 4.
24. Congressional Budget Office, *op. cit.* note 5, p. 21.
25. Daniel S. Hamermesh, *Jobless Pay and the Economy* (Baltimore: Johns Hopkins University Press, 1977), p. 64.
26. "Labor Department Seeks Comments on Qaulity Control for UI Program," *BNA's Employee Relations Weekly*, August 19, 1985, p. 1048; Paul L. Burgess, Jerry L. Kingston, and Robert D. St. Louis, *The Development of an Operational System for Detecting Payment Errors Through Random Audits: The Results of Five Statewide Pilot Tests* (Washington: Unemployment Insurance Service, U.S. Department of Labor, 1982).
27. Congressional Budget Office, *op. cit.* note 5, pp. 62–68.
28. "Restructuring Unemployment Insurance," *op. cit.* note 20, p. 76.

Chapter 9

1. Council of Economic Advisors, *Economic Report of the President, 1985* (Washington: Government Printing Office, 1985), p. 159.

2. Robert J. Meyers, *Social Insurance and Allied Government Programs* (Homewood, Ill.: Richard Irwin, Inc., 1965), pp. 11–13.

3. *Report to the President of the Committee on Economic Security* (Washington: Government Printing Office, January 15, 1934), p. 24.

4. Robert M. Ball, "The 1939 Amendments to the Social Security Act and What Followed," in *Project on the Federal Social Role, 50th Anniversary Edition: The Report of the Committee on Economic Security of 1935* (Washington: National Conference on Social Welfare, 1985), pp. 161–72.

5. *Congressional Quarterly Almanac,* 1977, p. 162.

6. Richard V. Burkhauser and Robert H. Haveman, *Disability and Work* (Baltimore: Johns Hopkins University Press, 1982), p. 42.

7. Ralph Teitel, *Disability Claimants Who Contest Denials and Win Reversals Through Hearings,* Washington, Department of Health, Education, and Welfare, Social Security Administration, Working Paper Series No. 3, February 1979.

8. U.S. Congress, Senate Committee on Finance, 96th Cong., 1st Sess., *Issues Related to Social Security Disability Programs* (Washington: Government Printing Office, 1979), p. 61.

9. David Koitz, "Social Security: Reexamining Eligibility for Disability Benefits," Library of Congress, Congressional Research Service, October 18, 1982, p. 6; *Congressional Quarterly Almanac,* 1979, p. 504.

10. U.S. Congress, Senate Special Committee on Aging, 99th Cong., 1st Sess., *Developments in Aging: 1984,* Volume 1 (Washington: Government Printing Office, 1985), pp. 30–31; Spencer Rich, "Disability Reviews to Resume," *The Washington Post,* November 28, 1985, p. A17.

11. Robert Pear, "Senate Study Calls for New Laws to Protect Aged Hospital Patients," *The New York Times,* September 26, 1985, p. A20.

12. Peter Henle, "Recent Trends in Retirement Benefit Related to Earnings," *Monthly Labor Review,* June 1972, p. 18; Alicia H. Munnell, "ERISA: Is It Consistent With Other National Goals?" in U.S. Congress, Senate Special Committee on Aging, 98th Cong., 2d Sess., *The Employee Retirement Income Security Act of 1974: The First Decade* (Washington: Government Printing Office, 1984), p. 192.

13. Susan Grad, U.S. Health and Human Services, Social Security Administration, *Income of the Population 55 and Over,* Table 47 (in press).

14. U.S. Congress, Senate Special Committee on Aging, 98th Cong., 2d Sess., *Medicare and the Health Costs of Older Americans: The Extent and the Effects of Cost Sharing* (Washington: Government Printing Office, 1984), p. v.

15. Martin J. Feldstein, "Social Security, Induced Retirement, and Aggregate Capital Accumulation," *Journal of Political Economy,* September-October 1974, pp. 905–926.

16. Joseph A. Pechman, Henry J. Aaron, and Michael K. Taussig, *Social Security: Perspectives for Reform* (Washington: Brookings Institution, 1968).

17. Alicia Munnell, *The Effect of Social Security on Personal Savings* (Cambridge: Ballinger, 1974).

18. Bruno Stein, *Social Security and Pensions in Transition,* pp. 161–170; Selig D. Lesnow and Dean R. Leimer, "Social Security and Private Savings: Theory and Historical Evidence," *Social Security Bulletin,* January 1985, pp. 14–30.

19. Richard V. Burkhauser and Karen Holden, eds., *A Challenge to Social Security* (New York: Academic Press, 1983); Gail B. King, "Social Security and the Changing Role of Women," in U.S. Congress, Senate Special Committee on Aging, 99th Cong., 1st Sess., *Fifty Years of Social Security* (Washington: Government Printing Office, 1985), pp. 60–72.

20. Bureau of the Census, *Economic Characteristics of Households in the United States: Second Quarter 1984,* Current Population Reports, Series P-70, Table A.

21. Bureau of the Census, *Estimates of Poverty Including the Value of Noncash Benefits: 1984,* Technical Paper 55 (Washington: Government Printing Office, 1985), Table 2.

22. Council of Economic Advisors, *op. cit.* note 1, p. 167.

23. "Social Security Insecurity," *Public Opinion,* August-September 1981, pp. 35–73.

24. Harry C. Ballantyne, "Actuarial Status of the OASI and DI Trust Funds," *Social Security Bulletin,* June 1985, pp. 27–31.

25. Peter J. Ferrara, ed., *Social Security: Prospects for Real Reform* (Washington: Cato Institute, 1985).

Chapter 10

1. Council of Economic Advisors, *Economic Report of the President, 1985* (Washington: Government Printing Office, 1985), p. 177.

2. Employee Benefit Research Institute, "New Survey Findings on Pension Coverage and Benefit Entitlement," *EBRI Issue Brief* No. 3, August 1984.

3. Alicia Munnell, *The Economics of Private Pensions* (Washington: The Brookings Institution, 1982), p. 53.

4. General Accounting Office, *Effects of the 1980 Multiemployer Pension Plan Amendments Act on Plan Participants Benefits,* GAO/HRD-85-58 (1985), p. 1; Dallas L. Salisbury, "What Impact Has ERISA Had on Different Types of Pension Plans," in *The Employee Retirement Income Security Act of 1974: The First Decade,* An Information Paper prepared for the U.S. Congress, Senate Special Committee on Aging, 98th Cong., 2d Sess., August 1984, p. 108.

5. Dan M. McGill, "Post-ERISA Legislation," *The Employee Retirement Income Security Act of 1974: The First Decade, op. cit.* note 4, p. 63.

6. "Two-thirds of All Eligible Employees Covered by 401(k) Plans, Survey Finds," *BNA's Employee Relations Weekly,* August 26, 1985, p. 1067.

7. Sumner H. Slichter *et al., The Impact of Collective Bargaining on Management* (Washington: The Brookings Institution, 1960), pp. 373–74.

8. John Dunlop, "Appraisal of Wage Stabilization Policies," in *Problems and Policies of Dispute Settlement and Wage Stabilization During World War II,* Bureau of Labor Statistics, Bulletin 1009 (Washington: Government Printing Office, 1950).

9. Alicia H. Munnell, "The Future of the U.S. Pension System," in Colin D. Campbell, ed., *Financing Social Security* (Washington: American Enterprise Institute, 1979), p. 256.

10. *Inland Steel Co. v. NLRB,* 366 U.S. 960 (1949).

11. Alfred M. Skolnick, "Private Pension Plans, 1950–1974," *Social Security Bulletin,* June 1976, p. 4.

12. General Accounting Office, *op. cit.* note 4, p. 3.

13. Spencer Rich, "Most Multiemployer Pension Plans Seen Healthy," *The Washington Post,* October 9, 1985, p. F3.

14. Department of Labor, *Findings From the Survey of Private Pension Benefit Amounts* (Washington: Government Printing Office, 1985).

15. *City of Los Angeles v. Manhart,* 435 U.S. 702 (1978).

16. *Norris v. Arizona Governing Comm.,* 463 U.S. 1073 (1983).

17. Council of Economic Advisors, *op cit.* note 1, p. 177.

18. Linda D. Maxfield, "Income of New Retired Workers by Age at First Benefit Receipt: Findings From the New Beneficiary Survey," *Social Security Bulletin,* July 1985, p. 13.

19. Daniel Beller, "Coverage and Vesting Status in Private Pension Plans," in *Pension Facts,* U.S. Department of Labor, Pension and Welfare Benefits Administration, Table 19 (in press).

20. Employee Benefit Research Institute, "Impact of Retirement Equity Act," *EBRI Issue Brief* No. 39, February 1985.

21. Pension Benefit Guaranty Corporation, *1984 Annual Report, The Tenth Anniversary,* p. iv.

22. Department of Labor, *Findings From the Survey of Private Pension Benefit Amounts* (Washington: Office of Pension and Welfare Benefit Programs, 1985).

23. General Accounting Office, *Effect of the Employee Retirement Income Security Act on the Termination of Single Employer Defined Benefit Plans,* HRD-78-90 (1978).

24. Ray Marshall, "The Multiemployer Pension Plan Amendments Act of 1980," A Report to the Council on Multiemployer Pension Security, Inc. (University of Texas at Austin, 1985, unpublished).

25. Thomas C. Woodruff, "The Goals of ERISA and the Impact of ERISA on Plan Participants," in *The Employee Retirement Income Security Act of 1974: The First Decade, op. cit.* note 4, p. 35.

26. Dallas L. Salisbury, "ERISA at Ten: Where Are We?" *Benefits Quarterly,* First Quarter 1985, p. 62.

27. "Costs of Defined Contribution Plans Can Exceed Defined Benefit Plan Costs," *BNA's Employee Relations Weekly,* March 18, 1985, p. 33.

28. Salisbury, *op. cit.* note 4, pp. 123–24.

29. Janet Hook, "Established to Resolve Crisis, Federal Pension Corporation Finds Itself in Financial Straits," *Congressional Quarterly,* March 10, 1984, p. 561.

30. Ronald Brownstein, "Federal Pension Insurance System Teetering on the Financial Brink," *National Journal,* September 3, 1983, p. 1777.

31. Congressional Budget Office, *Work and Retirement: Options for Continued Employment of Older Workers* (Washington: Government Printing Office, 1982), pp. 21–22; U.S. Department of Labor, *op. cit.* note 14, p. 4.

268 NOTES TO PAGES 214–232

32. Stephen R. McConnell, "Age Discrimination in Employment," in Herbert S. Parnes, ed., *Policy Issues in Work and Retirement* (Kalamazoo: The W.E. Upjohn Institute for Employment Research, 1983), pp. 176–77.

33. Employee Benefits Research Institute, "Individual Retirement Accounts: Characteristics and Policy Implications," *EBRI Issue Brief* No. 32, July 1984, Table 3.

34. Office of Management and Budget, *Budget of the United States Government, Fiscal Year 1985* (Washington: Government Printing Office), Special Analysis G.

35. Sophie M. Korczyk, *Retirement Security and Tax Policy* (Washington: Employee Benefit Research Institute, 1985); Richard Ippolito, "Public Policy Toward Private Pensions," *Contemporary Policy Issues*, April 1983, p. 57.

36. Clyde Farnsworth, "Pension Plans' Surplus Assets," *The New York Times*, August 12, 1985, p. D2.

Chapter 11

1. *Wieman v. Updegraff*, 344 U.S. 183 (1952).

2. *Perry v. Sindermann*, 408 U.S. 593 (1972).

3. Jack Stieber, "Recent Developments in Employment-At-Will," *Labor Law Journal*, August 1985, p. 558.

4. "Employment-at-Will Doctrine Undergoing Gradual Modification," *BNA's Employee Relations Weekly*, October 28, 1985, p. 1315.

5. *Petermann v. Teamsters Local 396*, 174 Cal.2d 184, 344 P.2d 25 (1959).

6. *Tameny v. Atlantic Richfield Co.*, 27 Cal.3d 167, 620 P.2d 1330 (1980).

7. *Sides v. Duke Hosp.*, 120 LRRM 2091 (1985).

8. *Toussaint v. Blue Cross and Blue Shield of Mich.*, 408 Mich. 579 (1980).

9. *Pugh v. See's Candies, Inc.*, 116 Cal. App.3d 311, 171 Cal. Rept. 917 (1981).

10. John Hoerr, "Beyond Unions," *Business Week*, July 8, 1985, p. 76.

11. Harihar Krishnan, "Courts Restricting Power of Employers to Fire Employees," *The Washington Post*, September 9, 1985, Business Supplement, p. 11.

12. Jack Stieber, "Employment-At-Will: An Issue for the 1980s," in *Industrial Relations Research Association 36th Annual Proceedings* (Madison: Industrial Relations Research Association, 1984), pp. 7–8.

13. Clyde Summers, "Protecting All Employees Against Unjust Dismissal," *Harvard Business Review*, January-February 1980, pp. 132–39.

14. Henry H. Perritt, Jr., *Employee Dismissal Law and Practice* (New York: John Wiley & Sons, 1984), pp. 353–57.

15. AFL-CIO Committee on the Evolution of Work, *The Changing Situation of Workers and Their Unions* (Washington: AFL-CIO, 1985).

16. "Employment-at-Will Doctrine Undergoing Gradual Modification," *op. cit.* note 4, 1315–16; Stieber, *op. cit.* note 3, 559–61; Theodore J. St. Antoine, "The Revision of Employment-At-Will Enters a New Phase," *Labor Law Journal*, August 1985, pp. 564–65.

17. H.R. 7010, 96th Cong., 2d Sess., reprinted in *The Employment-At-Will Issue*, BNA Special Report (Washington: Bureau of National Affairs, Inc., 1982), p. 9.

18. Barry Bluestone and Bennett Harrison, *The Deindustrialization of America* (New York: Basic Books, 1982), Ch. 1.

19. Candee Harris, "Plant Closings and the Replacement of Manufacturing Jobs: 1978–1982," The Brookings Institution, Washington, D.C., November 1983, cited in Barry Bluestone, Bennett Harrison, and Lucy Gorham, *Storm Clouds on the Horizon: Labor Market Crisis and Industrial Policy* (Brookline, MA: Economic Education Project, 1984), p. 8.

20. Paul O. Flaim and Ellen Sehgal, "Displaced Workers, 1979–1983," *Monthly Labor Review*, June 1985, p. 3.

21. House Debate on H.R. 1616, *Congressional Record* (daily ed., November 14, 1985), pp. H10213-H10242.

22. U.S. Congress, Office of Technology Assessment, *Technology and Structural Unemployment: Reemploying Displaced Adults* (Washington: Government Printing Office, 1986), pp. 221–22.

23. Bennett Harrison, "Plant Closures: Effects to Cushion the Blow," *Monthly Labor Review*, June 1984, p. 41.

24. *Ibid.*

25. Gary B. Hansen, "The San Jose Shutdown: Closing the Door Gently," *World of Work Report*, Work in America Institute, May 1985.

26. John V. Hickey, "Plant Closing: Electrolux Program a Model," *World of Work Report*, Work in America Institute, October 1985.

27. "Plant Closings: How Many? How Regulated?" *World of Work Report*, Work in America Institute, May 1985.

28. Nancy R. Follere, Julia L. Leighton, and Melissa R. Roderick, "Plant Closings and Their Regulation in Maine, 1971–1982," *Industrial and Labor Relations Review*, January 1984, pp. 190–91.

29. Mark Levenson, "Plant Closing Laws: Assessing the Options," *Pennsylvania Outlook*, Winter 1985, p. 7.

30. Office of Technology Assessment, *op. cit.* note 22, Ch. 5.

31. Earl F. Mellor, "Investigating the Differences in Weekly Earnings of Women and Men," *Monthly Labor Review*, June 1984, p. 26; "BLS: Earnings Gap Between Men, Women Narrows to 69 Percent, New High," *BNA's Employee Relations Weekly*, September 9, 1985, p. 1094.

32. Mark S. Seiling, "Staffing Patterns in Female-Male Earnings Gap," *Monthly Labor Review*, June 1984, p. 29.

33. Andrea H. Beller, "Occupational Segregation and the Earnings Gap," in *Comparable Worth: Issues for the 1980s* (Washington: U.S. Commission on Civil Rights, June 1984), pp. 27–28.

34. Janice Shack-Marquez, "Earnings Differences Between Men and Women: An Introductory Note," *Monthly Labor Review*, June 1984, p. 15.

35. Solomon William Polachek, "Women in the Economy: Perspectives on Gender Equality," in *Comparable Worth: Issues for the 1980s, op. cit.* note 33, pp. 34–52.

36. Cited in Peter Perl, "Lower Pay for Women Blamed on Job Barriers," *The Washington Post*, December 15, 1985, p. A14.

37. *County of Washington v. Gunther,* 452 U.S. 161 (1981).

270 NOTES TO PAGES 243–245

38. Marilyn Marks, "State Legislators, Judges and Now Congress Examining Comparable Worth," *National Journal,* September 8, 1984, pp. 1666–70.

39. U.S. Congress, House Committee on Post Office and Civil Service, Subcommittee on Compensation and Employment Benefits, 99th Cong., 1st Sess., *Options for Conducting a Pay Equity Study of Federal Pay and Classification Systems* (statement of Nina Rothchild, Commissioner of Employer Relations for the State of Minnesota) (Washington: Government Printing Office, 1985), pp. 104–116.

40. "Pay Equity System Not Costly, Surveys Say," *St. Paul Press and Dispatch,* October 19, 1985, p. 9.

41. Joann S. Lublin, "Big Fight Looms Over Gap in Pay for Similar 'Male' 'Female' Jobs, *The Wall Street Journal,* September 10, 1982.

42. "State Employees Sue California Charging Sex Bias," *The Washington Post,* November 22, 1984, p. A–7.

43. Communications Workers of America, *Newsletter,* October 1984, p. 8.

44. U.S. Congress, Senate Committee on Governmental Affairs, Subcommittee on Civil Service, Post Office, and General Services, 99th Cong., 1st Sess., *Report of the General Accounting Office,* "Options for Conducting a Pay Equity Study of Federal Pay and Classification Systems," May 22, 1985 (Washington: Government Printing Office, in press).

Index

Health, Education and Welfare,
Department of 106-07
Heritage Foundation 25-26, 31
*Hines v. Anchor Motor Freight,
Inc.* 135
Holt, Rush Dew 101
Howard University 61

I

Immigration 52ff.
illegal immigration 52-53
labor supply 36, 52
Immigration and Naturalization
Service 55
Income support (*see also* Social
security) 5
Work Incentive (WIN)
program 49-50
Individual retirement accounts (*see*
Pensions)
Individual training accounts 172
Inland Steel Co. v. NLRB 142, 200
Internal Revenue Code 216
Internal Revenue Service 205-06,
208
International Harvester Co. 213
International Labor
Organization 232
Interstate Commerce
Commission 22

J

Javits, Jacob 106
Job Corps 9, 48-49, 89
Job creation programs 47-48
Job service (*see* U.S. Employment
Service)
Job training (*see also*
Comprehensive
Employment and Training
Act (CETA); Job Training
Partnership Act
(JTPA)) 9, 47-48
Job Training Partnership Act
(JTPA) 47-48, 237
Johnson administration 6, 16
Johnson, Lyndon Baines 30, 60,
61, 105
*Jones & Laughlin Steel Corp.,
NLRB v.* 133
J.P. Stevens Co. 18
Justice, Department of 63, 66-67,
76

K

Kaiser Aluminum & Chemical
Co. 63
Kennedy administration 139, 140,
143
Kennedy, John F. 59
Keogh retirement accounts 199,
201, 216
Keynesian theory 5

L

Labor, Department of
affirmative action goals 43
Bureau of Apprenticeship and
Training 42-43
ERISA administration 205-06
FLSA enforcement 98
Landrum-Griffin Act 134, 135,
149-50
minimum wage 86
Office of Federal Contract
Compliance (OFCC) 61,
64, 68, 70-71
pension surveys 208, 209
plant closings 237-38
subminimum wage 86
unemployment insurance
study 160, 170
Labor and Human Resources
Committee 27
Labor Law Reform Bill of
1977 146
Labor-liberal coalition 8, 27-28
Labor Management Reporting and
Disclosure Act (*see*
Landrum-Griffin Act)
Labor movement (*see also* Unions)
AFL-CIO 28-29
collective bargaining 5
comparable worth 29
growth 4, 5, 132, 133
immigration 55
Labor Law Reform Bill of
1977 146
lobbies 27-29
OSHA 115
subminimum wage 88
unemployment insurance 162,
168
workplace deregulation 16, 26ff.
workplace regulation 8
Landrum-Griffin Act 134, 135,
149-50